The Baby Name Book

2,222+ Popular, Unique, & Spiritual Baby Names

Their Meanings, Origins, and Significance

THE PUBLISHERS

© **Copyright 2024 - All rights reserved.**

The content contained within this book may not be reproduced, duplicated or transmitted without direct written permission from the author or the publisher.

Under no circumstances will any blame or legal responsibility be held against the publisher, or author, for any damages, reparation, or monetary loss due to the information contained within this book, either directly or indirectly.

Legal Notice:

This book is copyright protected. It is only for personal use. You cannot amend, distribute, sell, use, quote or paraphrase any part or the content within this book, without the consent of the author or publisher.

Disclaimer Notice:

Please note the information contained within this document is for educational and entertainment purposes only. All effort has been executed to present accurate, up to date, reliable, complete information. No warranties of any kind are declared or implied. Readers acknowledge that the author is not engaged in the rendering of legal, financial, medical, or professional advice. The content within this book has been derived from various sources. Please consult a licensed professional before attempting any techniques outlined in this book.

By reading this document, the reader agrees that under no circumstances is the author responsible for any losses, direct or indirect, that are incurred as a result of the use of the information contained within this document, including, but not limited to, errors, omissions, or inaccuracies.

Table of Contents

INTRODUCTION 1

CHAPTER 1: TOP TRENDING NAMES 3
    Trending Boys' Names 3
    Trending Girls' Names 10

CHAPTER 2: MOST POPULAR NAMES 16
    Most Popular Boys' Names 16
    Most Popular Girls' Names 23

CHAPTER 3: UNISEX NAMES 30

CHAPTER 4: SPIRITUAL NAMES 39
    Male and Female Biblical Names 39
    Male and Female Mythological Names 51
    Male and Female Celestial Names 59

CHAPTER 5: UNIQUE AND UNCOMMON NAMES 64
    Unique and Rare Boys' Names 64
    Unique and Rare Girls' Names 72

CHAPTER 6: INTERNATIONAL NAMES 82
    Boys' Names from Different Cultures 82
    Girls' Names from Different Cultures 92

CHAPTER 7: CELEBRITY AND CELEBRITY KID NAMES 96
    Celebrity Names 96
    Boys' Celebrity Kid Names 101
    Girls' Celebrity Kid Names 108

CHAPTER 8: FICTIONAL NAMES 115

CHAPTER 9: OLD-FASHIONED NAMES 134
    Vintage Boys' Names 134
    Vintage Girls' Names 141

CHAPTER 10: MODERN NAMES 148
    Contemporary Boys' Names 148
    Contemporary Girls' Names 153

CHAPTER 11: TWIN NAMES 158
   TWIN BOY NAMES 158
   TWIN GIRL NAMES 169
   TWIN BOY AND GIRL NAMES 179

CONCLUSION 185

REFERENCES 187

INTRODUCTION

What is a name? Is it simply a word or a sound that we attach to certain things so we can all agree on what we're talking about? Is it that one word you use when you're *really* mad at your spouse? Or is there more to it than what meets the eye? Well, to put it simply, a name is what we're all known by. It carries incredible importance in terms of our identity, and in many cases, it can have a much deeper significance. A name gives you a sense of who you are, where you belong, and what you're known as. It almost represents who you are deep within your core. That's probably why choosing a name for your child is no easy task.

I feel like there are two kinds of people in this world: Those who know what they want to call their children years before they have a baby and those who have a baby and still struggle to decide. One of my favorite examples of this, even though it's fictional, can be found in the popular sitcom *Friends*. Monica is in the first category and chose names for her children when she was still in school, while Rachel had her baby and didn't know what to call her yet. Neither is wrong! As human beings, we're all different. It's okay if you've had a name planned for ages or didn't think about it until the last minute. However, based on the nature of this book, I'm guessing you're with me and Rachel, not Monica.

The truth is that choosing a name for your child is a huge decision, and it can be intimidating. The name you choose for your child will remain for their entire lives! Do you keep it simple and add another Ryan or Chloe to the mix, or do you choose something so unique that your child ends up hating it until they are adults? Well, that's what this book is here for, right? To help you choose the perfect name for your little one.

Let's debunk a few myths before we get started: There's no such thing as a perfect name. Why? Because there's no such thing as a perfect person. We all have certain names that we know we'll never choose because we knew someone with that name back when we were in high school, and they were awful (I'm looking at you, Bianca). So, let's remove the pressure of being perfect as we embark on this journey of seeking the right name.

Every name carries a meaning and an origin. It's more than just something that sounds cute, although some names are adorable! The goal is to find a name that you like that your partner is happy with, and that you think would fit well with your little one. That's why it's important not to overlook the meaning of a name before assigning it to your child forever. As an example, Cecilia is a very cute name for a baby girl. It sounds vintage and has a pretty vibe to it, but did you know that "Cecilia" is derived from the Latin word "Caecilius," which means "blind." Yup, you read that right blind! So, let's agree to not only choose names on how they sound but perhaps also on what they mean.

Before we jump in and look at names from different categories, here are a few things to keep in mind when choosing a name for your child (Murray, 2023).

- **Don't be scared to break tradition:** Many families have traditional names that get passed on from generation to generation, and you end up with five people with the same name and a sixty-year-old man named "Junior." It's okay to break away from tradition and give your child a name that is unique and special to them, even if it might upset a great-grandfather or an angry mother-in-law. Eventually, they'll come around, and your child will thank you for your sacrifice.

- **Be careful with initials:** If you're choosing a second name for your baby, do yourself a favor and check the initials. I had a friend called Camilla Olivia Wilson, and throughout her school life, she was mocked because her initials were spelled COW. So, double-check before you register those initials forever.

- **Get creative with spelling:** Sometimes, you can have a common name but spell it with a twist. This is a fun way to elevate a name and make it more unique. This trend is quite popular in fantasy novels, so let those creative juices flow.

- **Think of the rest of the family:** If the name of every member of your starts with a specific letter, consider choosing a name for your child that starts with that letter as well. Why? Because it will allow them to feel like they are part of the family, not on the outside looking in.

- **Consider the nickname:** Most people want a nickname that their friends can use. But some names can be really hard to create a nickname for. This might, therefore, be something you want to consider as you choose a name for your child.

I have a friend who wanted to name her little boy Aston but decided against it because she didn't want his nickname to be "Ashie," "Ass," or "Tony."

- **Think about the location:** Some names are geographically bound, meaning they might have significance to where you live, but they could have negative connotations in other parts of the country or world. Take this into account when naming your child something very specific to one location.

- **Be considerate of your child:** Your little one will not always be so little. What seems cute for them right now may hinder their personal lives and, eventually, their professional lives. I have a friend who, as soon as she became an adult, legally changed her embarrassing first name to just its first initial. Although she had always been called by her middle name, her parents, doctors, school records, and other legal documents used her given name. She kept the initial to honor her parents but never wanted to answer to that name again. So, choose a name your child wouldn't want to change at some point in their lives.

With all of this advice in mind, are you ready to embark on a journey of discovery and delve into the exciting world of baby names? As I mentioned earlier, we'll explore different categories for names, so feel free to jump to a specific section if you know that you're looking for a name in that category. In each section, we'll list names for boys and girls. In Chapter 1, we'll explore trending names that are currently all the buzz! After that, we'll explore the most common or popular names worldwide. In Chapter 3, we'll pay special focus to unisex names, so if you're looking for something more gender-neutral, that's a great chapter to start with.

We'll continue by exploring spiritual names in Chapter 4, followed by unique and uncommon names. Later, we'll dive into international as well as celebrity names, followed by fictional names in chapter 8. Certain classics never go out of style, which is why we'll look at classic names and old-fashioned names in Chapters 9. In Chapter 10, we'll transition into the world of modern names, where we explore contemporary trends and emerging favorites. Finally, we'll end the book by exploring names that work well for twins. Even though twins are unique, it can be special for their names to be connected somehow or complement each other.

So, get ready to highlight your favorite names, write down some cute ideas, and feel inspired to give your baby a name that will be just right for them.

CHAPTER 1: TOP TRENDING NAMES

A trendy name rides a wave of popularity during a particular time period. It's distinct from either a popular or common name. Common names might stay consistently popular across decades, like *Elizabeth* or *William*. Trendy names, however, capture the current zeitgeist and reflect what parents find appealing in a specific era. Names like *Moon Unit* or *Sunshine* would be trendy in the 1960s due to a focus on counterculture, while names like *River* or those with earthy vibes like *Jasper* would be trendy today due to a focus on nature. The key is that trendy names are tied to a specific era's interests and aesthetics, giving them a unique flair that fades over time. Using these names, you can stay ahead of the curve, taking the world by storm.

Trending Boys' Names

Choosing a trendy name for boys can be tricky since you don't want to sound gimmicky and want a name that will age well with your child. For example, maybe don't call your child "Tik-Tok" or "Stanley" based on the popular app and trending Stanley cups. Rather, choose meaningful names that are also trendy and cool. Here are a few names for boys that fit this category perfectly!

Adrian
Meaning and Origin: Man of Adria (Latin)
Significance: Refers to someone from the northern port region of Italy; it's commonly used as a sea-themed name.

Aiden
Meaning and Origin: Little; fiery (Irish)
Significance: Someone with a lot of pep and energy. Naming a child Aiden can reflect a hope for him to be bold, energetic, and enthusiastic in his pursuits.

Alastair
Meaning and Origin: Defender of men (Scottish)
Significance: Derivative of Alexander, indicating military might and leadership. Alastair also suggests qualities of protection and courage. Naming a child Alastair can reflect a hope for him to stand up for others and to be a source of strength and support.

Atlas
Meaning and Origin: Enduring; to endure (Greek)
Significance: This name evokes strength, adventure, and resilience. Atlas also can reflect hope for him to possess traits to withstand challenges and carry burdens with determination.

Arlo
Meaning and Origin: Fortified hill; army hill (English)
Significance: This name suggests a sense of protection and strength. Arlo can also reflect a hope for him to be resilient, courageous, and capable of defending others.

Asher
Meaning and Origin: Happy; blessed (Hebrew)
Significance: A positive name that speaks of joy, prosperity, and strong family ties. Asher has a sense of joy, contentment, and divine favor. Naming a child Asher can reflect a hope for him to lead a happy and fulfilling life, blessed with goodness and prosperity.

Austin
Meaning and Origin: Great; magnificent (Latin)
Significance: Short for Augustine, Austin refers to a man of great power. Austin suggests qualities of dignity, respect, and honor. Naming a child Austin can reflect a hope for him to embody these noble traits, to carry himself with grace and authority.

Basil
Meaning and Origin: Royal; kingly (Greek)
Significance: A name that demands respect as that of a king. Basil suggests qualities of nobility, leadership, and dignity. Naming a child Basil can reflect a hope for him to embody these regal traits, to inspire respect and admiration.

Beckett
Meaning and Origin: Little stream (Irish)
Significance: A name for a creative genius that sparks inspiration. Beckett suggests a connection to nature and community. A child named Beckett can reflect a hope for him to be industrious, cooperative, and productive, like bees in a hive.

Brayden
Meaning and Origin: Salmon; wise (Irish)
Significance: From the Irish mythological "Salmon of Knowledge." A fish that ate hazelnuts that had fallen into the Well of Wisdom, thus possessing all the wisdom in the world.

Brooks
Meaning and Origin: Small stream (British)
Significance: A nature-inspired name that speaks to strength and being refreshed. Brooks signifies a connection to the natural world, specifically to streams and waterways. Naming a child Brooks can reflect a calm and peaceful presence

Callum
Meaning and Origin: Dove (Latin)
Significance: Callum suggests a symbol of peace, harmony, and gentleness. Naming a child Callum can reflect a hope for him to embody these qualities, to be a calming presence and to promote unity among others.

Carter
Meaning and Origin: Transporter of goods by cart; sojourner (English)
Significance: Someone who is responsible and reliable. Carter is associated with a practical and industrious occupation. A child who is named Carter can reflect a hope for him to possess qualities of hard work, responsibility, and reliability.

Caspian
Meaning and Origin: From the sea (English)
Significance: Caspian is associated with the Caspian Sea, the world's largest lake between Asia and Europe. Caspian also represents Strong-willed people who enjoys nature and the ocean.

Connor
Meaning and Origin: Lover of hounds (Irish)
Significance: In Irish mythology, dogs are revered, so anyone who adores them also embodies the loyalty and good luck that hounds possess.

Crew
Meaning and Origin: Group of people working together (English)
Significance: Modern name emphasizing teamwork and camaraderie. Crew suggests a sense of community and collaboration. Naming a child Crew can reflect a hope for him to value relationships, work well with others, and contribute positively to his community.

Cyrus
Meaning and Origin: Sun (Persian)
Significance: Someone who is the light and focus of those around them. Cyrus suggests qualities of brightness, power, and authority. Naming a child Cyrus can reflect a hope for him to embody these regal traits, to lead with wisdom and strength.

Dylan
Meaning and Origin: Son of the sea (Welsh)
Significance: A name that references tranquility, peace, and the ability to face storms. This name has a strong connection to the elements of water and nature. Dylan can also reflect a wish for him to have a calm yet powerful presence, akin to the sea.

Easton
Meaning: Easter tower (British)
Significance: Someone who stands tall and firm in the face of adversity. Easton represents a sense of orientation and aspiration towards new beginnings and opportunities. Easton can also reflect a hope for him to embrace change, growth, and optimism.

Emmett
Meaning and Origin: Whole; universal (German)
Significance: This name refers to someone who is complete and fits within the larger universe perfectly. Emmett represents a name with broad and timeless significance. Naming a child Emmett can reflect a desire for him to embody values of truthfulness and inclusivity.

Ethan
Meaning and Origin: Strong; enduring; firm (Hebrew)
Significance: Someone who is very strong, stands up for their beliefs, and isn't easily thrown off course. Naming a child Ethan can reflect a hope for him to possess these strong traits and to overcome challenges with resilience.

Evan
Meaning and Origin: Youth (Welsh)
Significance: This name represents youth, grace, and vigor. Evan suggests qualities of bravery, strength, and honor. Naming a child Evan can reflect a hope for him to embody these warrior-like traits, to face challenges courageously and to uphold noble values.

Everett
Meaning and Origin: Wild boar; bravery (British)
Significance: This masculine name is connected to strength, nature, and courage. Everett signifies courage, fortitude, and determination. A child named Everett can reflect a hope for him to possess these brave and resilient traits in facing life's challenges.

Felix
Meaning and Origin: Lucky; happy (Latin)
Significance: Someone who is cheerful, optimistic, and fortunate. Naming a child Felix can reflect a hope for him to lead a joyful and fulfilling life, blessed with good fortune.

Forest
Meaning and Origin: A wooded area (French)
Significance: Someone who is close to nature, at peace with themselves, and offers emotional safety.

Gael
Meaning and Origin: Father rejoices (Hebrew)
Significance: Given to someone who brings great pleasure to their father and who has strong family ties.

Garrith
Meaning and Origin: Spear; brave (British)
Significance: A physically strong and brave man who is good at using tools. Garrith suggests qualities of leadership, strength, and authority. Garrith also can reflect a hope for him to possess these commanding traits, to lead with determination and to make impactful decisions.

Grey
Meaning and Origin: Gray; wisdom (British)
Significance: This name represents wisdom, respect, and playfulness. Naming a child Grey can reflect a hope for him to embody these qualities, to grow into a person respected for his insight and understanding.

Griffon
Meaning and Origin: Strong lord (Welsh)
Significance: A royal name given as a token of respect. It also refers to nobility, courage, and strength.

Hugo
Meaning and Origin: Heart; mind; spirit (German)
Significance: Hugo represents intelligence, wisdom, and emotional depth. Naming a child Hugo can reflect a hope for him to possess these qualities, to approach life with curiosity and analytical thinking.

Hunter
Meaning and Origin: One who hunts; pursuer (British)
Significance: A powerful name for someone ambitious and relentless in their pursuit. Hunter also suggests qualities of bravery, resourcefulness, and a love for the outdoors.

Indigo
Meaning and Origin: A deep blue; an Indian dye (British)
Significance: A color of joy, like a rainbow after the rain, Indigo represents hope and beauty. This name also suggests qualities of uniqueness, creativity, and vibrancy. Naming a child Indigo can reflect a hope for them to stand out, to be creative, and to bring color and vitality to their surroundings.

Ilias
Meaning and Origin: My God is Yahweh (Hebrew)
Significance: A name that speaks of identity and suggests qualities of faith, devotion, and spiritual strength. A child named Ilias can reflect a hope for them to have a strong spiritual foundation and a deep connection to their faith.

Jasper
Meaning and Origin: Bringer of treasure (Persian)
Significance: Positive meaning with a gemstone reference. Jasper suggests qualities of value, worth, and importance. Naming a child Jasper can reflect a hope for them to be cherished and valued, bringing joy and richness to the lives of others.

Jordan
Meaning and Origin: To flow; to descend (Hebrew)
Significance: A name that instills confidence and pride. Jordan signifies fluidity, adaptability, and continuity. Naming a child Jordan can reflect a hope for them to navigate life with ease and grace, adapting to changes and overcoming obstacles smoothly.

Justin
Meaning and Origin: Just; upright; righteous (Latin)
Significance: Someone who stands firm in their beliefs and who protects justice. This name suggests qualities of righteousness, integrity, and balance. Naming a child Justin can reflect a hope for them to embody these just traits, to act with fairness and to uphold ethical standards.

Kai
Meaning and Origin: Earth; keeper of the keys (Welsh)
Significance: This name is deeply connected to the fundamental elements of joy and fulfillment in life, representing nourishment and nature.

Kingsley
Meaning and Origin: King's Meadow (British)
Significance: Kingsley suggests qualities of nobility, dignity, and grace. This name can reflect a hope for them to possess these regal traits, to carry themselves with dignity and to inspire respect.

Knox
Meaning and Origin: Round hills (Scottish)
Significance: Strong name with Scottish roots, referencing hills or hillocks. Naming a child Knox can reflect a hope for them to possess these strong traits, to stand firm in the face of challenges and to be a solid foundation for others.

Landon
Meaning and Origin: Long hill (British)
Significance: Represents grace, longevity, and endurance. Naming a child Landon can reflect a hope for them to possess these enduring traits, to navigate life with grace and to achieve lasting success.

Liam
Meaning and Origin: Protection; strong-willed warrior (Irish)
Significance: Embodies courage, determination, and a protective nature. Liam may represent warrior-like traits to stand up for what is right and to protect those they care about.

Logan
Meaning and Origin: Hollow (Scottish)
Significance: A name of inspiration, loyalty, and creativity. Naming a child Logan can represent peaceful traits and signifies appreciation for the natural world.

Lucas
Meaning and Origin: Bringer of light (Latin)
Significance: This name represents a bringer of good news and joy. Naming a child Lucas can reflect a hope for them to bring light and joy to others, illuminating the world around them.

Mason
Meaning and Origin: Stone worker (British)
Significance: An industrious name, Mason conveys thoughts of building, reliability, and strength. A child named Mason can reflect a hope for them to build and create, using their skills and talents to make a lasting impact.

Max
Meaning and Origin: Greatest (German)
Significance: A name that means greatness and suggests qualities of excellence, ambition, and high achievement. Max can also reflect a hope for them to strive for greatness and to excel in their endeavors.

Milo
Meaning and Origin: Soldier; merciful (German)
Significance: Milo is a Strong name with a possible connection to warriors and compassion.

Nash
Meaning and Origin: At the ash tree (English)
Significance: Nature-inspired name with a specific location reference. Nash connects to a cultural tradition of appreciating the natural world and its enduring beauty. It evokes images of serene landscapes and the strength of nature.

Nolan
Meaning and Origin: Champion; little noble (Irish)
Significance: Name that suggests nobility and victory, also someone who is strong-willed. Nolan connects to a cultural tradition of valor and distinction. It symbolizes the rich history and proud heritage of Ireland, often associated with warriors and leaders.

Oliver
Meaning and Origin: Olive tree (Latin)
Significance: Name with a connection to the Mediterranean. Oliver suggests qualities of peace, harmony, and resilience. The olive branch has long been a symbol of peace and reconciliation, so naming a child Oliver can reflect a hope for them to foster peace and to live harmoniously with others.

Owen
Meaning and Origin: Noble-born (Welsh)
Significance: A name to encourage youth and embrace a childlike spirit. Owen suggests qualities of bravery, nobility, and leadership.

Parker
Meaning and Origin: Park keeper (British)
Significance: This name represents an adventurous, kind spirit that enjoys the outdoors.

Presley
Meaning and Origin: Priest's Meadow (British)
Significance: This name represents priesthood and being honesty. Naming a child Presley can reflect peaceful traits and foster a serene environment around them.

Paxton
Meaning and Origin: Peace (Latin)
Significance: Sweet name with a powerful message of peace and tranquility. This name also suggests qualities of harmony, unity, and community spirit.

Quinton
Meaning and Origin: Fifth (British)
Significance: It might hold special significance for families that traditionally name children in numerical order.

Quill
Meaning and Origin: Wood; writing implement (British)
Significance: Evokes a creative and literary connection. It's a trendy choice for parents who appreciate a name with a unique sound and a subtle symbolic meaning related to writing and expression.

Reese
Meaning and Origin: Enthusiasm (Welsh)
Significance: This name suggests passion and excitement. Reese can reflect a hope for them to live life with excitement and to pursue their dreams.

Rowan
Meaning and Origin: Red-haired; rusty (Irish)
Significance: Strong, protective, and someone with a strong connection to nature. Rowan represents qualities of vibrancy, natural beauty, and connection to the earth.

Ryan
Meaning and Origin: Little king (Irish)
Significance: A positive name with great leadership potential and nobility. A child named Ryan can reflect a hope for them to lead with honor and to possess a dignified and noble character.

Ryder
Meaning and Origin: Horseman; rider (British)
Significance: Someone who is adventurous and values freedom and mastery. This name symbolizes the spirit of the medieval knights and messengers who played crucial roles in their societies.

Ryker
Meaning and Origin: Rich; powerful (Dutch)
Significance: A name that suggests strength, leadership, wealth, and success. Ryker connects to a cultural tradition of resilience and determination. It symbolizes the strength and fortitude of individuals who overcome challenges.

Saylor
Meaning and Origin: Boatman; acrobat (French)
Significance: Evokes a sense of adventure and confidence. It can also be seen as a way to express individuality with a non-traditional name.

Sebastian
Meaning and Origin: Venerable; revered (Roman)
Significance: This name celebrates respect and honor. A child named Sebastian can reflect a hope for them to be respected for their character, wisdom, and contributions.

Silas
Meaning and Origin: The woods; forest dweller (Latin)
Significance: This name suggests a connection to the outdoors, strength, and grounded ness. It is associated with the rugged beauty
of forests and the tranquility found within nature.

Skylar
Meaning and Origin: Scholar; sky (Dutch)
Significance: This name connects to a sense of limitlessness, openness, or vastness. Its unique and scholarly sound makes it a rare choice among parents seeking a name that stands out while embodying intellectual pursuits.

Spencer
Meaning and Origin: Steward; administrator (French)
Significance: It conveys a sense of responsibility, management, and possibly historical importance.

Tatum
Meaning and Origin: Homestead (British)
Significance: Tatum is often associated with the concept of home and belonging. It can symbolize a wish for the child to feel rooted and cherished in their family and community.

Travis
Meaning and Origin: Place of passage; to cross over (French)
Significance: This name suggests someone who crosses over and is perhaps adventurous or adaptable.

Troy
Meaning and Origin: Fighter; foot soldier (Gaelic)
Significance: Its Gaelic origin suggests a lineage of warriors, while its connection to the city of Troy adds a touch of legend and epic battles.

Tyler
Meaning and Origin: Tile maker (British)
Significance: It suggests a connection to craftsmanship. Naming a child Tyler can reflect a hope for them to excel in their chosen endeavors and to approach tasks with diligence.

Usher
Meaning and Origin: Doorkeeper (French)
Significance: Distinctive name with a historical connotation and potential for a sense of responsibility or leadership.

Ulf
Meaning and Origin: Wolf (Norse)
Significance: Strong and symbolic name with Viking heritage, representing power, independence, and a connection to nature.

Valor
Meaning and Origin: Worthiness; bravery (Latin)
Significance: Directly signifies bravery and courage. It can also imply a sense of worthiness and nobility.

Victor
Meaning and Origin: Conqueror (Latin)
Significance: A strong and powerful name that signifies achievement, success, and overcoming challenges.

Vincent
Meaning and Origin: Winning; conquering (Latin)
Significance: Vincent suggests victory and overcoming challenges. It is associated with individuals who conquer challenges and emerge victorious.

Walker
Meaning and Origin: One who walks; fuller (British)
Significance: This name evokes a sense of movement, exploration, and possibly a connection to a family history in the textile industry.

Wesley
Meaning: Western meadow (British)
Significance: Nature-inspired name suggesting open space and peacefulness. Wesley can reflect a hope for them to appreciate the beauty of nature and to find peace in their surroundings.

Wyatt
Meaning and Origin: Strong fighter (English)
Significance: Wyatt symbolizes resilience and courage, embodying the strength and determination needed to overcome challenges.

Xaiden
Meaning and Origin: Increase; abundance (Arabic)
Significance: A unique name that has a strong, masculine sound and promises abundance.

Xander
Meaning and Origin: Defender (Greek)
Significance: As a shortened form of Alexander, Xander inherits the connotations of strength, protection, and leadership.

Xavier
Meaning and Origin: Bright; shining (Basque)
Significance: Xavier represents Positivity, intelligence, and potential for success. Xavier is often associated with excellence and leadership. It can also symbolize a wish for the child to excel in their endeavors and to inspire others through their achievements.

Zayn
Meaning and Origin: Beauty; grace (Arabic)
Significance: Zayn connects to a cultural tradition of poetic beauty and sophistication. It is associated with qualities admired in art, literature, and personal character.

Zeke
Meaning and Origin: God strengthens (Hebrew)
Significance: This name can suggest qualities of resilience, fortitude, and spiritual empowerment. Zeke connects to a cultural tradition of faith and belief in the divine.

Trending Girls' Names

A trendy name for your baby girl can be a fun way to break from tradition and choose a name that means something to you and your partner. Whether a beautiful meaning, a reference to your favorite movie, or a name that sounds fun and classy, a trendy name can be just what you need.

Abigail
Meaning and Origin: Cause of joy (Hebrew)
Significance: Joyful and uplifting, suggesting the bearer brings happiness. This name is also associated with virtues of kindness, compassion, and nurturing qualities.

Addison
Meaning and Origin: Son of Adam (British)
Significance: Addison suggests a familial bond and connection to heritage. It can also symbolize a wish for the child to honor their
family heritage and to carry forward the values instilled by previous generations. Naming a child Addison can reflect a celebration of family lineage and continuity.

Adeline
Meaning and Origin: Nobility (German)
Significance: It is a beautiful name with a classic feel. It carries a sense of nobility, grace, and gentleness. Naming a child Adeline can reflect a hope for them to embody these refined qualities.

Adora
Meaning and Origin: Adored; worshipped (Latin)
Significance: It expresses deep love and admiration for the bearer. It can also suggest a connection to something divine or highly valued. Naming a child Adora can reflect a desire for them to be cherished and loved dearly.

Alexis
Meaning and Origin: Defender; protector (Greek)
Significance: This name suggests qualities of courage, protection, and honor. Naming a child Alexis can reflect a hope for them to embody these qualities and to stand up for what is right.

Allison
Meaning and Origin: Noble (Scottish)
Significance: Allison connects to a cultural tradition of nobility and refinement. It is associated with qualities of leadership and respect. It can also symbolize a wish for the child to navigate life's challenges with grace and to embrace their inherent nobility.

Alyssa
Meaning: Noble; light (German)
Significance: It is a beautiful and trendy name with a potentially noble or protective connotation. Alyssa suggests qualities of dignity and honor.

Amelia
Meaning and Origin: Work; industrious (German)
Significance: It conveys a sense of diligence and hard work. Naming a child Amelia can reflect a hope for them to pursue their goals with dedication and perseverance.

Angelie
Meaning and Origin: Messenger of God (French)
Significance: Its divine connotation, implying a connection to spiritual guidance and communication. It also evokes a sense of purity, purpose, and a higher calling.

Anna
Meaning and Origin: Gracea; favor (Hebrew)
Significance: It signifies favor and grace bestowed upon the bearer. Anna can also reflect a hope for them to embody gracefulness and to be blessed with favor in life.

Aria
Meaning and Origin: Air; melody (Italian)
Significance: It can be chosen for its connection to music and the arts or for its suggestion of strength and nobility. Aria can also reflect a hope for them to bring joy and music into the lives of others.

Ava
Meaning and Origin: Bird; voice (Hebrew)
Significance: It has a connection to nature and is a symbolic reference to good communication. This name can also symbolize freedom and grace.

Avery
Meaning and Origin: Ruler of the elves; wise counselor (French)
Significance: Elves in folklore are often linked to nature and possess knowledge beyond humans. This name suggests a deep connection with the natural world and intelligence.

Bella
Meaning and Origin: Beautiful (Spanish)
Significance: Simple and straightforward, this name directly conveys inner and outer beauty. Bella can also suggest qualities of elegance, charm, and aesthetic appeal.

Brianna
Meaning and Origin: Noble; high; exalted (Irish)
Significance: It has the connotations of nobility and strength. This name also suggests qualities of resilience, honor, and moral integrity.

Brooklyn
Meaning and Origin: Small stream (Dutch)
Significance: Peaceful and calm, this name makes space for creativity and dreaming. Brooklyn also connects to a cultural tradition of exploration and discovery.

Charlotte
Meaning and Origin: Free; petite (French)
Significance: Traditional yet modern, this name suggests qualities of independence, strength, and self-reliance. Naming a child Charlotte can reflect a hope for them to embody these qualities and to pursue their aspirations freely.

Chloe
Meaning and Origin: New life; growth (Greek)
Significance: It is closely linked with nature and youth. Chloe connects to a cultural tradition of fertility and vitality. It is associated with the springtime and the renewal of life.

Claire
Meaning and Origin: Bright; clear (French)
Significance: This name evokes a sense of purity, intelligence, and optimism. It suggests someone who brings light and clarity to situations.

Dallas
Meaning and Origin: Water of the valley; meadows (Scottish)
Significance: It carries a strong connection to beauty and tranquility. It is associated with landscapes of meadows and fields, symbolizing a connection to the earth and its natural rhythms.

Drew
Meaning and Origin: Wise (Welsh)
Significance: It carries a major theme of wisdom while also hinting at inner strength. Naming a child Drew can reflect a hope for them to embody these qualities and to face their challenges.

Ella
Meaning and Origin: Goddess; oak tree (Hebrew)
Significance: Timeless and elegant, this name is connected to "Goddess" which implies a sense of divinity and power. Naming a child Ella can signify a wish for her to embody qualities associated with goddesses, such as strength, wisdom, and grace.

Eloise
Meaning and Origin: Healthy; wide (French)
Significance: Unique but well-known, this name exudes strength and elegance. Eloise connects to a rich tradition of resilience and cultural diversity.

Evelyn
Meaning and Origin: Desired child (French)
Significance: It has strong connotations of inspiration and achievement. Naming a child Evelyn can reflect a hope for them to be deeply desired and loved.

Fallon
Meaning and Origin: Supremacy; leadership (Gaelic)
Significance: It evokes a sense of success, and achievement. Fallon connects to a cultural tradition of resilience and determination. It is associated with stories of leadership and fortitude. Naming a child Fallon can reflect a hope for them to possess these qualities and to influence others positively.

Freya
Meaning and Origin: Lady; noblewoman (Norse)
Significance: Freya is often associated with feminine power and strength. This name has the connotations of power, beauty, and mystery.

Grace
Meaning and Origin: Goodness; kindness (Latin)
Significance: It signifies beauty, blessing, and charm. Grace connects to a tradition of refinement and poise. It is associated with virtues of kindness, compassion, and inner beauty.

Hailey
Meaning and Origin: Hay's meadow (British)
Significance: Familiar and stylish, this name carries the feelings of peace, tranquility, and new beginnings.

Harper
Meaning and Origin: Harp player (British)
Significance: Distinct and stylish, this name conveys musicality, creativity, and harmony. Harper connects to a tradition of creativity and innovation.

Hazel
Meaning and Origin: Strength; resilience; warmth (British)
Significance: Timeless and unique, this name is an effortless blend of strength and sophistication. Hazel connects to a tradition of
strength and endurance.

Isla
Meaning and Origin: Island (Gaelic)
Significance: Simple and elegant, it evokes images of idyllic island paradises. Isla is often associated with peacefulness and harmony.

Ivy
Meaning and Origin: Resilience; steadfastness; growth (English)
Significance: With a strong connection to nature, this name also carries a sense of loyalty and commitment.

Jade
Meaning and Origin: Precious stone (British)
Significance: It carries the connotations of rarity, beauty, and strength. Jade connects to a tradition of elegance and uniqueness.

Julia
Meaning and Origin: Descended from Jupiter (Latin)
Significance: Timeless and sophisticated, this name evokes legacy, nobility, and grandeur.

Kaitlyn
Meaning and Origin: Pure (Greek)
Significance: A stylish name with strong roots. It is also associated with virtues of integrity, kindness, and compassion.

Kayla
Meaning and Origin: Crown of laurels (Hebrew)
Significance: It symbolizes victory, achievement, and honor. Kayla connects to a tradition of resilience and determination. It is also associated with virtues of strength, courage, and leadership.

Kaylee
Meaning and Origin: Meadow (British)
Significance: Cheerful and friendly, this name has a deep connection to nature and purity. Kaylee also connects to a tradition of strength and resilience. It is associated with virtues of integrity, kindness, and compassion.

Kylie
Meaning and Origin: Graceful; beautiful (Irish)
Significance: Charming yet resilient, this name carries grace along with deep strength. Kylie can reflect a hope for them to embody these graceful qualities in their character and actions.

Lauren
Meaning and Origin: Victory (Latin)
Significance: Strength and elegance combine in this name to assure victory and success.

Layla
Meaning and Origin: Night beauty (Arabic)
Significance: Tied to ancient poems of love, this name brings a history of romance few names can match.

Lillian
Meaning and Origin: Peace; tranquility (Latin)
Significance: This name is delicate and graceful. Lillian connects to a tradition of grace and elegance. It is also associated with virtues of kindness, compassion, and inner strength.

Lily
Meaning and Origin: Purity; innocence (Latin)
Significance: Wholesome and good with connotations of simplistic elegance. Lily connects to a tradition of beauty and elegance. It is also associated with virtues of grace, charm, and inner peace.

Lucy
Meaning and Origin: Light bringer (Latin)
Significance: Representing light, this name brings strength, independence, and cheerfulness to all she does.

Madison
Meaning and Origin: Son of Matthew (British)
Significance: This name conveys a sense of righteousness and strength while being modern and stylish.

Malia
Meaning and Origin: Calm; serene (Hawaiian)
Significance: Peaceful and strong, it is connected to the tranquility and beauty of nature. Naming a child Malia can reflect a hope for them to embody these peaceful qualities.

Maya
Meaning and Origin: Illusion; magic (Sanskrit)
Significance: Mysterious and strong. It has a depth and richness that makes her shine.

McKenzie
Meaning: Strength; bravery (Scottish)
Significance: A modern name with deep historical roots. It means strong and independent. Its strong and spirited sound makes it a popular choice among parents seeking a name that is both distinctive and meaningful.

Mia
Meaning and Origin: Of the sea (Italian)
Significance: With a strong connection to the sea, this name is strong and untamable.

Mila
Meaning and Origin: Gracious; dear (Slavic)
Significance: Someone who is kind, affectionate, loving, and cherishes those around her.

Morgan
Meaning and Origin: Guardian of the sea (Welsh)
Significance: Wild and strong. Someone who is fiercely protective of those they love.

Natalie
Meaning and Origin: Christmas; the day of birth (Latin)
Significance: Bringing celebration and joy, this name has a classic beauty that never fades.

Nora
Meaning and Origin: Honor; light (Irish)
Significance: A shining light to those around. Someone who carries hope with her wherever she goes.

Oakley
Meaning and Origin: Oak tree meadow (British)
Significance: It means persevering through any challenge and conveys deep inner strength.

Olivia
Meaning and Origin: Olive tree; peace (Latin)
Significance: A symbol of peace. Someone always gracious and steady. Its soft and melodious sound makes it a popular choice among parents.

Paislee
Meaning and Origin: Patterned fabric (Scottish)
Significance: This name embodies someone colorful, bright, and connected to Scottish heritage.

Penelope
Meaning and Origin: Weaver (Greek)
Significance: Loyal and patient, this name means intelligence, patience, and creativity. Naming a child Penelope can reflect a hope for them to embody these qualities in their endeavors.

Peyton
Meaning and Origin: Warrior's domain (British)
Significance: Determined to see their way. Someone who is both strong-willed and charming.

Quinn
Meaning and Origin: Wise (Irish)
Significance: Intelligent and wise, this person is a strong and capable leader. It is associated with virtues of courage, independence, and resilience.

Riley
Meaning and Origin: Rye clearing; rye meadow (Old English)
Significance: Symbolizing new life, this name has connotations of bravery and energy.

Ruby
Meaning and Origin: The red gemstone (Latin)
Significance: A classic name linked to health, wealth, and success in love. Its bold and vibrant sound makes it a popular choice among parents.

Rory
Meaning and Origin: Red king (Irish)
Significance: This name represents strength, power, and a fiery spirit. Rory is also often associated with leadership and power.

Savannah
Meaning and Origin: Treeless plain (Spanish)
Significance: With a deep connection to nature, this name is elegant and charming. A child named Savannah can reflect a hope for them to embody these qualities and to appreciate the beauty of nature.

Scarlett
Meaning and Origin: Red; luxury (English)
Significance: Scarlett represents passion, boldness and someone who has a strong zest for life.

Stella
Meaning and Origin: Star (Latin)
Significance: Stella symbolizes brilliance, guidance, and hope. Naming a child Stella can reflect a hope for them to shine brightly and to be a source of inspiration.

Sydney
Meaning and Origin: From Saint-Denis (French)
Significance: Sydney, originating from Saint-Denis, a city north of Paris, is full of enthusiasm and vitality. Naming your child Sydney can signify one who stands firm on their beliefs without compromise.

Tate
Meaning and Origin: Cheerful (Norse)
Significance: This person is optimistic and cheerful while also being incredibly determined.

Taylor
Meaning and Origin: One who cuts (French)
Significance: With strong connotations of creativity and skill, this name means resourcefulness and easy adaptability under pressure.

Trinity
Meaning and Origin: Triad; three (Latin)
Significance: Deeply connected to the Christian faith, this name means devotion and balance.

Uma
Meaning and Origin: Splendor; tranquility; fame (Sanskrit)
Significance: A shining star, this person can maintain peace in all circumstances.

Valeria
Meaning and Origin: Strong; healthy (Latin)
Significance: A noble name with ancient roots, this name is a symbol of feminine strength.

Valkyrie
Meaning and Origin: Chooser of the slain (Norse)
Significance: Linked to Norse mythology. This person is a noble and brave warrior.

Violet
Meaning and Origin: Purple flower (Latin)
Significance: Violet is directly derived from the name of the flower, symbolizing beauty, creativity, and grace. Naming a child Violet can reflect a hope for them to embody these qualities and to bring elegance and charm into their surroundings.

Winter
Meaning and Origin: The coldest season (British)
Significance: Direct and bold. This person is unphased by any challenge they face.

Waverly
Meaning and Origin: Meadow of quivering aspens (British)
Significance: This name has connotations of openness and freshness with a strong connection to nature.

Wynn
Meaning and Origin: Joy; delight (British)
Significance: Always looking on the bright side, this person shares their positivity and cheer with everyone they meet.

Xavia
Meaning and Origin: New house; bright (Basque)
Significance: Representing new possibilities, this name is a reminder of the hope for a brighter future.

Xia
Meaning and Origin: Dawn; glow of sunrise (Chinese)
Significance: Delicate and beautiful, this name represents a fresh start. Xia also connects to a tradition of beauty, nature, and cultural richness.

Yasmin
Meaning and Origin: Jasmine flower (Persian)
Significance: Sweet and innocent. A delicate beauty, full of innocence and purity. Naming a child Yasmin can reflect a hope for them to embody these qualities and to bring joy and beauty into their surroundings.

Yvette
Meaning and Origin: Yew tree (French)
Significance: Elegant and mysterious, this person adapts quickly when faced with difficulty.

Zoe
Meaning and Origin: Life (Greek)
Significance: It embodies energy and dynamism, representing hope, growth, and potential.

These trendy names are fun, popular, and sure to stand the test of time, but if you're looking for something less adventurous and more common and classic, the next chapter is for you. There, we'll explore the most common names that are still pretty and not snooze-worthy. I'll catch you in the next chapter!

CHAPTER 2: MOST POPULAR NAMES

Giving your baby a popular name isn't a bad thing. In a sea of people looking for the most unique name, I bet there are many children out there who would prefer a basic name instead. One of my best friends from school had a name so unique that she often lied about it at camps or parties. She always explains it like this: It takes so much courage and energy to explain my name to others, just for them to laugh or make fun of it, that it's really not worth it. So, instead of explaining her name, she would introduce herself as Sarah or Michelle, which needed no explanation. If you're looking for a popular name that you know would still be beautiful and timeless in 30 years, this is the list for you.

Most Popular Boys' Names

These evergreen choices for boys' names are safe options to ensure your child's name is timeless. They are familiar and often cherished by others due to their prevalence. So, if you want your baby boy to be able to find his name on a keychain at a gift shop, these names should do the trick!

Alexander
Meaning and Origin: Defender of men (Greek)
Significance: From the Greek Alexandros, this name was given to the god Paris as a nickname when he defended shepherds' flocks against thieves.

Andrew
Meaning and Origin: Strong; manly; courageous (Greek)
Significance: Indicative of a confident, upstanding individual. Andrew is also associated with virtues of bravery, leadership, and resilience.

Anthony
Meaning and Origin: Flower (Greek)
Significance: Originated from an ancient Greek name Antonios which meaning flower.

Arthur
Meaning and Origin: Bear (English)
Significance: Indicates someone who is strong, sturdy, and can hold their own. Naming a child Arthur can reflect a hope for them to embody strength and nobility.

Ashton
Meaning and Origin: Ash tree town (English)
Significance: Ashton is of English origin and signify greatness and growth. Ashton represents a connection to nature.

Benjamin
Meaning and Origin: Son of the right hand (Hebrew)
Significance: Someone who is a beloved son. It is often associated with strength. Naming a child Benjamin, wishes for their child to embody strength, cultural heritage, loyalty, and a name that resonates with favor and blessing.

Brandon
Meaning and Origin: Beacon-topped hill (English)
Significance: A shining light of direction and protection.

Brady
Meaning and Origin: Spirited (Irish)
Significance: Brady signifies vitality and heritage. Brady also represents energy and enthusiasm.

Brody
Meaning and Origin: Ditch; muddy place (Irish)
Significance: It suggests a strong and perhaps adventurous spirit. Brody can reflect resilience and the capability of thriving even in challenging conditions.

Cameron
Meaning and Origin: Crooked nose (Scottish)
Significance: Indicates a rugged, outdoorsy characteristic. Naming a child Cameron can reflect a hope for them to embrace their unique qualities and to stand out.

Caleb
Meaning and Origin: Faithful; loyal (Hebrew)
Significance: It can suggest strength and the ability to guard loved ones with fierce loyalty.

Chance
Meaning and Origin: Good fortune (French)
Significance: Chance is of French origin and convey a sense of adventure and luck. Chase signifies pursuit and determination.

Charlie
Meaning and Origin: Free man (English)
Significance: Short for Charles, it often refers to someone with a good sense of humor and an easy nature.

Connor
Meaning and Origin: Lover of hounds; wise (Irish)
Significance: Emphasizes loyalty and a strong connection with animals, as well as bravery.

Cooper
Meaning and Origin: Barrel maker (English)
Significance: Cooper is of English origin and are occupational surnames, reflecting industriousness and skill. Cooper evokes images of craftsmanship and hard work.

Derek
Meaning and Origin: Ruler of the people (German)
Significance: Derek signifies leadership and courage. Derek also represents authority and protection.

Dustin
Meaning and Origin: Brave warrior (English)
Significance: Dustin shows leadership, strength and courage, while representing bravery and resilience.

Dylan
Meaning and Origin: Sea (Welsh)
Significance: A strong connection to the ocean and its vastness, possibly suggesting a free spirit or adventurous nature.

Dominic
Meaning and Origin: Successor; heir (Latin)
Significance: Implies someone lordly or sovereign, hinting at strength and nobility.

Diego
Meaning and Origin: Agile; quick; teachable (Spanish)
Significance: Someone who is quick-witted, adaptable, and eager to learn. Naming a child Diego can reflect a hope for them to be adaptable and resourceful.

Dante
Meaning and Origin: Enduring; steadfast; everlasting (Latin)
Significance: This name's core meaning emphasizes strength, resilience, and the ability to withstand challenges.

Edward
Meaning and Origin: Wealthy protector; guardian of riches (British)
Significance: Traditionally associated with royalty and aristocracy, this name suggests a sense of strength, leadership, and nobility.

Edgar
Meaning and Origin: A wealthy spearman (British)
Significance: The spear is a weapon associated with warriors and defense. This name suggests a strong and protective nature.

Elliot
Meaning and Origin: Noble (British)
Significance: It signifies faith in a higher power or a noble lineage. Elliot connects to a tradition of wisdom, faith, and cultural richness. It is also associated with virtues of belief, guidance, and resilience.

Eric
Meaning and Origin: Eternal ruler (Norse)
Significance: It carries a strong connotation of leadership and lasting power. Its robust name makes it a popular choice among parents.

Ethan
Meaning and Origin: Strong (Hebrew)
Significance: Ethan connects to a tradition of wisdom, faith, and cultural richness. It is associated with virtues of strength, reliability, and resilience.

Evan
Meaning and Origin: God is gracious (Welsh)
Significance: Evan suggests grace. Evan is often associated with grace and kindness. It can symbolize a wish for the child to be compassionate and to bring goodness into the lives of others.

Finley
Meaning and Origin: Fair hero (Irish)
Significance: Finley is often associated with heroism and fairness. It can symbolize a wish for the child to act with integrity and to inspire others through their courageous actions.

Francis
Meaning and Origin: Free one (Latin)
Significance: Its core meaning suggests independence and individuality. Francis is often associated with freedom and nobility. It can symbolize a wish for the child to live an independent and honorable life, free to pursue their dreams.

Franklin
Meaning and Origin: Free landholder (British)
Significance: The meaning directly connects owning land freely, suggesting a spirit of independence and self-sufficiency.

Frederick
Meaning and Origin: Peaceful ruler (German)
Significance: The meaning suggests the qualities of a strong and just leader who prioritizes peace.

George
Meaning and Origin: Farmer; earth-worker (Greek)
Significance: Suggests qualities like strength, perseverance, and dedication. George is often associated with diligence and hard work. It can symbolize a wish for the child to approach life with commitment and to contribute positively to their community.

Gilbert
Meaning and Origin: Bright pledge (German)
Significance: The meaning "bright pledge" suggests trustworthiness and keeping one's word.

Grant
Meaning and Origin: High; great (French)
Significance: Conveys a sense of achievement, nobility, and potential for greatness. Grant is often associated with ambition and achievement. It can symbolize a wish for the child to pursue their dreams boldly and to strive for excellence in all they do.

Grayson
Meaning and Origin: Son of the steward (English)
Significance: Grayson conveys nobility and strength, while representing responsibility and honor.

Gregory
Meaning and Origin: Watchful; awake (Greek)
Significance: This name Suggests qualities of alertness, protectiveness, and being aware. Gregory is also often associated with wisdom and intellect, while symbolizing a wish for the child to seek knowledge and to approach life with discernment.

Harrison
Meaning and Origin: Son of the ruler (British)
Significance: It suggests legacy, leadership, and power. Harrison is often associated with family and lineage. It also can symbolize a wish for the child to honor their roots and to cherish the bonds of family.

Harvey
Meaning and Origin: Battle-worthy (French)
Significance: Its core meaning evokes courage, resilience, and the ability to overcome challenges.

Henry
Meaning and Origin: House ruler (German)
Significance: Someone who takes charge and commands respect within their domain. Henry can also symbolize a wish for the child to lead with compassion and to inspire others through their actions.

Hudson
Meaning and Origin: Son of Hugh (British)
Significance: This name carries a sense of honoring one's heritage, particularly the father's side of the family.

Idris
Meaning and Origin: Fiery; element (Welsh)
Significance: In Welsh legends, this name is associated with learning and wisdom. It can symbolize a wish for the child to pursue learning and to excel in their academic or professional endeavors.

Jackson
Meaning and Origin: Son of Jack (British)
Significance: This is a classic example of a patronymic surname, meaning it originated as a way to identify someone as the son of someone else.

Jaden
Meaning and Origin: Flowing down (Hebrew)
Significance: Jaden is of Hebrew origin and convey a sense of gratitude and fluidity. Jaden also represents thankfulness.

Jensen
Meaning and Origin: Son of Jens (Danish)
Significance: The patronymic meaning signifies a connection to family heritage.

Juan
Meaning and Origin: Gift from above (Spanish)
Significance: Signifies a blessing and someone who has a lot of faith. Juan can also be associated with virtues of compassion and generosity.

Kennedy
Meaning and Origin: Chieftain with a helmet (Irish)
Significance: The name suggests strength, leadership qualities, and potential protection.

Kevin
Meaning and Origin: Beautiful; gentle and Origin (Irish)
Significance: A positive and complimentary name that signifies beauty and gentleness in character.

Kyle
Meaning and Origin: Narrow place; body of water (Scottish)
Significance: Evokes a connection to nature, particularly rivers or coastal areas. Naming a child Kyle can reflect a connection to nature.

Leonardo
Meaning and Origin: Lion-hearted; bold as a lion (German)
Significance: The association with lions implies bravery, strength, and leadership qualities.

Lincoln
Meaning and Origin: From the place by the pool ?(British)
Significance: Evokes a sense of leadership, integrity, and dedication to freedom.

Lorenzo
Meaning and Origin: Laurel (Latin)
Significance: The laurel wreath symbolized victory in ancient Rome, so this name suggests success and accomplishment.

Liam
Meaning and Origin: Strong-willed warrior (Irish)
Significance: Liam signifies strength and courage, while representing determination and warrior spirit.

Louis
Meaning and Origin: Famous warrior (German)
Significance: The meaning directly connects to a warrior, suggesting courage and valor.

Lucas
Meaning and Origin: Bringer of light (Italy)
Significance: A positive and hopeful name, suggesting the child will bring joy and illumination to the world.

Martin
Meaning and Origin: Martial; war-like (Latin)
Significance: The association with Mars suggests bravery and a warrior spirit. It is also associated with virtues of courage, resilience, and integrity.

Malcolm
Meaning and Origin: Devotee of Saint Columba (Scottish)
Significance: A name that represents pride and someone who entertains. It can symbolize a wish for the child to uphold principles of honor and to lead by example.

Maxwell
Meaning and Origin: Great well; mighty spring (Scottish)
Significance: Its meaning suggests qualities like strength, stability, and the ability to become a source of life or abundance.

Miles
Meaning and Origin: Soldier (English)
Significance: Miles signify strength and valor while representing courage and determination.

Muhammad
Meaning and Origin: Praiseworthy (Arabic)
Significance: Muhammad signifies someone commendable, admirable, and deserving of praise.

Myles
Meaning and Origin: Soldier; warrior (Latin)
Significance: Due to its connection to "soldier," this name suggests strength, bravery, and a fighting spirit.

Nathan
Meaning and Origin: He gave (Hebrew)
Significance: Nathan conveys a sense of generosity and heroism, while representing giving and benevolence.

Neil
Meaning and Origin: Champion; cloud (Irish)
Significance: The name suggests strength, determination, and a fighting spirit. Naming a child Neil can reflect a hope for them to embody qualities of strength and fervor.

Nelson
Meaning and Origin: Son of Neil; victorious (British)
Significance: It suggests "champion" and represents strength, victory, and achievement.

Nico
Meaning and Origin: Perseverance; to conquer (French)
Significance: The various meanings associated with this name carry positive messages of victory, perseverance, and success.

Oscar
Meaning and Origin: Champion warrior (Irish)
Significance: A sense of strength, bravery, and potential success. It can symbolize a wish for the child to face challenges boldly and to defend what they believe in.

Oswald
Meaning and Origin: Divine ruler (British)
Significance: A strong religious connection and leadership qualities. Oswald is also often associated with authority and divine guidance.

Patrick
Meaning and Origin: Nobleman (Latin)
Significance: Carries a strong connotation of nobility and social standing due to its Latin roots coming from the word "patrician."

Peter
Meaning and Origin: Rock; stone (Greek)
Significance: The meaning itself suggests a solid and dependable nature. It can symbolize a wish for the child to face challenges with resilience and to provide a stable foundation for others.

Philip
Meaning and Origin: Lover of horses (Greek)
Significance: Horses are often associated with strength, freedom, and nobility.

Richard
Meaning and Origin: Strong in rule (German)
Significance: The meaning directly conveys power, leadership, and potential to rule. Richard is often associated with authority. It can also symbolize a wish for the child to lead with integrity and to inspire others through their actions.

Robert
Meaning and Origin: Bright fame; shining glory (German)
Significance: The meaning suggests a potential to be great, to achieve success, and to leave a lasting mark.

Romeo
Meaning and Origin: Pilgrim (Italian)
Significance: Strongly tied to Shakespeare's tragic love story, this name signifies passion and romance.

Russell
Meaning and Origin: Red-haired (French)
Significance: It literally means red hair, but it can also speak of passion or someone who is feisty.

Sawyer
Meaning and Origin: Woodcutter (British)
Significance: Connects the bearer to a specific historical trade, suggesting a strong work ethic and connection to craftsmanship.

Sean
Meaning and Origin: God is gracious (Irish)
Significance: Sean is of Irish origin and convey a sense of divine favor. Sean signifies kindness and grace.

Seth
Meaning and Origin: Appointed; placed (Hebrew)
Significance: Seth is often associated with purpose and destiny. It can symbolize a wish for the child to embrace their unique path in life and to make a positive impact on others.

Spencer
Meaning and Origin: Steward; dispenser of provisions (French)
Significance: It can be associated with dependability, organization, and resourcefulness.

Sterling
Meaning and Origin: high quality; genuine (British)
Significance: The primary meaning directly suggests something of excellent quality, high price, or value.

Tanner
Meaning and Origin: Leatherworker (British)
Significance: Connects the bearer to a skilled trade and a practical approach to life.

Theodore
Meaning and Origin: Gift (Greek)
Significance: Suggests someone who is a gift to others and embodies positive qualities.

Trevor
Meaning and Origin: Large village (Welsh)
Significance: Trevor signifies industriousness and community. Trevor also represents nobility and tradition.

Tristan
Meaning and Origin: Tumult (Celtic)
Significance: Tristan signifies strength and resilience, while representing adventure and romanticism.

Tucker
Meaning and Origin: Fuller of cloth (British)
Significance: Evokes a sense of practicality and a connection to skilled trades. Naming a child Tucker can reflect a connection to craftsmanship or a wish for them to embody qualities of diligence and skill.

Tyson
Meaning and Origin: Firebrand (French)
Significance: The name has a strong and modern sound, making it a popular choice for parents.

Vaughn
Meaning and Origin: Small harbor; dweller (Welsh)
Significance: Harbors can represent safe havens, potentially signifying a sense of security and resilience.

Vikram
Meaning and Origin: Valorous (Hindi)
Significance: Its core emphasizes courage and heroism.

Walter
Meaning and Origin: Army commander; ruler (German)
Significance: Its meaning directly suggests qualities like leadership, authority, and strength.

Warren
Meaning and Origin: Guard (English)
Significance: Warren is of English origin and convey a sense of protection and tranquility. Warren signifies defense and strength.

William
Meaning and Origin: Determined guardian (German)
Significance: The meaning conveys a sense of safety, reliability, and the ability to become a dependable guardian.

Winston
Meaning and Origin: Joyful stone (British)
Significance: Stones are often seen as symbols of strength and stability, which the name can also convey, along with a happy and optimistic disposition.

Most Popular Girls' Names

We all know a Chloe or Rachel; these names are just so classic yet timeless. Many names are popular and common yet still carry loads of charm and sound like they are given to someone who is beautiful and has their life sorted out. These names are popular for a reason, so if you don't want your little girl to have a name so unique she only learns how to spell it in the third grade, choosing one from this list is the way forward for you.

Abby
Meaning and Origin: My father is joy (Hebrew)
Significance: Abby comes from Abigail, and it is known for her wisdom and beauty in the Hebrew Bible, becoming the wife of King David.

Alice
Meaning and Origin: Noble; kind (British)
Significance: Alice signifies high moral qualities, dignity, and integrity. Naming a child Alice can reflect a wish for her to embody these esteemed qualities, aspiring to live a life marked by honor and virtue.

Amanda
Meaning and Origin: Worthy of love (Latin)
Significance: Amanda conveys endearment and admiration. Naming a child Amanda can signify a wish for her to always feel cherished and valued, recognizing her innate worth and the love she deserves.

Anastasia
Meaning and Origin: Resurrection (Greek)
Significance: Beautiful name with a strong meaning, signifying rebirth or a new beginning.

Ariel
Meaning and Origin: Lion of God (Hebrew)
Significance: It suggests strength and bravery. Naming a child Ariel can reflect a wish for them to possess both physical and spiritual strength, embodying courage, leadership, and protection.

Audrey
Meaning and Origin: Wise ruler; noble strength (British)
Significance: Its meaning suggests qualities like leadership, power, and a sense of fairness.

Autumn
Meaning and Origin: Season of fall (British)
Significance: Named after the fall season, Autumn symbolizes the beauty of nature's transformation. It evokes images of vibrant foliage, a sense of change and renewal.

Bailey
Meaning and Origin: Court official (French)
Significance: The connection to a bailiff suggests a capable and authoritative figure.

Bianca
Meaning and Origin: White; fair (Italian)
Significance: Its meaning potentially evokes a sense of purity, goodness, and virtue.

Bonnie
Meaning and Origin: Pretty; beautiful (Scottish)
Significance: Primarily associated with beauty and pleasantness. This may highlight a desire for your child to possess physical beauty as well as inner charm and grace.

Beatrice
Meaning and Origin: Blessed; bringer of happiness (Latin)
Significance: Beatrice is often associated with joy and blessings. It can symbolize a wish for the child to spread happiness and to live a life filled with grace and positivity.

Brittany
Meaning and Origin: Region in France (French)
Significance: The name Brittany signifies a connection to this historical and cultural region. It reflects a sense of heritage and place, often associated with Celtic traditions and coastal beauty.

Camila
Meaning and Origin: Noble youth (Latin)
Significance: It is an elegant name with historical connotations and a suggestion of nobility.

Caroline
Meaning and Origin: Free man (German)
Significance: A popular choice for girls, suggesting independence and strength. Naming a child Caroline can reflect a desire for her to embody strength of character and the ability to make her own choices.

Casey
Meaning and Origin: Vigilant (Irish)
Significance: It suggests a sense of alertness and attentiveness. Naming a child Casey can reflect a desire for them to be aware of their surroundings, thoughtful in their actions, and protective of others.

Clara
Meaning and Origin: Clear; bright; famous (Latin)
Significance: Classic and positive name suggesting clarity, intelligence, and potential fame.

Cleo
Meaning and Origin: Glory; fame (Greek)
Significance: Classic name with a strong and glamorous connotation (due to its association with Cleopatra, a famous queen). It suggests achievement, recognition, and possibly a bit of regality.

Daphne
Meaning and Origin: Laurel tree (Greek)
Significance: Represents a connection to nature and the beauty of the laurel tree. In Greek mythology, laurel wreaths were symbols
of victory and achievement.

Delilah
Meaning and Origin: Delicate; languishing (Hebrew)
Significance: Its meaning of "delicate" suggests a connection to beauty and feminine charm.

Demi
Meaning and Origin: Half (Greek)
Significance: Its meaning of "half" can add a touch of intrigue or suggest a multifaceted personality.

Diana
Meaning and Origin: Divine; heavenly; huntress (Roman)
Significance: Diana is the Roman goddess of the hunt, the moon, and the wilderness. This association imbues the name with a sense of strength, independence, and connection to nature.

Elena
Meaning and Origin: Shining light (Greek)
Significance: It carries a beautiful meaning, suggesting someone who is radiant, illuminating, and brings light to others.

Eliza
Meaning and Origin: Oath to God (Hebrew)
Significance: Eliza suggests a divine promise or commitment. Naming a child Eliza can reflect a hope for her to embody faithfulness, trustworthiness, and a strong connection to spirituality.

Emma
Meaning and Origin: Whole; universal (German)
Significance: Strong and meaningful, suggesting a sense of completeness and inclusivity. Naming a child Emma can reflect a desire for her to possess a well-rounded personality, embracing all aspects of life.

Emily
Meaning and Origin: Rival (Latin)
Significance: Emily meaning "rival" suggesting a strong and determined personality.

Felicity
Meaning and Origin: Happiness; good fortune (Latin)
Significance: A virtuous name that directly refers to a positive quality. It conveys a wish for happiness and good luck for the bearer.

Fiona
Meaning and Origin: Fair; white (Scottish)
Significance: A beautiful name with a connection to purity. Fiona also represents a sense of fairness and justice.

Florence
Meaning and Origin: From Florence (Italian)
Significance: It refers to the beautiful city of Florence in Italy, known for its Renaissance art and architecture. This name evokes a sense of history, culture, and beauty.

Francesca
Meaning and Origin: French man (Italian)
Significance: This name signifies beauty and sophistication. Francesca also reflects a sense of elegance, and artistic flair often associated with France.

Gabby
Meaning and Origin: God is my strength (Hebrew)
Significance: Gabby comes from Gabrielle, representing its divine strength and support, with Gabriel being an archangel appearing in the books of Daniel and Luke.

Gale
Meaning and Origin: Strong; wind (British)
Significance: A powerful name with a direct link to the natural world, specifically strong winds. It can evoke a sense of adventure, strength, and independence.

Georgia
Meaning and Origin: Worker of the earth (Greek)
Significance: Its meaning suggests hard work, dedication, and a connection to the land.

Gracie
Meaning and Origin: Grace (British)
Significance: A familiar and affectionate form of the name Grace, signifying the virtue of gracefulness, elegance, and beauty.

Gwen
Meaning and Origin: Blessed; holy (Welsh)
Significance: The Welsh meaning of this name suggests fairness and beauty, creating a connection to purity and innocence.

Harmony
Meaning and Origin: Concord; agreement; a pleasing arrangement (Greek)
Significance: Harmony signifies peace, balance, and cooperation. It suggests someone who strives for unity and creates a sense of calm.

Helen
Meaning and Origin: Torch; bright shining (Greek)
Significance: Helen suggests a sense of illumination and clarity. Naming a child Helen can reflect a hope for her to bring light and positivity into the world, to be a guiding beacon for others.

Holly
Meaning and Origin: Plant with red berries (British)
Significance: Symbolizes resilience and hope as the holly plant thrives during winter.

Hope
Meaning and Origin: A feeling of expectation and desire for a positive future or a better outcome (British)
Significance: A straightforward name that directly conveys a hopeful and optimistic outlook on life.

Irene
Meaning and Origin: Peace (Greek)
Significance: Irene is often associated with harmony and unity. It can symbolize a wish for the child to promote peace and understanding in their interactions with others.

Iris
Meaning and Origin: Rainbow (Greek)
Significance: Choosing this name evokes a connection to beauty, communication, and connection between the divine and human realms.

Ida
Meaning and Origin: Mountain; worker (German)
Significance: It can represent strength, stability, and a connection to nature, similar to a mountain.

Jamie
Meaning and Origin: Supplanter (Scottish)
Significance: Traditionally used as a boy's name but increasingly popular for girls in recent times.

Jasmin
Meaning and Origin: From the Jasmin flower (Persian)
Significance: Named after the jasmine flower, Jasmin symbolizes beauty, grace, and elegance. It evokes images of delicate blossoms with a sweet and enchanting fragrance.

Jocelyn
Meaning and Origin: Joyous (German)
Significance: Jocelyn conveys joy and vitality. Jocelyn also represents happiness and delight.

June
Meaning and Origin: Juno (Roman)
Significance: Linked to Juno, this name suggests qualities associated with the goddess, like marriage, family, and women's issues.

Juliette
Meaning and Origin: Youthful (French)
Significance: Strongly linked to the famous Shakespearean character Juliet from "Romeo and Juliet," evoking a sense of romance, passion, and possibly tragedy.

Kate
Meaning and Origin: Pure; clean (Greek)
Significance: It can be seen as a strong and independent name due to its short and direct form.

Katherine
Meaning and Origin: Pure (Greek)
Significance: Associated with innocence, cleanliness, and moral integrity. Naming a child Katherine can reflect a desire for her to embody these qualities, aspiring to lead a life marked by honesty and virtue.

Kelly
Meaning and Origin: Bright-headed; warlike (Irish)
Significance: Kelly suggests a sense of strength, courage, and resilience. Naming a child Kelly can reflect a desire for them to possess these qualities, to face challenges bravely, and to protect others.

Kelsey
Meaning and Origin: Island of the ships (English)
Significance: Kelsey signifies uniqueness and resilience. Kelsey also represents adaptability and strength.

Khloe
Meaning and Origin: Blooming; victorious (Greek)
Significance: This name is a relatively recent invention, rising in popularity in the late 20th century. It offers a fresh and contemporary feel.

Lana
Meaning and Origin: Gentle; soft; tender (Arabic)
Significance: Its meanings of "gentle" and "bright" suggest positive qualities. It also symbolizes charm, beauty, and inner peace.

Laura
Meaning and Origin: Triumph; victory (Latin)
Significance: Classic and enduring name with a positive connotation of success and achievement.

Lilah
Meaning: Night; darkness (Arabic)
Significance: Its association with night can suggest peacefulness, tranquility, and beauty (like the starry night sky).

Lydia
Meaning and Origin: Lydian woman (Greek)
Significance: Lydia refers to an ancient kingdom in Asia Minor. Choosing this name suggests a connection to history and a specific region.

Margaret
Meaning and Origin: Pearl (Greek)
Significance: "Pearl" suggests beauty, rarity, and value. It's a lovely name for someone considered precious.

Melanie
Meaning and Origin: Black; dark (Greek)
Significance: While its literal meaning is "black" or "dark," the color black can hold various connotations depending on the context. In ancient Greece, it could not only represent mourning or death but also fertility and protection against evil spirits.

Melody
Meaning and Origin: Song (Greek)
Significance: Directly connects to music and the beauty of songs, which evokes a sense of sweetness, harmony, and creativity.

Miley
Meaning and Origin: Proud chief (Irish)
Significance: Miley signifies leadership and dignity. Naming a child Miley can reflect a hope for her to bring joy and positivity to those around her.

Millie
Meaning and Origin: Work; gentle strength (Latin)
Significance: Millie is often associated with gentle strength and diligence. It can symbolize a wish for the child to approach challenges with resilience and to excel in their endeavors.

Miranda
Meaning and Origin: Admirable; wonderful (Latin)
Significance: Miranda is popularized by Shakespeare's "The Tempest," signifies someone worthy of admiration and amazement.

Nadia
Meaning and Origin: Hope (Russian)
Significance: It has a strong and positive connotation, suggesting optimism and a hopeful outlook on life.

Nancy
Meaning and Origin: Favor; grace (British)
Significance: Nancy signifies "Favor" which suggests someone who is blessed or well-regarded.

Nicole
Meaning and Origin: Victory of the people (French)
Significance: Its meaning "victory of the people" suggests strength achieved through collective effort.

Nina
Meaning and Origin: Little girl (Spanish)
Significance: This is a versatile name with a sweet and delicate feel due to its meaning of "little girl" in some interpretations.

Octavia
Meaning and Origin: Eight (Latin)
Significance: A Roman name derived from the Latin word "octavus," meaning "eighth." It was traditionally given to the eighth-born child in a family.

Odette
Meaning and Origin: Wealthy arrow; defender's wealth (German)
Significance: The potential meaning of "wealthy arrow" suggests a connection to wealth and possibly protection or strength.

Paula
Meaning and Origin: Small; humble (Latin)
Significance: Its meaning of "small" or "humble" suggests a connection to modesty and simplicity.

Penny
Meaning and Origin: Weaver (British)
Significance: As a diminutive of Penelope, this name carries some of the mythological significance of the name that was given to the faithful wife who waited for Odysseus' return.

Phoebe
Meaning and Origin: Radiant; pure; shining (Greek)
Significance: Its primary meaning suggests qualities of radiance, brightness, and purity.

Polly
Meaning and Origin: Star of the sea (Latin)
Significance: A Friendly and informal name, suggesting approachability and warmth.

Queenie
Meaning and Origin: Queen (British)
Significance: This name carries a strong association with royalty and suggests regality, confidence, and leadership.

Rachel
Meaning and Origin: Female sheep (Hebrew)
Significance: Rachel suggests the meaning "ewe" which means female sheep and can be interpreted as representing gentleness, nurturing, and care.

Rebecca
Meaning and Origin: To tie; snare (Hebrew)
Significance: Its meaning of "to tie" can be seen as suggesting connection, loyalty, or destiny.

Rosie
Meaning and Origin: Like a rose (British)
Significance: This name is a diminutive form of Rose, which symbolizes love, passion, and beauty.

Sadie
Meaning and Origin: Princess (Hebrew)
Significance: Sadie is often associated with grace and leadership. It can symbolize a wish for the child to lead with kindness and to inspire others through their actions.

Sophia
Meaning and Origin: Wisdom (Greek)
Significance: A classic and enduring name symbolizing intelligence, knowledge, and learning.

Summer
Meaning and Origin: The warmest season of the year (British)
Significance: A trendy and evocative name with a connection to sunshine, warmth, and growth.

Tatiana
Meaning and Origin: Arranged; ordained (Russian)
Significance: Tatiana has long been associated with princesses and nobility in Slavic nations, particularly Russia.

Tessa
Meaning and Origin: To reap; gather (Dutch)
Significance: Its meaning connects it to ideas of productivity and success, reaping the rewards of one's efforts.

Tiana
Meaning and Origin: Princess
Origin: (Latin)
Significance: This is a beautiful and versatile name with positive connotations that suggest royalty.

Uma
Meaning and Origin: Light; people; nation (Sanskrit)
Significance: A meaningful name in Sanskrit with a few possible interpretations. It can suggest inner peace and light or represent a sense of community and belonging.

Vanessa
Meaning and Origin: Butterfly (British)
Significance: Given its meaning of "butterfly," this name can be connected to nature, beauty, and change.

Vera
Meaning and Origin: Truth; faith (Latin)
Significance: Its meanings of "truth" and "faith" carry positive associations with honesty, trust, and loyalty.

Vivian
Meaning and Origin: Lively; vivacious (Latin)
Significance: This name suggests someone full of life and energy. Naming a child Vivian can reflect a hope for her to live life to the fullest, with enthusiasm and vitality.

Wendy
Meaning and Origin: Friend; white (German)
Significance: Wendy suggests a warm and inviting personality. Naming a child Wendy can reflect a hope for her to cultivate meaningful friendships and to be a loyal companion to others.

Whitney
Meaning and Origin: White Island; white meadow (British)
Significance: Possible meanings suggest a connection to nature, potentially referring to purity or innocence.

Yvonne
Meaning and Origin: Yew tree (German)
Significance: Its meaning directly connects to nature, with the yew tree being a symbol of longevity and resilience.

Zara
Meaning and Origin: Blooming; radiant (Arabic)
Significance: This name can be interpreted in various ways, offering a range of positive connotations like radiance, royalty, or a new beginning.

Zoey
Meaning and Origin: Life (Greek)
Significance: Zoey, derived from the Greek word for life, embodies liveliness and energy. Naming a child Zoey can reflect a hope for her to embrace life with energy, passion, and a zest for living.

Zola
Meaning and Origin: Earth (Italian)
Significance: It can be seen as a name that has been inspired by nature. Naming a child Zola can reflect a wish for her to have a strong grounding in life, and to be connected to her roots.

These popular names can be a fun twist to traditional names while still keeping them within certain boundaries of familiarity. In the next chapter, we'll look at names that can work for both boys and girls. So, if you want to choose a gender-neutral name, be sure to check it out!

CHAPTER 3: UNISEX NAMES

Choosing a unisex name for your child can be a way to break free from traditional expectations and offer them more freedom of expression. It allows them to explore their identity and avoid feeling confined to gender stereotypes. A unisex name can be strong and beautiful regardless of who wears it, letting your child decide what the name means to them as they grow up. It can also be a fun way to express your own unique style as a parent, choosing a name that feels special and reflects your hopes for your child's future, regardless of the path they take. So, in this chapter, let's celebrate inclusivity and individuality with names that defy traditional gender norms. Over the last decade, unisex names have become more and more popular, so some of the names on this list might sound familiar to you, while others might be a bit more out there. Regardless of what you're looking for, this list of unisex names is sure to provide exactly what you're searching for.

Acer
Meaning and Origin: Maple (Latin)
Significance: Strong and resilient, this name refers to someone unmoved by the winds of change.

Ainsley
Meaning and Origin: One's own meadow; Clearing (Scottish)
Significance: Ainsley suggests a connection to the natural world. Naming a child Ainsley can reflect a wish for her to have a serene and peaceful presence, akin to a tranquil meadow or clearing.

Albany
Meaning and Origin: White; fair (Latin)
Significance: Albany represents Purity and strength. People with this name value integrity.

Alec
Meaning and Origin: Defender of men (Greek)
Significance: Protective and strong, people with this name have an ingrained sense of loyalty.

Alex
Meaning and Origin: Defender of the people (Greek)
Significance: A name associated with strength and protection, suitable for all genders, embodying the qualities of a guardian who stands up for and safeguards others.

Amari
Meaning and Origin: Promised by God; God said (Hebrew)
Significance: Representing spiritual blessing, this person has a clear drive and ambition.

Andy
Meaning and Origin: Brave (Greek)
Significance: This person is strong yet approachable and friendly. Andy is also often associated with courage and resilience. It can symbolize a wish for the child to face challenges bravely and to persevere in difficult times.

Aqua
Meaning and Origin: Water; sea blue (Latin)
Significance: Deeply connected to water, this name represents purity, adaptability, and life.

Arin
Meaning and Origin: Enlightened; mountain of strength (Hebrew)
Significance: This person is blessed with both strength and wisdom, bringing reliability and insight.

Ash
Meaning and Origin: The ash tree (British)
Significance: Ash is derived from the name of the ash tree, known for its strength and resilience. This name has the connotation of adaptability, change, and growth.

Ashley
Meaning and Origin: Ash tree meadow (British)
Significance: Originally a surname, Ashley became a popular unisex given name, denoting nature and tranquility. It symbolizes peace and a connection to the natural world.

Aubrey
Meaning and Origin: Elf ruler (German)
Significance: Aubrey conveys leadership and mystical charm, associated with mythical beings, symbolizing a person of profound influence and enchanting qualities.

Avery
Meaning and Origin: Ruler of the elves (Old English)
Significance: Avery has medieval roots and is associated with leadership and magical beings, reflecting an enchanting and authoritative presence.

Beck
Meaning and Origin: The stream (British)
Significance: Beck is often associated with tranquility and peace. It can symbolize a wish for the child to navigate life's challenges with calmness and to appreciate the beauty of simplicity.

Bellamy
Meaning and Origin: Good friend (French)
Significance: Highlighting the importance of friendship, this name speaks of someone reliable and trustworthy.

Bevan
Meaning and Origin: Son of Evan; God is gracious (Welsh)
Significance: Originally a masculine name, it has become more popular as a unisex name in recent years. Representing grace and strong family bonds, this is a good name when looking to honor one's heritage.

Billy
Meaning and Origin: Protector; defender (German)
Significance: This name refers to someone friendly and approachable while still representing safety and security.

Blair
Meaning and Origin: Dweller on the plain (Scottish)
Significance: It refers to someone who loves the outdoors and the peace that comes with being connected to the land.

Blake
Meaning and Origin: Dark-haired; pale (British)
Significance: Due to the contrast of the possible meanings, this name contains the possibility of breaking away from expectations or holding opposing characteristics in balance.

Blaze
Meaning and Origin: Bright fire (British)
Significance: Closely linked to fire, this name refers to someone passionate and bold.

Bobbie
Meaning and Origin: Bright; fame (German)
Significance: A follower of tradition, this name holds fast to cultural heritage while remaining friendly and approachable.

Bowie
Meaning and Origin: Yellow-haired; fair-haired (Scottish)
Significance: An on-the-nose name for any child with light hair. It can pay homage to a child's heritage and family connections.

Capri
Meaning and Origin: Wild boars; goat (Italian)
Significance: Associated with the island of Capri in Italy. This island is situated in the Gulf of Naples in southern Italy. As a habitational term, it indicates someone from Capri Island.

Carson
Meaning and Origin: Son of Carr (British)
Significance: Respected and well-established, this name also has a connection to nature.

Charlie
Meaning and Origin: Free man; man of the army (German)
Significance: Its close link to freedom means that this name evokes feelings of a free spirit and a love of adventure.

Chandler
Meaning and Origin: Candlestick maker (French)
Significance: Representing skill and reliability, this person brings light wherever they go.

Chris
Meaning and Origin: Christ-bearer (Greek)
Significance: Deeply linked with the Christian faith, this name carries a sense of service to and sacrifice for others.

Corey
Meaning and Origin: Heart; inner strength (British)
Significance: This person carries strength and the ability to motivate and support others.

Dakota
Meaning and Origin: Friend; ally (Native American)
Significance: This person invokes a sense of friendship in everyone they meet. Naming a child Dakota can reflect a wish for them to embody qualities of friendship, loyalty, and camaraderie.

Dale
Meaning and Origin: Valley (British)
Significance: Dale is often associated with peaceful landscapes and the beauty of nature. It can symbolize a wish for the child to appreciate simplicity and to find harmony in life.

Darcy
Meaning and Origin: Descendant of the free man (Irish)
Significance: Firm and good, this person has deep moral strength and unwavering resolve.

Dallas
Meaning and Origin: Meadowland (Scottish)
Significance: Carrying connotations of nature and openness. This name speaks of a love for the outdoors and freedom.

Devon
Meaning and Origin: From Devonshire (British)
Significance: This name is perfect to allude to ancestry and heritage.

Dorian
Meaning and Origin: Descendant of Dorus; the sea (Greek)
Significance: Due to the connection with the Greek hero, this name speaks of the potential for greatness, achievement, and success.

Dylan
Meaning and Origin: Born from the sea (Welsh)
Significance: This person's strength comes from the ability to flow and adapt in creative ways.

Eden
Meaning and Origin: Place of delight; paradise (Hebrew)
Significance: Holding a deep spiritual connection. This name also represents peace, innocence, and beauty.

Eilian
Meaning and Origin: Second (Welsh)
Significance: A clear-cut name for a second child. This name indicates that the bearer is comfortable and content with their place in the world.

Emerson
Meaning and Origin: Child of Emery; Brave; Powerful (German)
Significance: Emerson conveys strength and bravery, derived from the German name Emery, symbolizing a lineage of courage and resilience.

Emery
Meaning and Origin: Industrious ruler; powerful worker (German)
Significance: Representing strength and diligence, this name refers to the potential of being a powerful leader.

Ezra
Meaning and Origin: Help; helper (Hebrew)
Significance: Always ready to help and support, this name speaks of a sense of renewed hope.

Fable
Meaning and Origin: Story; a moral lesson (British)
Significance: A modern and unique name with connotations of creativity, wisdom, and imagination.

Fenix
Meaning and Origin: Deep red; crimson (Greek)
Significance: Signifying rebirth and transformation (like the mythical bird, phoenix), this name can never be counted out.

Finn
Meaning and Origin: Fair; white (Irish)
Significance: Finn signifies purity, honesty, and transparency. Naming a child Finn can reflect a desire for him to embody these traits, to be just and clear-minded in his actions.

Francis
Meaning and Origin: Frenchman; a free man (Latin)
Significance: An independent thinker and free spirit who can't wait to be part of this world.

Frankie
Meaning and Origin: Sincere; truthful (Latin)
Significance: While playful and relaxed, this name evokes a sense of trustworthiness and honesty.

Garnet
Meaning and Origin: Seed-like; a dark red gemstone (British)
Significance: Passionate and fiery, this name represents strength and a connection to the natural world.

Glen
Meaning and Origin: Valley (British)
Significance: Intricately related to nature, this name carries a sense of seclusion and peace.

Hao
Meaning and Origin: Good; excellent (Chinese)
Significance: Kind and well-behaved, this name carries the implication of a good life.

Harlow
Meaning and Origin: Rock hill; army hill (British)
Significance: Reliable and resilient, the child with this name may can face any challenge with unrelenting determination.

Harley
Meaning and Origin: Hare's meadow (British)
Significance: Quick-witted and calm, this name has connotations of peace, tranquility, and safety.

Hayden
Meaning and Origin: Valley with hay (Old English)
Significance: Hayden symbolizes pastoral beauty and tranquility, associated with rural landscapes, reflecting a person who is peaceful and connected to nature.

Henley
Meaning and Origin: From high meadows; from Henley (British)
Significance: Connected to both nature in general and a specific location, this name evokes a sense of openness, calmness, and honesty.

Jazz
Meaning and Origin: Lively; energetic (American)
Significance: Creativity and improvisation are characteristics that this name embodies to the fullest.

Jean
Meaning and Origin: God is gracious (French)
Significance: Jean suggests a sense of divine favor and kindness. Naming a child Jean can reflect a hope for her to embody these qualities, to be compassionate, generous, and understanding towards others.

Jessie
Meaning and Origin: To behold; the Lord exists; gift (Hebrew)
Significance: Relatable and friendly, this person can adapt to life's unexpected twists and turns with ease.

Jody
Meaning and Origin: Jehovah increases; praised (Hebrew)
Significance: Friendly and carefree, this name is down-to-earth and grounded.

Jordan
Meaning and Origin: To go down; descend (Hebrew)
Significance: Reflecting the nature of a river, this person is constantly moving forward to the next big thing.

Kade
Meaning and Origin: Warrior (Scottish)
Significance: Kade is often associated with strength and stability. It can symbolize a wish for the child to face challenges with determination and who faces challenges head-on.

Kami
Meaning and Origin: Spirit; deity (Japanese)
Significance: Representing the connectedness of the natural and spiritual world, this name evokes a sense of balance and order.

Kane
Meaning and Origin: Warrior; battler (Scottish)
Significance: Strong and courageous, this person has a certain kind of tenacity that others may lack.

Kendall
Meaning and Origin: and Origin King's valley (British)
Significance: With a sense of nobility and grandeur, this person carries a strong potential for leadership.

Lake
Meaning and Origin: Body of water (English)
Significance: Lake is derived directly from the English word for a body of water. Naming a child Lake can reflect a connection to nature or a wish for them to embody qualities of tranquility and fluidity.

Lane
Meaning and Origin: Narrow Road; Pathway (English)
Significance: Lane signifies direction and journey, symbolizing progress and exploration, reflecting a person who is on a path to discovery.

Lennon
Meaning and Origin: Lover; sweetheart (Irish)
Significance: Warm and affectionate, this person has a deep love of family and community. Lennon is often associated with love and connection. It can also symbolize a wish for the child to nurture meaningful relationships and to bring love into the lives of others.

Lotus
Meaning and Origin: Lotus flower (Greek)
Significance: It signifies grace and carries a sense of beauty. The lotus flower symbolizes purity and spiritual awakening in many Eastern traditions. It can symbolize a wish for the child to embrace their inner beauty and to achieve enlightenment in life.

Luca
Meaning and Origin: Bringer of light; illuminator (Latin)
Significance: Positive and optimistic, this person can brighten up the darkest of times. Luca is also often associated with wisdom and clarity of thought.

Lyric
Meaning and Origin: Songlike; lyre (Greek)
Significance: This person is intimately connected to their emotions and uses creativity to express them.

Mani
Meaning and Origin: Gem; jewel
Origin: (Sanskrit)
Significance: Highly valued and sought after. Someone who is used to being the center of attention and shines in this position.

Maple
Meaning and Origin: One who lives by the maple tree
Origin: (British)
Significance: Strong, beautiful, and courageous. This person is renowned for sweetness and supportiveness.

Marcel
Meaning and Origin: Martial; warlike
Origin: (Latin)
Significance: Someone who is strong and courageous, as well as highly skilled and controlled.

Marley
Meaning and Origin: Pleasant meadow (British)
Significance: Easy-going and relaxed, creating a calm atmosphere for those around them.

Maverick
Meaning and Origin: Independent; non-conforming (American)
Significance: This name signifies Confident and self-assured. Maverick also represents someone who is unafraid of following their own path.

Max
Meaning and Origin: Greatest (Latin)
Significance: Someone with unlimited potential and likely to achieve great things.

Meredith
Meaning and Origin: Great ruler; sea lord (Welsh)
Significance: The name Meredith is rooted in Welsh culture, originally used as a masculine name before becoming unisex. It combines the elements "Maur" (great) and "rid" (ruler), thus meaning "great ruler" or "sea lord." The name conveys a sense of leadership, strength, and authority.

Monroe
Meaning and Origin: From the hill; the mouth of the river Roe (Scottish)
Significance: This name has a strong connection to nature, specifically the hills and rivers of Scotland and Ireland.

Morgan
Meaning and Origin: Sea-born; sea defender (Welsh)
Significance: A defender of both nature and people, this person loves the sea and has a strong sense of right and wrong.

Nat
Meaning and Origin: Gift of God (Hebrew)
Significance: A true gift to everyone in their life. Bring joy and happiness wherever they go.

Nell
Meaning and Origin: Bright; shining one (Greek)
Significance: This person can be relied upon to always see the positive in a situation, bringing contagious optimism and hope.

Noel
Meaning and Origin: To be born; Christmas (French)
Significance: Noel carries holiday connotations and symbolizes joy and celebration, reflecting a person who brings happiness and festivity.

Nova
Meaning and Origin: New (Latin)
Significance: It evokes a sense of wonder at the universe and carries the possibility of new beginnings and untapped potential.

Nox
Meaning and Origin: Night (Latin)
Significance: Unique and mysterious. It contains a depth that most will never fully explore.

Ocean
Meaning and Origin: Sea; great river (Greek)
Significance: Linked to the Greek titan, Oceanus, who represented the seas, this name represents an internal power that is unrivaled and the potential to achieve many different things.

Page
Meaning and Origin: Youthful; child; attendant (Greek)
Significance: Caring and helpful, this person is playful and young at heart. Page can also be associated with roles of service and responsibility. It can symbolize a wish for the child to approach life with a sense of duty, integrity, and commitment.

Pat
Meaning and Origin: Noble (Latin)
Significance: Pat signifies dignity and honor, chosen for its regal associations, reflecting a person who is esteemed and respected.

Pax
Meaning and Origin: Peace (Latin)
Significance: This person isn't just peaceful by nature but values peace and strives to create and uphold it.

Poet
Meaning and Origin: Maker; creator (Greek)
Significance: While it would be easy to focus on a poet's use of words, their true strength lies in their ability to empathize with others and help them process their emotions.

Quest
Meaning and Origin: Trial; search (French)
Significance: With a sense of adventure and a love of the journey, this person will be right at home in an outgoing family.

Quincy
Meaning and Origin: The fifth (French)
Significance: The perfect name for a fifth child. It could also be a good choice depending on your culture's understanding of the meaning of the number five.

Reagan
Meaning and Origin: Little king (Irish)
Significance: Reagan signifies leadership and bravery. Reagan also represents royalty and strength.

Rebel
Meaning and Origin: Revolutionary; challenger (French)
Significance: A fiery personality. This name has connotations of challenging authority and defying oppression.

Reese
Meaning and Origin: Enthusiasm; ardor (Welsh)
Significance: Passionate and driven, this person enjoys life to the fullest and embraces every opportunity.

Regan
Meaning and Origin: Descendant of a king (Irish)
Significance: With a strong potential to be a highly effective leader and the ambition to go with it, this person is intelligent and a cut above the rest.

Ripley
Meaning and Origin: Strip of clearing in the woods (British)
Significance: Bound to be a lover of the outdoors. It has a strong connection to nature, specifically woodland areas.

River
Meaning and Origin: A large stream (British)
Significance: A source of life for those around them, rivers carry a sense of peace while also possessing an unyielding strength.

Robin
Meaning and Origin: Bright; fame (German)
Significance: Cheerful and friendly. Someone not afraid to stand up for what is right and fight for those who can't fight for themselves.

Rory
Meaning and Origin: Red king; red ruler (Irish)
Significance: This name represents a leader and a fighter. It can also symbolize a wish for the child to lead with integrity and to honor their cultural roots.

Rumi
Meaning and Origin: Beauty; lapis lazuli (Japanese)
Significance: Rumi is often associated with beauty of thought and spiritual insight. It can symbolize a wish for the child to appreciate beauty in all aspects of life and to seek spiritual fulfillment.

Ryan
Meaning and Origin: Little king (Irish)
Significance: A noble and honest personality. This name has connotations of confidence and leadership.

Sailor
Meaning and Origin: Boatman; seafarer (German)
Significance: Independent and adventurous. It carries a sense of wanderlust and a love of the oceans.

Sage
Meaning and Origin: Wise one; healer (Latin)
Significance: Intricately connected to wisdom. Sages can be found wherever there is knowledge to be gained, especially where that knowledge will empower them to help others.

Sam
Meaning and Origin: God has heard; told by God (Hebrew)
Significance: Sam signifies Wisdom and insightfulness. This name also has a playful nature that helps others accept its wisdom.

Shannon
Meaning and Origin: Old River (Irish)
Significance: Shannon is a river name that signifies continuity and natural beauty, reflecting a person who is enduring and connected to nature.

Shaun
Meaning and Origin: God is gracious (Irish)
Significance: A reminder of the goodness of God. Someone optimistic and always ready to lend a helping hand.

Shea
Meaning and Origin: Hawk-like; stately (Irish)
Significance: A noble and observant soul who can see into the heart of any issue.

Sky
Meaning and Origin: and Origin Sky; cloud (British)
Significance: This name means a sense of limitless potential and hope, inspired by the vastness of the sky we see every day.

Sloane
Meaning and Origin: Raider; explorer (Irish)
Significance: Determined and courageous, with an iron will and the strength to make it a reality.

Stevie
Meaning and Origin: Garland; crown (Greek)
Significance: Someone graceful and strong, capable of achieving great success and victory.

Storm
Meaning and Origin: Tempest (British)
Significance: Storm carries an intensity that few other names do, along with a deep sense of passion, determination, and resilience.

Sydney
Meaning and Origin: Wide meadow; at the wide island (British)
Significance: Sydney means Peace and being grounded. Someone who appreciates the simple things in life.

Tarian
Meaning and Origin: Shield (Welsh)
Significance: Brave and willing to bear the burdens of others. They can overcome challenges while protecting those they hold dear.

Terry
Meaning and Origin: Power of the tribe (British)
Significance: Terry signifies someone who is a natural leader who excels when guiding others and forging the path ahead.

Toby
Meaning and Origin: God is good (Hebrew)
Significance: Someone with a positive outlook and who believes that, with hard work, things will turn out for the best.

Toni
Meaning and Origin: Beyond praise; flower; flourishing (French)
Significance: This name represents someone who is a natural all-rounder, tackling new challenges with confidence and ease.

Umber
Meaning and Origin: Shade; shadow (French)
Significance: Umber Conveys a sense of mystery, sophistication, and hidden potential.

Valentine
Meaning and Origin: Strong; healthy (Latin)
Significance: Valentine has a strong connection to romance and love, this name also relates to health and strength.

Valo
Meaning and Origin: Light (Finnish)
Significance: Positive, hopeful, and pure. Valo is someone who seeks to illuminate the lives of those around them.

Vermont
Meaning and Origin: A green mountain (French)
Significance: It has an obvious connection to nature and represents the strength of the mountains as well as the verdant life that is found in them.

Vick
Meaning and Origin: Champion; settlement (Latin)
Significance: Strong and brave. Someone who strives for victory and success in the face of any odds.

Wallace
Meaning and Origin: Welshman (French)
Significance: While "Wallace" was initially synonymous with "foreigner," it has come to represent strength, bravery, and resistance.

Wren
Meaning and Origin: Small bird (British)
Significance: Lively and always on the go. Wren is a symbol of good luck and fortune. Naming a child Wren can reflect a connection to nature or a wish for them to embody qualities of beauty, freedom, and grace.

Xia
Meaning and Origin: Glow of the sunrise; welcoming (Chinese)
Significance: A truly ancient name that imbues a sense of tradition and heritage, as well as beauty and positivity.

Yael
Meaning: and Origin Ibex; mountain goat (Hebrew)
Significance: Strong, determined, and incredibly resourceful, a combination that will see them through many challenges others could not overcome.

Zephyr
Meaning and Origin: West wind (Greek)
Significance: Gentle and kind like a breath of fresh air to those blessed by their company.

If these unisex names aren't quite what you were looking for, don't lose hope! There are still many more wonderful, unique names to explore. Up next, let's look at different spiritual names and their meaning, including biblical, mythological, and celestial names.

CHAPTER 4: SPIRITUAL NAMES

There are several reasons parents might choose a spiritual name for their child. For some, it's a way to connect their child to their faith or belief system. A spiritual name can act as a bridge, fostering a lifelong connection to religious texts, traditions, and spiritual figures. These names can also transcend religious boundaries, carrying beautiful meanings that reflect universal concepts like hope, peace, or strength—qualities many parents would want for their child.

Beyond religious affiliation, spiritual names can also connect a child to their cultural heritage. Many cultures have naming traditions steeped in spiritual beliefs, with names chosen to honor ancestors, invoke blessings, or reflect a desired personality trait. Choosing a spiritual name for a child can, therefore, be a way of honoring their heritage and providing them with a deeper sense of their place in the world. Ultimately, a spiritual name can be a powerful way to express your deepest hopes and aspirations for your child. It can be a constant reminder of the values you hold dear, a source of inspiration on your life's journey.

In this chapter, we'll explore three different types of spiritual names, starting with biblical names, then exploring mythical names, and finally ending with celestial names. So, if you want to connect with the divine and imbue your child's life with names rich in spiritual significance, this is the chapter for you!

Male and Female Biblical Names

The Bible is rich with names of great meaning, some more popular than others. But what we might not know is that many of the common names we know today actually originated from the Bible or were derived from other biblical names. However, not all biblical names have a good meaning. Some names, like Mara, literally mean "bitter," which is why it's important to still look at the meaning and the significance. Many of these names gained their significance due to a biblical character that portrayed a certain set of characteristics. So, let's explore timeless names from the Bible that imply faith, courage, and even redemption.

Aaron
Meaning and Origin: Enlightened (Hebrew)
Significance: Aaron was the first High Priest of the Old Testament; it signifies someone in a high position who is committed to the work of God.

Abigail
Meaning and Origin: Father's joy (Hebrew)
Significance: Abigail is known for her wisdom and discernment, successfully preventing a war between David and her foolish husband. This name signifies qualities like intelligence, resourcefulness, and the ability to become a source of joy.

Abital
Meaning and Origin: My father is the dew (Hebrew)
Significance: Abital was one of King David's wives, noted for her role in the royal court. Her name's poetic meaning, "my father is the dew," symbolizes fertility and blessing, suggesting a connection to divine favor and natural abundance.

Adam
Meaning and Origin: Man; humanity (Hebrew)
Significance: Adam is the name of the first man created by God according to the Book of Genesis. Adam signifies the origin and essence of humanity.

Adlai
Meaning and Origin: Justice of God (Hebrew)
Significance: Adlai served as an overseer of King David's flocks, showcasing his responsibility and role in maintaining justice and order. The name's meaning, "justice of God," underscores his righteous character and the importance of divine justice in Hebrew culture.

Ammiel
Meaning and Origin: People of God (Hebrew)
Significance: Ammiel is noted in the Bible as a spy sent by Moses to explore the land of Canaan, reflecting bravery and commitment to God's mission. His name's meaning, "people of God," highlights his faithfulness and connection to the community of believers.

Amnon
Meaning and Origin: Faithful (Hebrew)
Significance: Amnon was one of King David's sons, known for his tragic story involving his sister Tamar. His name, meaning "faithful," may suggest irony or contrast, illustrating the complexities of human nature and familial relationships in biblical narratives.

Asherah
Meaning and Origin: Upright; Fortunate (Hebrew)
Significance: Asherah was a mother goddess worshipped in ancient Israel, associated with fertility, healing, and protection. Her name's meaning, "upright" or "fortunate," suggests divine favor and blessings bestowed upon her worshippers, illustrating the cultural significance of feminine deities in ancient religions.

Azariah
Meaning and Origin: Yahweh has helped (Hebrew)
Significance: This is a powerful name that expresses dependence on and faith in God's help. It highlights themes of divine intervention, protection, and deliverance.

Baara
Meaning and Origin: Burning (Hebrew)
Significance: Baara was the wife of Shaharaim, a Benjamite mentioned in the Bible. Her name, meaning "burning," symbolizes intensity and passion, reflecting characteristics valued in ancient Hebrew culture. Baara's role underscores familial ties and the importance
of lineage within the community.

Bathsheba
Meaning and Origin: Daughter of abundance (Hebrew)
Significance: The name itself holds positive connotations of abundance and divine favor.

Benaiah
Meaning and Origin: Yahweh has built (Hebrew)
Significance: Benaiah was one of King David's mighty warriors, known for his bravery and strength in battle. His name's meaning, "Yahweh has built," emphasizes divine intervention and support in his endeavors, illustrating the belief in God's providence and power among ancient Hebrews.

Benjamin
Meaning and Origin: Son of the right hand (Hebrew)
Significance: In Hebrew culture, the right hand is associated with strength, favor, and power. Therefore, this name signifies being favored by God, possessing strength, and occupying a position of honor.

Bethany
Meaning and Origin: House of figs and dates (Aramaic)
Significance: Bethany is most significantly known as the village near Jerusalem where Jesus' friends Mary, Martha, and Lazarus lived.

Boaz
Meaning and Origin: Swift; Strong (Hebrew)
Significance: Boaz was a kinsman-redeemer in the Book of Ruth, known for his kindness, generosity, and loyalty. His name, meaning "swift" or "strong," reflects his character traits and the role he played in securing the family lineage and providing for Ruth and Naomi, exemplifying principles of justice and compassion.

Cain
Meaning and Origin: To acquire (Hebrew)
Significance: This name represents ambition and someone hard-working.

Caleb
Meaning and Origin: Dog; devoted (Hebrew)
Significance: This name represents someone loyal and devoted to the cause—always faithful

Candace
Meaning and Origin: Queen mother (Ethiopian)
Significance: Candace was the title of the queen of the Ethiopians mentioned in the New Testament. The name, meaning "queen mother," underscores her royal authority and maternal role, highlighting cultural norms and the significance of matriarchal leadership in ancient Ethiopian society.

Castiel
Meaning and Origin: God is my shield (Hebrew)
Significance: Its biblical meaning implies someone who is strong and shows trust in the Lord.

Christian
Meaning and Origin: Follower of Christ (Greek)
Significance: Indicates someone of faith, who has a pure heart.

Christopher
Meaning and Origin: Bearer of Christ (Greek)
Significance: The name can suggest a strong moral compass and a willingness to help others.

Damaris
Meaning and Origin: Calf (Greek)
Significance: Damaris was a woman converted by Paul in Athens. Her name, meaning "calf," may symbolize innocence or gentleness, reflecting the transformative power of faith and evangelism in early Christian communities.

Daniel
Meaning and Origin: God is my judge (Hebrew)
Significance: The name itself signifies a reliance on God's judgment and guidance. It can also be interpreted as acknowledging God's ultimate authority in one's life.

David
Meaning and Origin: Beloved (Hebrew)
Significance: David is known for his bravery, leadership, and deep faith in God. His name can, therefore, signify qualities like courage, righteousness, and being a chosen leader.

Deborah
Meaning and Origin: Dove; bee (Hebrew)
Significance: In the Bible, Deborah is a strong and respected prophetess and judge who led the Israelites to victory over the Canaanites. The bee can also symbolize being hard-working, intelligent, and a symbol of sweetness.

Demetrius
Meaning and Origin: Devoted to Demeter (Greek)
Significance: Demetrius is a name derived from the Greek goddess Demeter, reflecting an ancient reverence for nature and agriculture. In the New Testament, Demetrius is mentioned as a silversmith in Ephesus who opposed the teachings of the Apostle Paul, illustrating cultural and religious conflicts of the time.

Dibri
Meaning and Origin: Word; Speaker (Hebrew)
Significance: Dibri was the father of Shelomith, a Levite mentioned in the Bible. His name, meaning "word" or "speaker," suggests a role involving communication or proclamation within the community, emphasizing the importance of verbal expression and leadership in ancient Hebrew culture.

Dinah
Meaning and Origin: Judged; Vindicated (Hebrew)
Significance: Dinah was the daughter of Jacob and Leah, known for her story in the Bible involving an incident of assault and its repercussions. Her name, meaning "judged" or "vindicated," reflects themes of justice and redemption, illustrating the challenges faced by women in ancient Hebrew society and the importance of familial honor.

Dorcas
Meaning and Origin: Gazelle (Greek)
Significance: Dorcas, also known as Tabitha, was known for her acts of charity and resurrection by Peter. Her name, meaning "gazelle," symbolizes grace and beauty, highlighting the virtues admired in women within early Christian traditions.

Ebed
Meaning and Origin: Servant (Hebrew)
Significance: Ebed was the father of Gaal, a figure mentioned in the Book of Judges. His name, meaning "servant," signifies humility and obedience, reflecting the values of service and devotion within ancient Hebrew society.

Eli
Meaning and Origin: Yahweh is my God (Hebrew)
Significance: The name emphasizes faith and devotion to God.

Elias
Meaning and Origin: God is the Lord (Hebrew)
Significance: This name embodies submitting to the authority of Divine power and being obedient to God's voice.

Eliezer
Meaning and Origin: God is my help (Hebrew)
Significance: Eliezer was Abraham's trusted servant, mentioned in the Bible for his role in securing a wife for Isaac. His name, meaning "God is my help," illustrates divine assistance and providence in fulfilling his master's wishes, highlighting faith and reliance on God's guidance.

Elijah
Meaning and Origin: The Lord is my God (Hebrew)
Significance: Elijah was known for unwavering faith. This is a name that embodies spiritual strength and resilience.

Eliot
Meaning and Origin: Sun; craftsmen (Hebrew)
Significance: This name carries a strong spiritual meaning for those who choose it based on its Hebrew origin. It signifies faith and a connection to a higher power.

Eliphelet
Meaning and Origin: God is deliverance (Hebrew)
Significance: Eliphelet was one of King David's sons, noted for his loyalty and support. His name, meaning "God is deliverance," signifies divine rescue or salvation, emphasizing the belief in God's protective presence and intervention in times of need.

Emmanuel
Meaning and Origin: God is with us (Hebrew)
Significance: Emmanuel signifies not only God's presence but also hope, salvation, and the fulfillment of a promise.

Enoch
Meaning and Origin: Dedicated (Hebrew)
Significance: Enoch was an ancestor of Noah, known for his righteousness and close relationship with God. His name, meaning "dedicated," underscores his commitment to spiritual devotion and living a life pleasing to God, illustrating the importance of faith and piety in ancient Hebrew culture.

Ephraim
Meaning and Origin: Fruitful (Hebrew)
Significance: Ephraim was one of Joseph's sons, representing a fruitful or prosperous future for the Israelite tribes. His name, meaning "fruitful," symbolizes abundance and blessings, reflecting the hopes and aspirations of ancient Hebrews for prosperity and growth.

Esther
Meaning and Origin: Star; hidden (Persian)
Significance: This name signifies courage, faith, and the power to stand up for what's right.

Eunice
Meaning and Origin: Good victory (Greek)
Significance: Eunice was the mother of Timothy, a disciple of the Apostle Paul. Her name, meaning "good victory," suggests triumph or success, highlighting her role in nurturing and supporting Timothy's faith journey, emphasizing the importance of maternal influence and spiritual guidance.

Eve
Meaning and Origin: Living; life (Hebrew)
Significance: In the Bible, Eve is the first woman created by God. The name itself reflects her role as the mother of all living things.

Ezekiel
Meaning and Origin: God strengthens (Hebrew)
Significance: Ezekiel is of Hebrew origin and have deep biblical connections. Ezekiel also signifies divine fortitude.

Felix
Meaning and Origin: Happy; lucky (Latin)
Significance: This name portrays favor and wealth.

Festus
Meaning and Origin: Joyful; festive (Latin)
Significance: Someone who is trustworthy and reasonable.

Gabriella
Meaning and Origin: God is my strength (Italian and Spanish)
Significance: This name offers a sense of security, protection, and divine guidance for those of faith.

Gershom
Meaning and Origin: Expulsion; exile (Hebrew)
Significance: Gershom was the firstborn son of Moses, named to commemorate his father's exile from Egypt. His name, meaning "expulsion" or "exile," reflects historical events and firsthand experiences, symbolizing resilience and adaptation in the face of adversity.

Gianna
Meaning and Origin: God is gracious (Italian and Hebrew)
Significance: Elegant and approachable, Gianna carries the added significance of a blessing from God.

Gideon
Meaning and Origin: Warrior (Hebrew)
Significance: Gideon's name reflects his role in the Bible as a courageous military leader. His name signifies the act of cutting down enemies and embodies the qualities of a strong and valiant warrior.

Haggith
Meaning and Origin: Festive; rejoicing (Hebrew)
Significance: Haggith was one of King David's wives, known for her place in the royal court. Her name, meaning "festive" or "rejoicing," suggests joy and celebration, highlighting her role in the cultural and social life of ancient Israel.

Hannah
Meaning and Origin: Favor; grace (Hebrew)
Significance: Hannah evokes positive qualities, such as kindness, compassion, and being chosen.

Haran
Meaning and Origin: Mountainous (Hebrew)
Significance: Haran was Abraham's brother, known for his familial ties and journey alongside Abraham. His name, meaning "mountainous," may symbolize strength or endurance, reflecting characteristics valued in ancient Hebrew culture and the challenges faced during nomadic life.

Hosea
Meaning and Origin: God is salvation
Origin: Hebrew
Significance: This name carries a powerful message about God's redemptive power and serves as a constant reminder of God's desire to save and restore his people.

Huldah
Meaning and Origin: Weasel; mole
Origin: Hebrew
Significance: Huldah was a prophet in ancient Israel, recognized for her spiritual insights and guidance. Her name, meaning "weasel" or "mole," may metaphorically denote keen perception or wisdom, illustrating the revered role of prophets in delivering divine messages and interpreting God's will.

Ian
Meaning and Origin: God is gracious (Scottish)
Significance: While rooted in faith, Ian also conveys a sense of strength.

Ira
Meaning and Origin: Watchful (Hebrew)
Significance: Ira was one of King David's mighty warriors, noted for his vigilance and dedication. His name, meaning "watchful," emphasizes alertness and readiness for action, illustrating the qualities valued in military leaders and defenders of ancient Israel.

Isaac
Meaning and Origin: He laughs; he rejoices (Hebrew)
Significance: The name Isaac reflects the joy and laughter that ultimately came with his birth.

Isabella
Meaning and Origin: God is my oath (Spanish and Hebrew)
Significance: Isabella, derived from Elizabeth, signifies strong faith and commitment to God, With an air of royalty and nobility, this name is connected to divine favor, blessing, and being chosen.

Isaiah
Meaning and Origin: God saves (Hebrew)
Significance: This name reflects the core message Isaiah delivered: God is the source of salvation and deliverance.

Ishmael
Meaning and Origin: God hears (Hebrew)
Significance: Ishmael was the son of Abraham and Hagar, known for his connection to the Arab nations. His name, meaning "God hears," reflects the divine promise and attention given to his birth, illustrating God's responsiveness to human prayers and concerns.

Jabez
Meaning and Origin: Sorrow (Hebrew)
Significance: Jabez was noted for his prayer for blessing and territory expansion. His name, meaning "sorrow," symbolizes the trials and challenges faced in life, illustrating the transformative power of faith and prayer in seeking God's provision and protection.

Jacob
Meaning and Origin: Supplanter (Hebrew)
Significance: A name from the Old Testament. Jacob was one of the key patriarchs of the 12 tribes of Israel.

Jake
Meaning and Origin: Supplanter; one who follows (Hebrew)
Significance: Jake is a modern-day, informal variation of Jacob. It represents leadership and reconciliation.

James
Meaning and Origin: Watcher; heed (Hebrew)
Significance: This name signifies someone who is protective and follows God wholeheartedly.

Jane
Meaning and Origin: God is gracious (British)
Significance: A classic and timeless name with a strong religious connotation (God's grace).

Jared
Meaning and Origin: Decent (Hebrew)
Significance: This name is often connected to someone bold, independent, inquisitive, and with strong family connections.

Jedidiah
Meaning and Origin: Beloved of Yahweh (Hebrew)
Significance: Jedidiah was the name given to Solomon by God through Nathan the prophet. His name, meaning "beloved of Yahweh," signifies divine favor and affection, highlighting Solomon's unique relationship with God and his role as a wise and prosperous king.

Jemima
Meaning and Origin: Dove (Hebrew)
Significance: Jemima was one of Job's daughters, known for her beauty and familial ties. Her name, meaning "dove," symbolizes peace and innocence, highlighting her gentle nature and the qualities admired in women within ancient Hebrew society.

Jeremiah
Meaning and Origin: Yahweh will exalt (Hebrew)
Significance: Jeremiah, a major prophet known for his prophecies and lamentations, emphasizes faithfulness and divine purpose.

Jethro
Meaning and Origin: Excellence (Hebrew)
Significance: Jethro was Moses' father-in-law, known for his wisdom and advice. His name, meaning "excellence," may symbolize leadership or honor, illustrating the importance of familial relationships and guidance in biblical narratives.

Joab
Meaning and Origin: Yahweh is father (Hebrew)
Significance: Joab was David's general and commander, recognized for his military prowess and loyalty. His name, meaning "Yahweh is father," underscores divine authority and leadership, illustrating the belief in God's guidance and protection in times of conflict.

Joaquin
Meaning and Origin: Established by God (Spanish)
Significance: Joaquin carries a connotation of God's grace and potentially a connection to John the Baptist. This name embodies creativity and unwavering faith.

Joel
Meaning and Origin: Yahweh is God (Hebrew)
Significance: In the Bible, Joel is the prophet who authored the Book of Joel. The book focuses on themes of judgment, repentance, and restoration. Choosing the name Joel can signify hope for a strong connection with God and a life of faith.

John
Meaning and Origin: God is gracious (Hebrew)
Significance: Choosing the name John signifies a connection to many important figures in the Bible and the values they represent, such as faith, devotion, and love. It also carries the broader meaning of receiving God's grace.

Jonah
Meaning and Origin: Dove (Hebrew)
Significance: The dove is a well-known symbol of peace and harmony. A name like Jonah can signify a desire for these qualities in your child's life.

Joseph
Meaning and Origin: He will add (Hebrew)
Significance: Joseph have strong biblical connections and signify divine favor. Joseph also represents growth and addition.

Joshua
Meaning and Origin: Salvation (Hebrew)
Significance: Choosing this name signifies hope for your child to be strong, courageous, and a leader who brings about positive change.

Josiah
Meaning and Origin: Yahweh supports or heals   (Hebrew)
Significance: Josiah, a king of Judah, symbolizes righteousness and reform through his religious reforms and efforts to restore the worship of Yahweh.

Judah
Meaning and Origin: Praised (Hebrew)
Significance: This name embodies strength, courage, and leadership.

Justin
Meaning and Origin: Just; fair (Latin)
Significance: Someone with this name is known for their righteousness and fairness.

Keturah
Meaning and Origin: Incense; fragrance (Hebrew)
Significance: The implied meanings of this name, "incense" or "fragrance," carry a symbolic connotation of something pleasing or precious.

Kezia
Meaning and Origin: Sweet-scented spice (Hebrew)
Significance: Kezia was one of Job's daughters, known for her beauty and virtue. Her name, meaning "cassia" or "sweet-scented spice," symbolizes preciousness and grace, reflecting the values of femininity and spiritual integrity in ancient Hebrew culture.

Keziah
Meaning and Origin: Fragrant spice (Hebrew)
Significance: This name holds a beautiful meaning associated with a pleasant fragrance. It is given to someone pleasing and joyful.

Korah
Meaning and Origin: Call; to proclaim (Hebrew)
Significance: Korah is a strong leader with a lot of ambition and intelligence.

Laban
Meaning and Origin: White (Hebrew)
Significance: Laban was the father of Leah and Rachel, known for his role in Jacob's life. His name, meaning "white," may symbolize purity or clarity, illustrating the complexities of familial relationships and the dynamics within ancient Hebrew households.

Leah
Meaning and Origin: Weary; worn out (Hebrew)
Significance: This name represents endurance, motherhood, and the importance of family.

Levi
Meaning and Origin: Joined; attached (Hebrew)
Significance: The name can also represent a desire for your child to be a unifying force or someone who brings people together.

Luke
Meaning and Origin: Grove; wood (Greek)
Significance: Choosing Luke signifies a connection to Christianity and the message of the Gospels. It can also represent a desire for your child to be a healer or someone who brings light to darkness.

Mahlah
Meaning and Origin: Sickness (Hebrew)
Significance: Mahlah was one of Zelophehad's daughters, known for her courage and initiative. Her name, meaning "sickness," may reflect challenges or hardships overcome, illustrating resilience and determination in securing her family's inheritance rights within ancient Hebrew society.

Malachi
Meaning and Origin: My messenger; my angel (Hebrew)
Significance: Choosing the name Malachi signifies the hope that your child will be a messenger of goodness, a communicator of faith, or a champion for what is right.

Mara
Meaning and Origin: Bitter (Hebrew)
Significance: Mara was Naomi's name meaning "bitter" after experiencing loss and hardship. Her name symbolizes the struggles faced in life, highlighting themes of sorrow and resilience, and illustrating the transformation from bitterness to hope and renewal.

Mariam
Meaning and Origin: Bitterness; rebellion (Hebrew)
Significance: The name means purity, devotion, and blessedness. Choosing Mariam signifies the hope that your child will embody these qualities or hold a special place in your faith.

Mark
Meaning and Origin: Warlike (Latin)
Significance: Mark has a strong biblical tie and signifies divine favor and strength. Mark also represents courage and resilience.

Mary
Meaning and Origin: Beloved; wished-for child (Hebrew)
Significance: Mary's significance stems primarily from her role in Christianity as the mother of Jesus Christ. The name represents obedience, motherhood, and God's favor.

Mateo
Meaning and Origin: Gift of God (Spanish)
Significance: Mateo signifies a child seen as a blessing or a precious gift from God. This meaning resonates with parents of many faiths who believe their children are a form of divine grace.

Matthew
Meaning and Origin: Gift (Hebrew)
Significance: It carries a beautiful meaning, signifying a child as a precious gift from God.

Micah
Meaning and Origin: Who can be like God? (Hebrew)
Significance: Micah's significance lies in its deep connection to faith. The name itself is a statement of belief in God's supremacy.

Milcah
Meaning and Origin: Queen (Hebrew)
Significance: Milcah was the wife of Nahor, noted for her familial ties and lineage. Her name, meaning "queen," symbolizes honor and authority, reflecting the esteemed position of matriarchs within ancient Hebrew households.

Moses
Meaning and Origin: Delivered from the water (Hebrew)
Significance: Moses' name embodies themes of deliverance, divine intervention, and faith.

Naaman
Meaning and Origin: Pleasantness (Hebrew)
Significance: Naaman was the commander of the army of the king of Aram, known for his encounter with the prophet Elisha. His name, meaning "pleasantness," suggests favor and grace, illustrating the transformative power of faith and obedience in receiving divine healing and redemption.

Naomi
Meaning and Origin: Pleasant one; sweetness (Hebrew)
Significance: Despite facing personal tragedy and hardship, Naomi exemplifies resilience and faith. Her name reflects the hope and optimism that can emerge even in difficult times.

Nathaniel
Meaning and Origin: Gift of God (Hebrew)
Significance: Nathaniel carries a powerful meaning, signifying a child viewed as a blessing from God. In the New Testament, Nathaniel appears as one of Jesus' disciples, known for his honesty and straightforwardness.

Neriah
Meaning and Origin: Lamp of Yahweh (Hebrew)
Significance: Neriah was the father of Baruch, Jeremiah's scribe and companion. His name, meaning "lamp of Yahweh," signifies enlightenment and divine guidance, illustrating the role of prophets and scribes in preserving and transmitting God's messages to the people.

Nimrod
Meaning and Origin: Rebel (Hebrew)
Significance: Nimrod was a mighty hunter and ruler mentioned in Genesis. His name, meaning "rebel," may symbolize defiance or ambition, illustrating the complexities of human ambition and the consequences of pride in biblical narratives.

Noah
Meaning and Origin: Rest; peace (Hebrew)
Significance: Noah holds immense significance in the Bible as the faithful man chosen by God to build an ark and save his family and animal pairs from the Great Flood. The name embodies themes of hope, renewal, and the promise of a new beginning.

Obadiah
Meaning and Origin: Servant of Yahweh (Hebrew)
Significance: Obadiah was a prophet in the Bible, known for his message against Edom. His name, meaning "servant of Yahweh," underscores his devotion and obedience to God's will, highlighting the prophetic tradition and the call to speak truth to power.

Obed
Meaning and Origin: Servant; worshipper (Hebrew)
Significance: Obed signifies devotion and faithfulness, particularly to God. In the Bible, Obed was the son of Ruth and Boaz and a significant figure in the lineage of King David. The name carries a sense of humility and dedication, reflecting a life lived in service to a higher purpose.

Orpah
Meaning and Origin: Back of the neck (Hebrew)
Significance: Orpah was Ruth's sister-in-law, known for her decision to return to Moab. Her name, meaning "back of the neck," may symbolize turning away or separation, illustrating the complexities of loyalty and choice in ancient Hebrew narratives.

Oshea
Meaning and Origin: Yahweh is salvation (Hebrew)
Significance: Oshea, or Hosea, carries a powerful message of hope and redemption. The name signifies God's role as the ultimate source of salvation. It evokes themes of forgiveness, divine love, and the promise of salvation.

Paul
Meaning and Origin: Small; humble (Latin)
Significance: While the literal meaning suggests smallness, over time it evolved to represent humility and modesty.

Peter
Meaning and Origin: Rock; stone (Greek)
Significance: Peter's name originates from the Greek word "petros," meaning "stone" or "rock." This name embodies qualities of stability, strength, and unwavering faith.

Rahab
Meaning and Origin: Broad, spacious (Hebrew)
Significance: Rahab was a woman who helped Israelite spies in Jericho, known for her courage and faith. Her name, meaning "broad" or "spacious," symbolizes liberation and opportunity, illustrating the transformative power of trust and obedience in God's promises.

Ruben
Meaning and Origin: Behold, a son! (Hebrew)
Significance: Ruben's story offers lessons about leadership, responsibility, and the complexities of family dynamics. He is also the founder of the Tribe of Reuben, one of the twelve tribes of Israel.

Ruth
Meaning and Origin: Friend; companion (Hebrew)
Significance: Ruth, the central character in the Book of Ruth, is a Moabite woman known for her unwavering loyalty and love. She exemplifies the qualities of faithfulness, kindness, and resilience.

Salome
Meaning and Origin: Peace (Hebrew)
Significance: The meaning of this name offers a beautiful sentiment for a child. It represents faithfulness to Christ and someone who brings peace to those around them.

Samuel
Meaning: and Origin Heard by God (Hebrew)
Significance: Samuel is of Hebrew origin and signify a connection to the divine. Samuel represents divine communication and faith.

Sapphira
Meaning and Origin: Precious (Greek)
Significance: Sapphira was the wife of Ananias, known for their deceit in the early Christian community. Her name, meaning "precious," may suggest value or esteem, highlighting the moral lessons and consequences of dishonesty and hypocrisy.

Sarah
Meaning and Origin: Princess; joyful (Hebrew)
Significance: Sarah's story embodies themes of faith, perseverance, and the promise of God's blessings. This name can represent nobility, joy, and a connection to one's heritage.

Serah
Meaning and Origin: Princess (Hebrew)
Significance: Serah was the daughter of Asher, noted for her lineage and genealogy. Her name, meaning "princess," symbolizes honor and distinction, reflecting the esteemed status of women in preserving ancestral histories and traditions.

Shadrach
Meaning and Origin: Command of Aku (Babylonian)
Significance: Shadrach was one of Daniel's friends who refused to worship the golden image. His name, meaning "command of Aku," reflects his Babylonian origin and the challenge of maintaining faithfulness to Yahweh amidst cultural pressures.

Shammah
Meaning and Origin: Desolation (Hebrew)
Significance: Shammah was one of David's mighty warriors, known for his defense of a lentil field. His name, meaning "desolation," may symbolize strength or perseverance, illustrating the courage and commitment of ancient Hebrew warriors in defending their land and resources.

Sharon
Meaning and Origin: Plain; flat area (Hebrew)
Significance: In the Bible, Sharon refers specifically to the fertile plain between the Samarian Hills and the Mediterranean coast, known as the Sharon plain. This region was renowned for its beauty and agricultural abundance.

Shem
Meaning and Origin: Name (Hebrew)
Significance: Shem was Noah's son, known for his lineage and descendants. His name, meaning "name," signifies reputation or identity, highlighting the importance of familial heritage and ancestral legacy within ancient Hebrew narratives.

Simon
Meaning and Origin: Hear; hearing (Hebrew)
Significance: This name signifies faith, discipline, attentiveness, and openness. It also embodies characteristics of commitment and zeal.

Stephen
Meaning and Origin: Crowned; garland (Greek)
Significance: Stephen's name reflects the concept of receiving a crown of glory in heaven for his faith. More broadly, the name carries connotations of victory, honor, and achievement.

Susanna
Meaning and Origin: Lily (Hebrew)
Significance: Susanna was a woman who followed Jesus, known for her devotion and support. Her name, meaning "lily," symbolizes purity and beauty, reflecting the virtues admired in women within Christian traditions.

Talia
Meaning and Origin: Dew of God (Hebrew)
Significance: Representing divine blessing, Talia always perseveres in the face of challenge.

Talitha
Meaning and Origin: Little girl (Aramaic)
Significance: Talitha was the young girl resurrected by Jesus. Her name, meaning "little girl," illustrates the compassion and miraculous power of Jesus, emphasizing the themes of healing and restoration in Christian faith.

Tamar
Meaning and Origin: Palm tree (Hebrew)
Significance: Tamar is a significant figure in the Bible, known for her courage and resourcefulness. By naming a child Tamar, parents may hope to honor biblical heritage.

Tertius
Meaning and Origin: Third (Latin)
Significance: Tertius was Paul's scribe who transcribed the Book of Romans. His name, meaning "third," may denote birth order or sequence, highlighting his role in documenting and preserving Paul's teachings for future generations.

Tiffany
Meaning and Origin: Manifestation of God (Greek)
Significance: Tiffany is historically associated with the Feast of Epiphany, which celebrates the revelation of Christ to the Gentiles. The name suggests a sense of clarity, divine presence, and illumination.

Timothy
Meaning and Origin: Honoring God (Greek)
Significance: Choosing this name signifies a desire for your child to be a person of faith and integrity.

Tobiah
Meaning and Origin: God is good (Hebrew)
Significance: Tobiah opposed Nehemiah during the rebuilding of Jerusalem's walls. His name, meaning "God is good," underscores the contrasting beliefs and conflicts encountered in biblical narratives, illustrating the challenges of leadership and perseverance in the face of opposition.

Uriah
Meaning and Origin: Yahweh is my light (Hebrew)
Significance: Choosing this name could signify hope for your child to be a person of strong faith and unwavering loyalty.

Uriel
Meaning and Origin: God is my fire (Hebrew)
Significance: Uriel signifies enlightenment, divine guidance, and the presence of God's light in one's life.

Uziel
Meaning and Origin: Strength of God (Hebrew)
Significance: Strong biblical name signifying divine power and protection. Uziel also reflects a deep belief in divine support and fortitude.

Vashti
Meaning and Origin: Beautiful; excellent (Persian)
Significance: She is viewed as a symbol of female strength and resistance to male authority.

Vaniah
Meaning and Origin: Nourishment; weapons, of the lord (Hebrew)
Significance: This name embodies strength and leadership. Vaniah is often chosen by parents to symbolize gratitude for God's blessings and mercy.

Yoel
Meaning and Origin: Jehovah is God (Hebrew)
Significance: This name directly connects to God, signifying faith and devotion. Yoel is often chosen by parents to symbolize faith in God's guidance and to express hope for the child to live a life dedicated to God's purpose and truth.

Zacharias
Meaning and Origin: Yahweh has remembered (Hebrew)
Significance: Zacharias was the father of John the Baptist, known for his faith and prophecy. His name, meaning "Yahweh has remembered," symbolizes divine favor and fulfillment of promises, highlighting the role of prophets in preparing the way for the Messiah.

Zachary
Meaning and Origin: Remembered by God (Hebrew)
Significance: Zachary reflects a belief in divine remembrance and providence. Zachary is also often chosen by parents to symbolize divine favor and faith. It can symbolize a wish for the child to live a life guided by faithfulness, trust in God's providence, and remembrance of spiritual values.

Zadok
Meaning and Origin: Righteous; just (Hebrew)
Significance: This name carries significant historical and religious weight, symbolizing righteousness, leadership, and a connection to Judeo-Christian tradition.

Zephaniah
Meaning and Origin: Yahweh has hidden (Hebrew)
Significance: Zephaniah was a prophet who delivered messages of judgment and hope. His name, meaning "Yahweh has hidden," suggests divine mystery and revelation, illustrating the prophetic tradition and the unfolding of God's plan for redemption.

Zillah
Meaning and Origin: Shadow (Hebrew)
Significance: Zillah was the wife of Lamech, noted for her role in early genealogies. Her name, meaning "shadow," may symbolize protection or companionship, reflecting the familial bonds and support valued within ancient Hebrew households.

Ziph
Meaning and Origin: Drought; coming (Hebrew)
Significance: "Drought" might symbolize overcoming hardship, and "coming" could suggest arrival, growth, or a new beginning.

Zipporah
Meaning and Origin: Bird (Hebrew)
Significance: Zipporah was Moses' wife, known for her courage and intervention. Her name, meaning "bird," may symbolize freedom or guidance, illustrating the supportive role of women in biblical narratives and their contributions to God's unfolding plan.

Male and Female Mythological Names

Delving into mythology for a baby name can be an enchanting adventure. Mythological names boast rich histories and captivating stories, instantly imbuing your child's name with meaning and intrigue. Imagine a daughter named Daphne, forever linked to the Greek myth of the swift nymph, or a son named Atlas, carrying the symbolic strength of the titan who held the world on his shoulders. These names spark curiosity and invite exploration, offering a unique connection to the captivating world of myths and legends. Let's explore names inspired by ancient myths and legends, evoking a sense of magic and wonder.

Achelous
Meaning and Origin: Flowing water; troubled (Greek)
Significance: As the Greek god of water and rivers, this name symbolizes the changing and unpredictable nature of rivers.

Achilles
Meaning and Origin: Without tears; no grief (Greek)
Significance: Achilles was the hero of the Trojan War and known for his bravery and courage.

Adonis
Meaning and Origin: Lord; pleasant; delightful (Greek)
Significance: Adonis was the human lover of Aphrodite, and his name carries connotations of beauty, passion, and the cyclical nature of life.

Aeacus
Meaning and Origin: Son of Zeus (Greek mythology)
Significance: Son of Zeus who became king of the island Aegina. Aeacus is often chosen to symbolize justice, fairness, and integrity. It reflects a wish for the child to embody qualities of righteousness, moral strength, and impartiality.

Aella
Meaning and Origin: Whirlwind (Greek)
Significance: Aella was an Amazon warrior, representing bravery and strength. This name also reflects themes of speed, power, and energy.

Aeneas
Meaning and Origin: Praiseworthy (Greek)
Significance: A Trojan hero and the protagonist of Virgil's "Aeneid," Aeneas symbolizes duty, piety, and the founding of Rome.

Ajax
Meaning and Origin: Eagle (Greek)
Significance: In Greek mythology, Ajax was the name of two heroes who fought for the Greeks in the Trojan war, the son of Telamon and the son of Oileus.

Amalthea
Meaning and Origin: To soothe; soften (Greek)
Significance: As the woman who nursed Zeus, this name carries nurturing qualities of care and love. Amalthea is often chosen to symbolize nurturing and protection. It reflects a wish for the child to embody qualities of care, gentleness, and protective strength.

Aoife
Meaning and Origin: Beauty (Irish)
Significance: Aoife is a prominent figure in Irish myths, known for her beauty and warrior spirit. It reflects a wish for the child to embody qualities of radiance, inner strength, and courage.

Aphrodite
Meaning and Origin: Foam-born (Greek)
Significance: The goddess of love, beauty, and desire, Aphrodite symbolizes passion, allure, and the power of attraction.

Apollo
Meaning and Origin: He who drives away evil; destroyer (Greek)
Significance: Apollo was associated with the sun and its life-giving properties. This name signifies light, creativity, and power.

Ares
Meaning and Origin: War (Greek)
Significance: Ares was the god of war who often let rage control him. This name signifies passion and protection.

Argo
Meaning and Origin: Builder; swift (Greek)
Significance: Argo is most famous as the name of the ship built by Jason and the Argonauts in their quest for the Golden Fleece. The ship itself became a symbol of courage, exploration, and the pursuit of knowledge.

Artemis
Meaning and Origin: Butcher (Greek)
Significance: Artemis was known for her independence, strength, and skill in archery. Her name evokes a sense of fierce protectiveness, nature, and the untamed wilderness.

Astraia
Meaning and Origin: Star (Greek)
Significance: This name belongs to the goddess of justice and innocence, connecting these qualities to the bearer.

Atalanta
Meaning and Origin: Equal in weights (Greek)
Significance: This name represents a strong and powerful woman and is based on the Greek maiden who refused to marry anyone who could not beat her in a race.

Athena
Meaning and Origin: Wealth (Greek)
Significance: Athena, the famed Greek goddess, embodied wisdom, handicraft, and strategic warfare. Her name thus signifies intelligence, strategic thinking, bravery, and prowess in various fields.

Aurora
Meaning and Origin: Dawn (Latin)
Significance: Aurora embodies new beginnings, hope, and the promise of a fresh start.

Bacchus
Meaning and Origin: To shout (Roman)
Significance: The god of wine, revelry, and ecstasy, Bacchus symbolizes celebration, freedom, and the transformative power of intoxication.

Bellerophon
Meaning and Origin: Slayer of Belleros (Greek)
Significance: A hero who tamed the winged horse Pegasus and defeated the Chimera, Bellerophon symbolizes ambition, courage, and the fallibility of pride.

Bridget
Meaning and Origin: Exalted one; the high one (Celtic)
Significance: Bridget is a prominent figure in Irish mythology, associated with fire, poetry, healing, and craft. Choosing the name Bridget signifies strength, creativity, and a connection to the natural world.

Brontes
Meaning and Origin: Thunder; roaring (Greek)
Significance: Brontes was one of the three Cyclopes, giant one-eyed beings known for their immense strength and skill as blacksmiths. Choosing the name Brontes signifies strength, power, and a connection to the raw forces of nature.

Cadmus
Meaning and Origin: One who excels; leader (Greek)
Significance: Cadmus was a legendary founder and king of Thebes, a prominent city in Greek mythology. His name signifies leadership, innovation, and the power of knowledge.

Caleus
Meaning and Origin: Sky; heaven (Latin)
Significance: It is associated with Caelus, the Roman god, and evokes the vastness and wonder of the celestial realm.

Cepheus
Meaning and Origin: Head; pointed (Greek)
Significance: Cepheus was the king of Ethiopia and the husband of Cassiopeia in Greek mythology. The constellation Cepheus is named after him, depicted as a kneeling king eternally facing his wife who is permanently fixed in the sky.

Chandra
Meaning and Origin: Moon (Hindu)
Significance: Chandra is the Hindu moon god, associated with creativity, intuition, and cycles of change.

Charon
Meaning and Origin: Fierce-eyed; bringer of joy (Greek)
Significance: Charon is the ferryman of the dead in Greek mythology. He was responsible for transporting the souls of the deceased across the River Styx, which separated the world of the living from the underworld. His name embodies the transition from life to death and serves as a reminder of mortality.

Clementia
Meaning and Origin: Kindness; mercy (Roman)
Significance: Clementia was the Roman personification of clemency and forgiveness. Her name represents the virtues of compassion, understanding, and the willingness to show mercy. Choosing Clementia as a name signifies hope that the child will embody these positive qualities.

Cronus
Meaning and Origin: Ruler of time (Greek)
Significance: Cronus was one of the twelve Titans, a powerful race of deities who ruled before the Olympians. He represents power and ambition.

Dalia
Meaning and Origin: Portion (Lithuanian)
Significance: She was the Baltic goddess of weaving, fate, and childbirth. Her name represents strong feminine qualities and balance.

Damion
Meaning and Origin: One who tames; heavenly messenger (Greek)
Significance: Saints Cosmas and Damian were twin brothers known as healers, making Damian a name linked to medicine and good health.

Daphne
Meaning and Origin: The laurel tree (Greek)
Significance: This name represents transformation, beauty, and the fleeting nature of desire. The laurel tree itself represents success, honor, and protection.

Dardanos
Meaning and Origin: Son of Darda (Greek)
Significance: Dardanos is linked to the founding myth of Troy. According to legend, he was the founder of Dardania, a city that later became Troy.

Dimitri
Meaning and Origin: Devoted to Demeter (Greek)
Significance: Dimitri is connected to Demeter, the Greek goddess of agriculture, grain, fertility, and sacred law. Choosing Dimitri signifies a connection to the bounty of the harvest and the cycle of life, death, and rebirth.

Dionysus
Meaning and Origin: The god of wine (Greek)
Significance: Dionysus is the Olympian god of wine, festivity, theatre, religion, and madness. He was known for his love of revelry, music, and dance.

Electra
Meaning and Origin: Amber; shining one (Greek)
Significance: She is best known for Sophocles' plays, particularly *Electra*, in which she becomes a symbol of unwavering loyalty and determination in the face of injustice.

Elysia
Meaning and Origin: Blissful (Greek)
Significance: Elysia refers to the Elysian Fields, the final resting place of the blessed souls, symbolizing paradise, peace, and eternal happiness.

Endeis
Meaning and Origin: In the Earth (Greek)
Significance: was the wife of King Aeacus and the mother of the heroes Telamon and Peleus.

Endymion
Meaning and Origin: To dive into (Greek)
Significance: Endymion symbolizes beauty and eternal youth, often linked to a captivating and timeless personality. The name suggests a person who is eternally charming and holds a special allure. Endymion evokes images of moonlit nights and mythological tales, reflecting a sense of romance and mystique.

Eros
Meaning and Origin: Love; desire (Greek)
Significance: He embodies not just romantic love but also passion, attraction, and desire. Choosing Eros as a name would evoke a connection to these powerful emotions.

Europa
Meaning and Origin: Wide face (Greek)
Significance: A princess abducted by Zeus in the form of a bull, Europa symbolizes exploration, the unification of cultures, and the naming of the continent Europe.

Freya
Meaning and Origin: Lady; mistress (Norse)
Significance: Freya is a major goddess in Norse mythology. She is associated with love, beauty, fertility, war, and magic. She is depicted as a powerful and alluring figure, often riding in a chariot pulled by cats. Freya's name reflects her high status and association with nobility.

Gaia
Meaning and Origin: Earth (Greek)
Significance: Gaia is the primordial goddess of the Earth itself. She is a powerful and nurturing figure, often depicted as a giant woman emerging from the earth. Her name directly reflects her role as the embodiment of the Earth.

Griffin
Meaning and Origin: Lion and eagle; majesty; wisdom (Greek)
Significance: The griffin is a powerful and majestic creature often depicted guarding treasure or sacred places. In some myths, it symbolizes vigilance, intelligence, and duality.

Hades
Meaning and Origin: Unseen; invisible (Greek)
Significance: His name signifies the hidden world of the afterlife and its power over the living. He embodies qualities of strength, power, and attention to rules.

Halcyon
Meaning and Origin: Kingfisher (Greek)
Significance: Halcyon is associated with the mythical Alcyone, a daughter of the wind god Aeolus. The name Halcyon carries connotations of peace, calmness, and conjugal love.

Harmonia
Meaning and Origin: Harmony (Greek)
Significance: Harmonia was the daughter of Ares, the god of war, and Aphrodite, the goddess of love and beauty. Harmonia embodies the concept of harmony itself, representing the potential for peace and balance even amidst conflict.

Hecate
Meaning and Origin: Worker from afar (Greek)
Significance: The goddess of magic, witchcraft, and crossroads, Hecate symbolizes mystery, transformation, and the unseen forces of the world.

Hector
Meaning and Origin: Slayer; keeper (Greek)
Significance: Hector is often depicted as a noble and courageous hero, fiercely loyal to his family and country.

Helios
Meaning and Origin: Sun (Greek)
Significance: Helios is the personification of the sun in Greek mythology. He was depicted as a handsome titan who rode a golden chariot across the sky each day, bringing light and warmth to the world.

Hera
Meaning and Origin: Protectress (Greek)
Significance: The queen of the gods and goddess of marriage and family, Hera symbolizes loyalty, power, and the sanctity of marriage.

Hercules
Meaning: Hera's glory (Greek)
Significance: His name reflects his dual nature: "Hera" refers to his jealous stepmother, the goddess Hera, who tormented him throughout his life, and "glory," highlighting his immense strength and accomplishments. Hercules embodies strength, perseverance, and the power to overcome seemingly insurmountable challenges.

Hermes
Meaning and Origin: Heap of stones; interpretation (Greek)
Significance: He is known for his incredible speed, thanks to his winged sandals, and his role as the messenger of the gods. He is also the god of travelers, thieves, merchants, athletes, and shepherds. Hermes embodies communication, resourcefulness, and the ability to navigate complex situations.

Hyperion
Meaning and Origin: The high one; he who walks above (Greek)
Significance: Hyperion embodies the vastness and power of the heavens, often depicted as the personification of the sun itself. The name carries connotations of strength, authority, and the passage of time.

Ianthe
Meaning and Origin: Violet flower (Greek)
Significance: Ianthe symbolizes delicacy and charm, often linked to a graceful and enchanting personality. The name suggests a person who is gentle and captivating, embodying a sense of natural beauty. Ianthe evokes images of blooming flowers and serene gardens, reflecting a soothing and picturesque presence.

Icarus
Meaning and Origin: Follower (Greek)
Significance: The myth of Icarus serves as a cautionary tale about the dangers of ambition, hubris, and going too far. Therefore, this name represents being humble and taking wise counsel.

Janus
Meaning and Origin: Doorway; beginning (Roman)
Significance: Janus is the Roman god of beginnings, endings, transitions, doorways, gates, passages, time, and fates. He symbolizes new beginnings, change, and looking toward the future while acknowledging the past.

Jason
Meaning and Origin: Healer; curer (Greek)
Significance: In Greek mythology, Jason was the leader of the Argonauts, a band of heroes who embarked on a perilous quest to retrieve the Golden Fleece. This name symbolizes courage, strategic thinking, and intelligence.

Larisa
Meaning and Origin: Pleasant; cheerful (Greek)
Significance: Larisa was the name of an ancient Greek city known for its beauty and prosperity. This name has a positive connotation of wealth and represents someone pleasant.

Leander
Meaning and Origin: Smooth man; lion-man (Greek)
Significance: The story of Leander represents devoted love and commitment to loved ones. Leander swam across stormy waters many nights to be with his love and was brave in facing the perils of nature.

Leda
Meaning and Origin: Lady (Greek)
Significance: A queen who was seduced by Zeus in the form of a swan, Leda symbolizes beauty, mystery, and the union of divine and mortal realms.

Lilith
Meaning and Origin: Storm; night creature (Mesopotamian)
Significance: Lilith represents a strong feminine power that challenges societal expectations. Lilith's portrayal can be both monstrous and sympathetic, highlighting the complexities of human nature.

Linus
Meaning and Origin: Artistic talent (Greek)
Significance: Linus is often portrayed as a young musician and the teacher of music to legendary figures like Hercules and Orpheus. Choosing Linus can symbolize a wish for the child to possess musical talent or a love for learning.

Maia
Meaning and Origin: Greater (Greek)
Significance: Choosing Maia can signify a wish for the child to possess beauty, grace, and a connection to the natural world (stars).

Medusa
Meaning and Origin: Guardian (Greek)
Significance: A Gorgon whose gaze could turn people to stone, Medusa symbolizes danger, transformation, and the power of the female.

Midas
Meaning and Origin: King (Greek)
Significance: A king who turned everything he touched into gold, Midas symbolizes wealth, greed, and the consequences of unchecked desire.

Mina
Meaning and Origin: Feminine version of Minos (Greek)
Significance: Symbolizes wisdom, knowledge, and good leadership skills. Mina is appreciated for its elegance and meaningful connotations.

Minos
Meaning and Origin: Son of Zeus (Greek)
Significance: Minos was a powerful and renowned king of Crete in Greek mythology. He was known for his lawmaking skills, association with the labyrinth, and the myth of the Minotaur. Choosing Minos can symbolize qualities like leadership, justice (lawmaking), or a connection to mazes and puzzles (labyrinth).

Morpheus
Meaning and Origin: Shaper; former (Greek)
Significance: Morpheus was the god of dreams in Greek mythology. The name carries connotations of creativity, imagination, and the transformative power of dreams.

Nemesis
Meaning and Origin: To give what is due (Greek)
Significance: The goddess of retribution, Nemesis symbolizes justice, revenge, and the balance of fortune.

Neo
Meaning and Origin: The one (Greek)
Significance: The name Neo emphasizes themes of new beginnings, awakening, and the potential for change.

Niobe
Meaning and Origin: Derived from the mythological Niobe who was turned into a stone (Greek)
Significance: Represents strength and resilience as a captain of the Logos. In *Matrix* Niobe is a skilled pilot and former lover of Morpheus, playing a key role in the human resistance.

Nyx
Meaning and Origin: Night (Greek)
Significance: Nyx is the primordial goddess of the night in Greek mythology. She is a powerful and independent figure, often depicted as cloaked in darkness and riding a chariot drawn by black horses. She is associated with sleep, dreams, and the stars, seen emerging from her every night.

Odysseus
Meaning and Origin: The man of pain; wrathful one (Greek)
Significance: His name, while potentially suggesting a troubled past, ultimately reflects his journey. Odysseus embodies perseverance, intellect, and the ability to overcome seemingly insurmountable obstacles.

Oilues
Meaning and Origin: Broad leather strap (Greek mythology)
Significance: Originally the name of an Arcadian Mountain god. In Greek mythology Oileus was the son of Hodoedocus and Agrianome, and was a king of the Locrian.

Orion
Meaning and Origin: He who rises; hunter (Greek)
Significance: Orion is a prominent constellation known for its bright stars, which form the outline of a hunter with a belt and raised sword. The name Orion carries connotations of strength, prowess, and a connection to the natural world.

Orpheus
Meaning and Origin: Darkened; the one who tames beasts (Greek)
Significance: Orpheus represents the power of music and art to move hearts and even influence the gods. The name Orpheus carries connotations of artistry, eloquence, and the ability to inspire.

Pallas
Meaning and Origin: Shaker; warrior (Greek)
Significance: This name is often connected with the symbol of an owl, which represents intelligence and peace.

Pan
Meaning and Origin: All; encompassing (Greek)
Significance: Pan is the god of the wild, nature, shepherds, flocks, and rustic music. His name signifies creativity and companionship.

Persephone
Meaning and Origin: Bringer of destruction (Greek)
Significance: The queen of the underworld and goddess of spring growth, Persephone symbolizes rebirth, duality, and the cycle of life and death.

Perseus
Meaning and Origin: Destroyer; breaker (Greek)
Significance: Perseus is a legendary hero known for slaying Medusa. His story is one of courage, resourcefulness, and divine favor. This name can be shortened to Percy.

Phoenix
Meaning and Origin: The purple-red bird (Greek)
Significance: Choosing the name Phoenix for a child signifies hope for them to overcome challenges, rise from adversity, and experience continuous growth throughout their life.

Poseidon
Meaning and Origin: Husband of the earth (Greek)
Significance: Choosing the name Poseidon for a child signifies a wish for them to be strong, courageous, and possess a powerful life force.

Prometheus
Meaning and Origin: Forethought (Greek)
Significance: A titan who stole fire from the gods and gave it to humanity, Prometheus symbolizes innovation, sacrifice, and the quest for knowledge.

Rama
Meaning and Origin: Dark and delightful (Sanskrit)
Significance: The name Rama carries strong connotations of heroism, virtue, and unwavering loyalty.

Rhiannon
Meaning and Origin: Great queen; divine queen (Irish)
Significance: Her stories often involve themes of redemption, resilience, and the importance of maintaining one's rightful place. Choosing the name Rhiannon evokes a sense of regality, otherworldly mystery, and connection to nature's bounty.

Selena
Meaning and Origin: Moon (Greek)
Significance: Her name is associated with themes of femininity, beauty, mystery, and the changing phases of the moon.

Silvia
Meaning and Origin: Forest; woods (Latin)
Significance: This name evokes a sense of nature, growth, and mystery. Silvia is often chosen to symbolize a deep connection to nature and the vitality of the natural world.

Telamon
Meaning and Origin: Support, enduring (Greek Mythology)
Significance: Telamon is a significant figure in Greek mythology. He was one of the Argonauts who accompanied Jason in his quest for the Golden Fleece and the father of the hero Ajax. Telamon's story is one of heroism and steadfastness. Telamon is often chosen to symbolize heroism, loyalty, and enduring strength.

Theseus
Meaning and Origin: To set (Greek)
Significance: A hero and king of Athens known for his many adventures, Theseus symbolizes bravery, justice, and the unity of Athens.

Triton
Meaning and Origin: Of the great sea; noisy (Greek)
Significance: He is a herald of the sea, using a conch shell to create thunderous sounds and control the waves. Triton embodies the untamed power and mystery of the ocean depths.

Troy
Meaning and Origin: Foot soldier (Greek)
Significance: Troy represents themes of human ambition, conflict, and the enduring power of stories.

Zephyr
Meaning and Origin: West wind (Greek)
Significance: Zephyrus is the Greek god of the west wind, known for bringing light spring and early summer breezes. Zephyrus is also associated with growth and renewal.

Zeus
Meaning and Origin: Sky; shine (Greek)
Significance: Zeus is the king of the gods in Greek mythology and ruler of the sky. Zeus is often chosen to symbolize power, authority, and leadership.

Male and Female Celestial Names

Gazing up at the night sky filled with twinkling stars and distant galaxies has sparked wonder for millennia. Choosing a celestial name for your baby taps into that very sense of awe and mystery. These names carry the weight of history, mythology, and scientific discovery. Imagine a daughter named Lyra, forever linked to the constellation of the harp, or a son named Orion, echoing the strength and prowess of the legendary hunter. Celestial names transcend cultures and languages, offering a timeless connection to the vast universe we inhabit. They spark curiosity and a sense of wonder, reminding your child of the infinite possibilities that life holds.

If you're looking for a name inspired by the cosmos, reflecting the awe and mystery of the universe, the following list of names contains the one for you!

Adhara
Meaning and Origin: Virgins (Arabic)
Significance: Adhara is the second brightest star in the constellation Canis Major, symbolizing beauty, purity, and brilliance.

Alcyone
Meaning and Origin: Kingfisher (Greek)
Significance: Alcyone is the brightest star in the Pleiades cluster, symbolizing tranquility and the mythological tale of transformation and peace.

Altair
Meaning and Origin: Flying eagle (Arabic)
Significance: Altair is the brightest star in the constellation Aquila, the Eagle. The name Altair evokes a sense of majesty, strength, and the ability to soar through the vastness of space.

Andromeda
Meaning and Origin: Ruler of men (Greek)
Significance: Andromeda is a constellation named after a mythological princess, symbolizing strength, beauty, and resilience.

Antares
Meaning and Origin: Rival of Mars (Greek)
Significance: Antares is the brightest star in the constellation Scorpius, symbolizing power, strength, and a deep, fiery passion.

Aries
Meaning and Origin: Ram (Latin)
Significance: Aries is a zodiac constellation representing leadership, courage, and a pioneering spirit.

Astrea
Meaning and Origin: Starry (Greek)
Significance: Astrea is linked to the Greek concept of divine justice and fairness. The name Astrea carries connotations of purity, righteousness, and a connection to the celestial realm.

Auriga
Meaning and Origin: Charioteer (Latin)
Significance: Auriga is a constellation representing a chariot driver, symbolizing guidance, protection, and a journey.

Aurora
Meaning and Origin: Dawn (Latin)
Significance: Aurora embodies the essence of new beginnings, hope, and the promise of a fresh start. The name also carries a touch of magic due to its association with the mesmerizing Aurora Borealis, or the Northern Lights.

Aquila
Meaning and Origin: Eagle (Latin)
Significance: Aquila has a strong and majestic connotation, embodying the powerful bird of prey. The eagle symbolizes freedom, leadership, strength, and sharp vision.

Bellatrix
Meaning and Origin: Warrior woman (Latin)
Significance: The name itself carries a strong and powerful connotation, embodying a female warrior. Choosing Bellatrix as a name evokes a sense of strength and determination and the ability to be a shining star.

Boone
Meaning and Origin: Good; companion (British)
Significance: This name evokes a sense of trust and partnership. By naming a child Boone, parents may hope to convey values of goodness and positivity.

Caelum
Meaning and Origin: Heaven; sky (Latin)
Significance: Caelum is a straightforward and beautiful name that directly connects to the vastness of the celestial realm, which evokes a general sense of awe and wonder associated with the cosmos.

Callisto
Meaning and Origin: Most beautiful (Greek)
Significance: Callisto is a nymph in Greek mythology and one of Jupiter's moons, symbolizing beauty and transformation.

Carina
Meaning and Origin: Keel of a ship (Latin)
Significance: Carina is a constellation, symbolizing navigation, exploration, and the journey through the celestial seas.

Cassiopeia
Meaning and Origin: Queen (Greek)
Significance: Cassiopeia is a constellation named after a mythological queen, representing vanity, beauty, and celestial grandeur.

Celeste
Meaning and Origin: Heavenly (Latin)
Significance: Celeste carries a direct meaning linked to the heavens. It also reflects themes of divinity and beauty.

Comet
Meaning and Origin: Ice rock (British)
Significance: Comet carries a sense of wonder and fleeting beauty. Comet is often chosen to symbolize brilliance, uniqueness, and a journey through the cosmos.

Cosmo
Meaning and Origin: Order; harmony (Greek)
Significance: Cosmo evokes a sense of connection to the universe as a whole. It suggests a child with a broad perspective and a deep appreciation for the natural world.

Cygnus
Meaning and Origin: Swan (Latin)
Significance: Cygnus is a constellation representing a swan, symbolizing grace, elegance, and transformation.

Delphinus
Meaning and Origin: Dolphin (Greek)
Significance: Delphinus is a constellation symbolizing playfulness, intelligence, and harmony.

Despina
Meaning and Origin: Ladyv (Greek)
Significance: Despina is a moon of Neptune, symbolizing nobility, grace, and a regal presence.

Draco
Meaning and Origin: Dragon (Latin)
Significance: In constellation mythology, Draco represents a large dragon that coils around the North Pole. Choosing Draco as a name evokes these qualities and a connection to the celestial realm.

Ember
Meaning and Origin: A small piece of glowing coal (British)
Significance: It evokes the image of glowing embers reminiscent of distant stars. This name suggests a child with a spark of brilliance and the potential to create something extraordinary.

Eridanus
Meaning and Origin: River (Greek)
Significance: Eridanus is a constellation symbolizing a river, representing continuity, flow, and life's journey.

Everest
Meaning and Origin: Dweller on the Eure River (English)
Significance: George and Amal Clooney named their son Alexander Everest Clooney, reflecting grandeur and aspiration.

Ganymede
Meaning and Origin: Prominent among men (Greek)
Significance: Ganymede is the largest moon of Jupiter, symbolizing beauty, youth, and the myth of the cupbearer to the gods.

Gemini
Meaning and Origin: Twins (Latin)
Significance: The name carries connotations of duality, partnership, and strong connections. In astrology, Gemini is also a zodiac sign associated with communication, intelligence, and adaptability.

Halley
Meaning and Origin: Ruler; commander (British)
Significance: The name carries a strong connection to astronomy, scientific discovery, and the awe-inspiring nature of comets.

Hesperus
Meaning and Origin: Evening star (Greek)
Significance: Hesperus is the personification of the evening star, symbolizing twilight, beauty, and the transition between day and night.

Indus
Meaning and Origin: Indian (Latin)
Significance: Indus is a constellation, symbolizing exploration, discovery, and the connection between different cultures.

Jupiter
Meaning and Origin: Father; shine (Roman)
Significance: A name associated with power, leadership, and benevolence, Jupiter embodies kingly authority, sky and thunder, and law and justice.

Leo
Meaning and Origin: Lion (Latin)
Significance: Leo carries the symbolism of the lion: bravery, royalty, and protection. It can also connect to the astrological sign Leo, known for its confidence and creativity.

Libra
Meaning and Origin: Scales; balance (Latin)
Significance: This name symbolizes balance, justice, and equality.

Lumi
Meaning and Origin: Snow (Finnish)
Significance: Lumi evokes the beauty and serenity of the night sky, offering a unique and less literal connection to the cosmos.

Luna
Meaning and Origin: Moon (Latin)
Significance: Choosing Luna for your child imbues them with a connection to these qualities and the moon's awe-inspiring presence.

Lynx
Meaning and Origin: Wildcat (Greek)
Significance: Lynx is a constellation, symbolizing sharp sight, stealth, and the elusive nature of the night sky.

Maia
Meaning and Origin: Mother (Greek)
Significance: One of the Pleiades stars, Maia symbolizes nurturing, growth, and maternal strength.

Mars
Meaning and Origin: God of war (Roman)
Significance: Choosing the name Mars can represent bravery, determination, and a passionate spirit.

Mercury
Meaning and Origin: God of messengers, travelers, and thieves (Roman)
Significance: Choosing the name Mercury can represent quick thinking, communication skills, and adaptability.

Mira
Meaning and Origin: Wonderful (Latin)
Significance: Mira is a binary star in the constellation Cetus, symbolizing wonder, change, and the marvels of the universe.

Nashira
Meaning and Origin: Bearer of good news (Arabic)
Significance: Nashira is a star in the constellation Capricornus, symbolizing hope, good fortune, and positive change.

Nova
Meaning and Origin: New (Latin)
Significance: Nova reflects a wish for the child to embody qualities of creativity, innovation, and a fresh start. Parents choosing Nova might hope their child brings a burst of light and energy into the world.

Oberon
Meaning and Origin: Elf king (German)
Significance: Oberon name embodies a sense of magic, mischief, and connection to the natural world.

Pandora
Meaning and Origin: All-gifted (Greek)
Significance: The name Pandora is a double-edged sword. It signifies beauty, potential, and the gifts bestowed upon humanity. However, it also carries a cautionary tale about curiosity and the potential for unintended consequences.

Rigel
Meaning and Origin: Foot (Arabic)
Significance: Rigel is a bright star in the constellation Orion, symbolizing strength, stability, and a guiding light.

Sagitta
Meaning and Origin: Arrow (Latin)
Significance: Sagitta is a constellation representing an arrow, symbolizing precision, direction, and swiftness.

Scorpius
Meaning and Origin: Scorpion (Latin)
Significance: Scorpius is a zodiac constellation representing mystery, intensity, and transformative power.

Sidereal
Meaning and Origin: Of the stars (Latin)
Significance: Sidereal signifies a deep connection to the cosmos and the vastness of space. It evokes a sense of wonder and mystery associated with the stars and the unknown.

Sienna
Meaning and Origin: Redish-brown color (Italian)
Significance: Sienna is often chosen to symbolize warmth, creativity, and a vibrant personality. It reflects a wish for the child to embody qualities of passion, artistic flair, and a sunny disposition.

Sirius
Meaning and Origin: Dark dog (Greek)
Significance: Choosing Sirius as a name imbues your child with a sense of strength, brilliance, and the ability to become a guiding light.

Skyla
Meaning and Origin: Belonging to the sky (Hebrew)
Significance: Skyla is a unique name with a beautiful celestial connection. It evokes images of vastness, wonder, and the delicate luminescence of the moon.

Solar
Meaning and Origin: Of the sun (Latin)
Significance: It represents warmth, light, energy, and the very spark of life. It's a bold and symbolic name, suggesting a bright future and a radiant personality.

Solstice
Meaning and Origin: Sun-standing (Latin)
Significance: It refers to the astronomical event where the sun reaches its highest or lowest point in the sky, marking the longest or shortest day of the year. As a name, it evokes a sense of change, transition, and the power of the sun.

Starr
Meaning and Origin: Star (American)
Significance: It evokes feelings of brilliance, hope, and guidance, just like a star in the night sky.

Taurus
Meaning and Origin: Bull (Latin)
Significance: Taurus is a zodiac constellation symbolizing strength, determination, and stability.

Titania
Meaning and Origin: Giant; the Titans (Greek)
Significance: Titania evokes images of both earthly power and otherworldly magic. It is appreciated for its poetic and imaginative connotations.

Ursa
Meaning and Origin: Bear (Latin)
Significance: As a celestial name, Ursa evokes strength, resilience, and a connection to the natural world.

Vega
Meaning and Origin: Falling eagle (Arabic)
Significance: Vega is one of the brightest stars in the constellation Lyra, symbolizing brightness, prominence, and a soaring spirit.

Vela
Meaning and Origin: Sails of a ship (Latin)
Significance: Vela is a constellation, symbolizing navigation, adventure, and the journey through the celestial ocean.

Venus
Meaning and Origin: Love; beauty; desire (Roman)
Significance: Named after the Roman goddess of love, Venus embodies charm, grace, and aesthetic beauty. As a celestial name, it signifies romance and allure.

Volans
Meaning and Origin: Flying fish (Latin)
Significance: Volans is a constellation representing a flying fish, symbolizing agility, adaptability, and a sense of wonder.

Vulcan
Meaning and Origin: God of fire and forge (Roman)
Significance: Vulcan is named after the Roman god of fire and metalworking, symbolizing creativity, craftsmanship, and strength.

Zaniah
Meaning and Origin: Corner (Arabic)
Significance: Zaniah is a star in the constellation Virgo, symbolizing precision, order, and a guiding light in the vastness of space.

Zaria
Meaning and Origin: Sunrise; blossom (Slavic)
Significance: This name evokes a sense of new beginnings, hope, and a promise of a bright future.

Zenith
Meaning and Origin: The highest point (Arabic)
Significance: Zenith represents the point in the sky directly above an observer, symbolizing the peak, excellence, and reaching the highest goals.

Zosma
Meaning and Origin: Girdle (Greek)
Significance: Zosma is a star in the constellation Leo, symbolizing dignity, strength, and leadership.

These spiritual names can be a beautiful and unique way to give your child a name that will stand the test of time while also giving them a sense of mystery and depth. However, if these names aren't quite unique enough for you, be sure to check out the next chapter!

CHAPTER 5: UNIQUE AND UNCOMMON NAMES

Bestowing your baby with a unique name can be magical. It sets them apart from the crowd, fostering a sense of individuality from the very beginning. Imagine a classroom where your child isn't one of several Eva's or Liam's but is the only Arlo or Elara. This uniqueness can spark confidence and a sense of being special. Beyond individuality, unique names often hold deeper meanings or interesting stories behind them. They can be a tribute to a cherished family member, a character from a beloved book, or a connection to a particular culture or heritage. Ultimately, a unique name becomes a conversation starter, a chance for your child to share the story behind their name and celebrate what makes them *them*. If you want to stand out from the crowd with names as special as your precious one, this chapter is for you!

Unique and Rare Boys' Names

Boys rarely get blessed with an exciting name. In a sea of Justins, Jasons, and Seans, these unique names will help your little boy make a statement and stand out from the crowd, ensuring he leaves a lasting impression wherever he goes. Choosing a unique name for your son can set him apart with style and substance.

Aeric
Meaning and Origin: Eternal ruler; the air (Norse)
Significance: This name reminds the baby of their high potential. As a respelling of Eric, it is creative and embodies leadership skills. A baby with this name is sure to soar high.

Arden
Meaning and Origin: Eagle valley (British)
Significance: Arden carries a nature-inspired meaning, referencing a place inhabited by majestic eagles. Eagles are often associated with strength, freedom, and keen vision.

Austin
Meaning and Origin: Magnificent (Latin)
Significance: Austin is a unique choice compared to more popular names. Choosing Austin for your son implies that you wish for him to be successful and respected and perhaps even leave a lasting mark on the world.

Barak
Meaning and Origin: Lightning (Hebrew)
Significance: The name carries connotations of courage, strength, and leadership. Additionally, "lightning" evokes swiftness, power, and a touch of the unexpected.

Barrett
Meaning and Origin: Strife; mighty bear (German)
Significance: Barrett embodies a strong-willed and determined boy. This name also symbolizes qualities of courage, resilience, and inner strength.

Blade
Meaning and Origin: Knife; sword (British)
Significance: This name signifies strength, sharpness, and power. It also embodies someone who cuts through obstacles and challenges with ease.

Branwen
Meaning and Origin: Blessed Raven (Welsh)
Significance: This name symbolizes protection and wisdom, often associated with mystery, intuition, and strength of character.

Brax
Meaning and Origin: From the brick town (British)
Significance: This name offers a sense of strength, determination, and tenacity. By naming a child Brax, parents may hope to set their child on a path of confidence, individuality, and uniqueness.

Brock
Meaning and Origin: Badger (British)
Significance: Badgers are known for their persistence and toughness, burrowing in intricate dens and defending themselves fiercely. Choosing Brock for your son suggests your hope for him to inherit these positive qualities.

Cian
Meaning and Origin: Ancient (Irish)
Significance: It evokes a connection to ancient Gaelic culture and the long lineage of Irish heritage. The meaning "ancient" can also be interpreted as wise, experienced, or enduring.

Cillian
Meaning and Origin: Little church (Irish)
Significance: Cillian has a unique and charming meaning. It refers to a small church or place of worship and suggests a connection to faith, spirituality, and a sense of community. The name could also be interpreted as someone who is devoted, peaceful, or a source of comfort for others.

Colton
Meaning and Origin: The coal town (English)
Significance: Colton is of English origin and signify industriousness and craftsmanship. Colton represents a strong work ethic.

Cove
Meaning and Origin: A small, sheltered inlet (British)
Significance: This name doesn't have a traditional meaning associated with a person, so its significance would be more personal. It could evoke a sense of being sheltered, protected, or nestled away.

Damien
Meaning and Origin: To tame (Greek)
Significance: Damien signifies strength and devotion, while Damien represents calmness and control.

Dashiell
Meaning and Origin: Young boy; page (French)
Significance: The name carries a sense of literary history and a touch of mystery. It also offers a sophisticated sound and the option of using the shorter nickname "Dash."

Daxton
Meaning and Origin: Warrior; overcomer (French)
Significance: This name signifies strength and resilience to overcome obstacles. It reflects a wish for the child to embody qualities of bravery, resilience, and a strong sense of identity.

Dean
Meaning and Origin: Valley (English)
Significance: Dean signifies strength and tranquility. Dean also represents peacefulness and leadership.

Deke
Meaning and Origin: Ruler of people (Dutch)
Significance: Deke offers a friendly and approachable feel while retaining a connection to a more traditionally powerful name. It refers to someone who is down-to-earth yet possesses leadership qualities.

Eero
Meaning and Origin: Everlasting (Finnish)
Significance: Eero is a unique and handsome name with a strong meaning. In Finnish culture, it can evoke a sense of resilience and enduring spirit.

Elowen
Meaning and Origin: Elm tree (Cornish)
Significance: Elowen symbolizes growth and strength, often linked to a nurturing and resilient personality. The name evokes images of nature and stability, suggesting a person who is deeply rooted and dependable. Elowen is chosen for its unique beauty and connection to the natural world, reflecting a harmonious and balanced character.

Elwin
Meaning and Origin: Elf-friend; noble friend (British)
Significance: Elwin offers a touch of whimsy and connotes loyalty and friendship. Elwin is often chosen to symbolize honor and integrity. It reflects a wish for the child to embody qualities of trustworthiness, kindness, and a strong sense of camaraderie.

Enzo
Meaning and Origin: Estate ruler (German)
Significance: Enzo is a short form of various German names beginning with "Heinz," meaning "estate ruler." It's also a strong name that speaks of flair and wealth.

Erwan
Meaning and Origin: Sea warrior; man of the sea (French)
Significance: The meaning "sea warrior" conjures images of strength, bravery, and a connection to the natural world.

Evander
Meaning and Origin: Bow warrior, strong man (Greek)
Significance: Represents strength and courage, often associated with a brave and resilient personality.

Ezra
Meaning and Origin: Help (Hebrew)
Significance: Symbolizes support and compassion, reflecting a helpful and kind personality.

Falcon
Meaning and Origin: Bird of prey (British)
Significance: Falcon is a name that evokes a sense of power, focus, and keen observation. These birds are admired for their intelligence and hunting skills. In some cultures, falcons are seen as symbols of nobility, freedom, and spiritual connection.

Florian
Meaning and Origin: Blooming; flowering (Latin)
Significance: Florian is a unique choice for a boy's name because it has a beautiful and positive meaning that isn't overly common. It evokes images of growth, potential, and vibrancy.

Fletcher
Meaning and Origin: Arrow maker (British)
Significance: It offers a glimpse into the history of skilled craftspeople and the tools they used. The association with arrows can also symbolize focus, precision, and ambition.

Gatsby
Meaning and Origin: Sting (British)
Significance: This masculine name signifies sunshine, hope, and a vibrant life. Gatsby can also symbolize ambition, charm, and a spirit of adventure.

Ginevra
Meaning and Origin: Fair One (Italian)
Significance: Represents beauty and fairness, often associated with elegance and grace.

Grove
Meaning and Origin: Small wood (British)
Significance: Literally refers to a small cluster of trees. Figuratively, it could evoke a sense of nature, peace, or a place of refuge.

Gunner
Meaning and Origin: Army defender; warrior (Norse)
Significance: It carries connotations of bravery, strength, and a willingness to fight for what's right. Historically, the name was associated with Vikings and Norse warriors, adding a touch of adventurous spirit.

Harlan
Meaning and Origin: Land by the forest; hare clearing (British)
Significance: Harlan evokes a sense of connection to nature, peacefulness, and a touch of mystery surrounding the "clearing."

Hesper
Meaning and Origin: Evening star (Greek)
Significance: Hesper symbolizes guidance and enlightenment, often associated with hope and direction in darkness. People with this name are seen as beacons of light, providing clarity and inspiration to those around them. The name evokes a sense of calm and serenity, reflecting a personality that is both wise and comforting.

Horizon
Meaning and Origin: Where the earth meets the sky (British)
Significance: Horizon is highly unique and evokes a sense of vastness, possibility, and new beginnings. It suggests a child who is curious about the world and always looking toward the future.

Imran
Meaning and Origin: Prosperity, happiness (Arabic)
Significance: A name with rich religious and cultural significance, symbolizing abundance and joy.

Ishaan
Meaning and Origin: The sun, Lord Shiva (Sanskrit)
Significance: A name of Indian origin, symbolizing brilliance, divinity, and positivity. This name is also often associated with prayers, rituals, and sacred places.

Izaiah
Meaning and Origin: God is salvation (Hebrew)
Significance: A contemporary variation of Isaiah, representing divine protection and deliverance.

Inigo
Meaning and Origin: Free man, noble (French)
Significance: Inigo offers a unique and handsome name choice. It evokes strength and determination, as well as independence, nobility, and a spirit of adventure.

Isolde
Meaning and Origin: Ice ruler (Welsh)
Significance: Isolde embodies strength and clarity, often linked to a powerful and resilient character. The name suggests a person who is unyielding and steadfast, able to face challenges with grace and determination. Isolde is historically tied to Arthurian legend, adding a sense of romantic heroism and enduring love.

Jagger
Meaning and Origin: Carter, peddler (English)
Significance: A name with a strong and edgy appeal, often associated with iconic cultural figures.

Jareth
Meaning and Origin: Bled of the jar (English)
Significance: Jareth signifies uniqueness and distinction, often associated with a charismatic and individualistic personality. The name evokes a sense of mystery and allure, suggesting a person who stands out from the crowd. Jareth gained popularity through the character in the film "Labyrinth," enhancing its association with charm and enigma.

Jericho
Meaning and Origin: Place of the moon; city of palms (Hebrew)
Significance: The name evokes a sense of history, mystery, and a connection to ancient cultures. It also carries a touch of beauty with the "city of palms" meaning.

Jura
Meaning and Origin: Yew tree (Irish)
Significance: It holds connotations of strength, longevity, or a connection to nature.

Kael
Meaning and Origin: Mighty warrior (Irish)
Significance: Kael embodies strength and valor, often linked to a bold and fearless personality. The name suggests a person who is powerful and courageous, capable of facing great challenges with determination. Kael evokes images of ancient warriors and heroic deeds, reflecting a sense of bravery and fortitude.

Kairo
Meaning and Origin: Victorious; triumphant (Arabic)
Significance: Kairo is a strong and positive name with a clear meaning. It signifies victory and triumph over challenges. This name carries a powerful message for a child, symbolizing the potential to achieve great things.

Kerensa
Meaning and Origin: Love (Cornish)
Significance: Kerensa is often chosen to symbolize love, kindness, and a nurturing spirit. It reflects a wish for the child to embody qualities of empathy, warmth, and a strong bond with others.

Koa
Meaning and Origin: Warrior; brave (Hawaiian)
Significance: In Hawaiian culture, Koa wood is known for its strength and resilience. Naming a child Koa carries the symbolic meaning of a strong, courageous warrior, someone who will face challenges with bravery.

Koda
Meaning and Origin: Small tiger; little field (Japanese)
Significance: This name represents someone with a powerful spirit, who is strong and stands up for what is right.

Lachlan
Meaning and Origin: Land; place (Scottish)
Significance: The meanings "land" and "place" evoke a sense of belonging, stability, and connection to one's roots.

Lawson
Meaning and Origin: Son of Lawrence (English)
Significance: Lawson signifies heritage and strength. Lawson also represents lineage and nobility.

Lawton
Meaning and Origin: Free from the estate (British)
Significance: Lawton remains a distinctive choice compared to more popular names. It offers a touch of sophistication and a connection to a bygone era.

Lorcan
Meaning and Origin: Little dark one (Irish)
Significance: Lorcan is a unique and relatively uncommon name with a strong Irish heritage. Its meaning suggests a quiet or mysterious nature with intelligence and strength.

Magnus
Meaning and Origin: Great (Latin)
Significance: Magnus represents greatness and nobility, often linked to a powerful and influential personality. The name suggests a person who is destined for significant achievements and commands respect. Magnus evokes images of historical leaders and grand achievements, reflecting a sense of majesty and importance.

Monet
Meaning and Origin: A French surname (French)
Significance: Monet is a truly unique name with a strong artistic connection. Choosing this name for your son signifies an appreciation of art and creativity. It also offers a touch of sophistication and elegance, referencing one of the most influential artists in history.

Monty
Meaning and Origin: Sharp Mountain (French)
Significance: Monty is a friendly and informal nickname that can be associated with various names. It doesn't carry a strong historical or cultural significance, but it offers a sense of warmth and informality.

Mori
Meaning and Origin: Forest (Japanese)
Significance: This name evokes a connection to nature and tranquility while also representing wisdom and guidance.

Nalu
Meaning and Origin: Surfing; wave (Hawaiian)
Significance: This name embodies the essence of the ocean and the power and strength of each wave.

Naoki
Meaning and Origin: Honest, straightforward (Japanese)
Significance: Naoki translates to "honest tree" or "straightforward tree." This signifies someone upright, honest, and dependable. In Japanese culture, these are highly valued traits. The name also connects to nature, with the "tree" symbolizing strength and growth.

Nerissa
Meaning and Origin: Sea nymph (Greek)
Significance: Nerissa embodies beauty and mystery, often associated with a captivating and enchanting personality. The name suggests a person who is graceful and alluring, capable of drawing others in with their charm. Nerissa evokes images of the sea and mythical creatures, reflecting a sense of wonder and enchantment.

Nevin
Meaning and Origin: Friendly; gracious (Scottish)
Significance: Nevin avoids the trend of overly common names while offering a friendly and approachable feel.

Omari
Meaning and Origin: Long-lived; flourishing (Swahili)
Significance: Omari is a vibrant name brimming with positive meaning. Derived from the Arabic word "Omar," it translates to "long-lived" or "flourishing" in Swahili. The name carries wishes for a blessed and prosperous life for the bearer.

Oswaldo
Meaning and Origin: Powerful ruler (German)
Significance: Oswaldo offers a rich tapestry of meaning. It embodies divine power, leadership qualities, and potentially a connection to nature.

Otis
Meaning and Origin: Wealthy (German)
Significance: It carries a certain air of strength and fortune due to its possible connection to wealth.

Paladin
Meaning and Origin: Court official; palace official (French)
Significance: In literature and fantasy, paladins became noble warriors and champions of justice and righteousness. They were often depicted as skilled fighters who upheld a strict moral code. Therefore, choosing Paladin for your son imbues him with a sense of chivalry, honor, and dedication to the greater good.

Peregrine
Meaning and Origin: Wanderer; traveler (Latin)
Significance: Peregrine refers to someone who travels long distances, often on foot, someone unafraid to explore and push boundaries. It also evokes a sense of adventure, freedom, and a determined spirit.

Phaedra
Meaning and Origin: Bright (Greek)
Significance: Phaedra represents radiance and intelligence, often associated with a brilliant and insightful personality. The name suggests a person who is enlightening and inspiring, capable of bringing clarity and understanding to those around them. Phaedra evokes images of light and wisdom, reflecting a luminous and wise character.

Presley
Meaning and Origin: Priest's meadow (British)
Significance: Presley is a unique name in the sense that it's not a common first name but rather a surname. This gives it a more vintage feel and a potential connection to family history if it was an ancestral surname.

Pryce
Meaning and Origin: Value; worth (Welsh)
Significance: Pryce is a fun name, and it represents someone of high worth. It also embodies qualities admired in Welsh history, such as resilience, loyalty, and a strong sense of identity.

Quillon
Meaning and Origin: Crossing swords (Latin)
Significance: Quillon represents protection and strength, often associated with a fierce and courageous personality. The name suggests a person who is brave and ready to defend their beliefs and loved ones. Quillon evokes images of a warrior, embodying valor, and honor.

Rhydian
Meaning and Origin: Red (Welsh)
Significance: Reflects a passionate and vibrant personality, bringing energy and enthusiasm.

Rhys
Meaning and Origin: Enthusiasm; ardor (Welsh)
Significance: Rhys is a name steeped in Welsh culture and history. It has been borne by many Welsh noblemen, princes, and rulers throughout the Middle Ages. Its meaning refers to someone passionate and energetic about their pursuits.

Roscoe
Meaning and Origin: Beautiful forests (Scottish)
Significance: Its meaning suggests a connection to nature. The name embodies beauty and gentle strength, just like in nature.

Rowena
Meaning and Origin: Fame, joy; famous friend (German)
Significance: Rowena embodies happiness and renown, often associated with a joyful and esteemed personality. The name suggests a person who brings joy and positivity to those around them, capable of achieving great recognition. Rowena evokes images of medieval courts and celebrated figures, reflecting a sense of joy and accomplishment.

Rush
Meaning and Origin: Storm (British)
Significance: This name signifies a violent weather condition with strong winds, rain, hail, thunder, and lightning. It embodies a strong and passionate character who is strong and bold.

Rylan
Meaning and Origin: Little king (Irish)
Significance: This name suggests a connection to Irish heritage and, potentially, leadership qualities of a king, including bravery.

Shephard
Meaning and Origin: Sheepherder (British)
Significance: Traditionally, Shephard was a surname given to those who herded sheep. It can represent a connection to family history or a rural way of life. The name embodies leadership qualities and someone who is responsible and caring.

Storm
Meaning and Origin: Violent weather (Dutch)
Significance: The name Storm evokes a sense of power, intensity, and the untamed force of nature. It suggests someone with a strong personality and a zest for life.

Sullivan
Meaning and Origin: Dark-eyed (Irish)
Significance: Its meaning suggests striking dark eyes or sharp eyesight, which could be a way parents honor a physical characteristic
of their child. In some cultures, dark eyes can symbolize strength or determination, adding another layer of meaning.

Sylas
Meaning and Origin: Forest; wood (Latin)
Significance: Sylas represents nature and resilience, often linked to a strong and enduring personality. The name suggests a person who is connected to nature and capable of withstanding challenges. Sylas evokes images of ancient forests and natural landscapes, reflecting a sense of strength and stability.

Taiga
Meaning and Origin: Great wilderness (Japanese)
Significance: Taiga refers to a subarctic biome characterized by coniferous forests. Choosing this name suggests a love for nature and wilderness.

Tiberius
Meaning and Origin: Near the Tiber River (Latin)
Significance: Tiberius represents power and leadership, often associated with a commanding and authoritative personality. The name suggests a person who is influential and respected, capable of making significant impacts. Historically, Tiberius is the name of Roman emperors, adding a sense of grandeur and historical significance.

Torian
Meaning and Origin: Thunder (Greek)
Significance: Torian is derived from the ancient Greek name "Torianos," which means "thunder." It symbolizes strength, power, and awe-inspiring presence.

Torin
Meaning and Origin: Chief (Irish)
Significance: Someone who is a leader or possesses strength and authority. This meaning connects to the Gaelic word "torfhinn," which translates to "chief."

Trent
Meaning and Origin: Gushing waters (English)
Significance: Trent signifies positivity and movement. Trent also represents strength and dynamic energy.

Ulric
Meaning and Origin: Wolf power (German)
Significance: Ulric embodies strength and resilience, often linked to a fierce and determined character. The name suggests a person who is powerful and unyielding, capable of overcoming great challenges. Ulric evokes images of wolves, reflecting a sense of loyalty and courage.

Urban
Meaning and Origin: Of the city (Latin)
Significance: The meaning "of the city" suggests a connection to urban life, culture, and possibly sophisticated or worldly air.

Vale
Meaning and Origin: Valley (French)
Significance: The meaning of "valley" connects Vale to nature and the beauty of the landscape. It could suggest someone grounded and peaceful.

Vesper
Meaning and Origin: Evening star (Latin)
Significance: Vesper symbolizes guidance and tranquility, often associated with a calm and reflective personality. The name suggests a person who brings peace and clarity, providing direction in times of uncertainty. Vesper evokes images of the evening sky, reflecting a serene and contemplative nature.

Viggo
Meaning and Origin: Worthy war (Scottish)
Significance: The meaning directly connects Viggo to strength and bravery in battle. It is also a name that resonates with a sense of heritage and a strong, independent spirit.

Winslow
Meaning and Origin: Hill of Victory (English)
Significance: Symbolizes success and achievement, often seen as a determined and ambitious figure.

Wolf
Meaning and Origin: Cunning man (German)
Significance: The name evokes power, intensity, and the untamed force of nature. It suggests someone who is strong-willed and the leader of a pack.

Wynell
Meaning and Origin: Joyful; blessed (Welsh)
Significance: The name Wynel has Welsh origins, meaning "joyful" or "blessed." It evokes a sense of happiness, positivity, and good fortune. Wynel suggests a person who brings joy to others and has an optimistic outlook on life. It carries connotations of being blessed and fortunate, reflecting a life filled with love and prosperity.

Wystan
Meaning and Origin: Battle stone (Old English)
Significance: Wystan represents strength and endurance, often linked to a steadfast and reliable character. The name suggests a person who is resilient and dependable, capable of withstanding difficult situations. Wystan evokes images of ancient warriors, reflecting a sense of historical valor and courage.

Zane
Meaning and Origin: God is gracious (Hebrew)
Significance: Zane is of Hebrew origin and convey a sense of divine remembrance and favor. Zane also signifies grace and kindness.

Zyke
Meaning and Origin: High energy (American)
Significance: This name signifies someone who is energetic, full of life, and a positive influence on everyone around them.

Unique and Rare Girls' Names

There's something magical about a girl with a unique name. These unusual choices exude charm and originality, so be sure to look if you're not interested in adding another Michelle or Alecia to the world.

Abilene
Meaning and Origin: Land of meadows (Hebrew)
Significance: Abilene is often chosen to symbolize serenity, natural beauty, and a harmonious environment. It reflects a wish for the child to embody qualities of peace, grace, and a deep connection with the natural world. Its most prominent meaning connects Abilene to the beauty and serenity of nature.

Adelina
Meaning and Origin: Noble (German)
Significance: Adelina represents nobility and grace, often associated with elegance and a refined character. Those named Adelina are often seen as embodying dignity and high moral standards, standing out in society for their poised and respectable nature. Historically, the name is tied to noble families and figures who have contributed positively to their communities.

Adina
Meaning and Origin: Delicate; luxurious (Hebrew)
Significance: The meaning "delicate" or "luxurious" imbues Adina with a sense of grace and elegance.

Adira
Meaning and Origin: Strong; splendid (Hebrew)
Significance: Adira carries a powerful meaning, suggesting someone with strength, nobility, and a touch of grandeur. It's a beautiful way to express hope for your child's future.

Aislinn
Meaning and Origin: Dream, vision (Irish)
Significance: Aisling embodies creativity and inspiration, often linked to a visionary and imaginative personality. The name suggests a person who is driven by their dreams and capable of bringing their visions to life. Aisling evokes images of poetic beauty and artistic expression, reflecting a profound and insightful character.

Anya
Meaning and Origin: Grace; limitless (Russian)
Significance: The name emphasizes kindness, elegance, and beauty. It also suggests someone with boundless potential and possibilities.

Arianell
Meaning and Origin: Silver (Welsh)
Significance: Symbolizes purity and clarity, often associated with a bright and sparkling presence.

Ashere
Meaning and Origin: Blessed (Hebrew)
Significance: Represents happiness and favor, reflecting a joyful and content personality. Ashere carries a sense of divine blessing and fulfillment, often associated with a life of peace and prosperity.

Avalon
Meaning and Origin: Island of apples (Welsh)
Significance: Avalon is most famous for being the mystical island in Arthurian legend, where King Arthur was taken to heal after his final battle. This association imbues the name with a sense of magic, mystery, and otherworldliness.

Avina
Meaning and Origin: Bird (Latin)
Significance: This name represents freedom, flight, and connection to nature.

Azalea
Meaning and Origin: Dry (Greek)
Significance: The name Azalea directly connects the child to a beautiful flowering plant, symbolizing beauty, resilience (due to its ability to thrive in dry conditions), and even delicate nature.

Blossom
Meaning and Origin: Bloom; flower (British)
Significance: Blossom evokes a sense of new beginnings, potential, and the beauty of a flower in bloom. It suggests someone who is flourishing or blossoming into their full potential.

Blythe
Meaning and Origin: Happy, Carefree (English)
Significance: Reflects a joyful and optimistic personality, bringing happiness and lightness to others.

Briar
Meaning and Origin: Thorny plant (British)
Significance: The association with a thorny bush refers to someone strong and able to withstand challenges by protecting themselves.

Cali
Meaning and Origin: Fairest, beautiful, or lovely (Latin)
Significance: Cali is often chosen to symbolize sunshine, optimism, and a positive outlook on life. It reflects a wish for the child to embody qualities of warmth, energy, and a joyful spirit.

Calix
Meaning and Origin: Very Handsome (Greek)
Significance: Suggests a striking and attractive presence, often seen as charming and charismatic.

Calliope
Meaning and Origin: Beautiful-voiced (Greek)
Significance: The meaning "beautiful voiced" suggests a connection to music, singing, or artistic expression in general. It might be chosen if you hope your child has a talent or passion for the arts.

Cambria
Meaning and Origin: Wales (Latin)
Significance: Cambria has a clear and direct connection to Wales. It's a great choice for parents of Welsh descent or those seeking a name with a specific geographical connection.

Carla
Meaning and Origin: Free woman; Strong (German)
Significance: Carla signifies independence and strength. It is a name that reflects power and resilience, often chosen to impart a sense of freedom and determination.

Claudette
Meaning and Origin: Protection (French)
Significance: Claudette inherits some meaning and history from Claudia. Claudia was a Roman family name, linked to the concept of "enclosure" or "protection."

Clover
Meaning and Origin: Meadow flower (English)
Significance: Clover is best represented as a luck flower. It also signifies luck and charm, often associated with the four-leaf clover symbol.

Comfort
Meaning and Origin: Consolation; relief (French)
Significance: This name embodies a peaceful nature and refers to someone kind and gentle.

Clover
Meaning and Origin: Meadow flower (English)
Significance: Represents luck and charm, often associated with the four-leaf clover symbol.

Coraline
Meaning and Origin: Coral (Latin)
Significance: Evokes images of the sea and natural beauty, symbolizing uniqueness and vibrancy.

Crimson
Meaning and Origin: A deep red color (French)
Significance: Crimson is often chosen to symbolize passion, determination, and a fiery spirit. It reflects a wish for the child to embody qualities of resilience, creativity, and a strong sense of self.

Cyra
Meaning and Origin: Sun (Persian)
Significance: Represents light and warmth, embodying a radiant and cheerful disposition.

Delphine
Meaning and Origin: Dolphin (French)
Significance: The "dolphin" meaning evokes intelligence, gracefulness, and a connection to the ocean.

Devika
Meaning and Origin: Little goddess; minor deity (Sanskrit)
Significance: Devika carries a strong association with divinity, referring to someone blessed or having a graceful and divine nature.

Dione
Meaning and Origin: Divine Queen (Greek)
Significance: Dione is often chosen to symbolize beauty, grace, and a connection to the divine. This name also represents divinity and power, often seen as a majestic and influential figure.

Dulcinea
Meaning and Origin: Sweet (Spanish)
Significance: Represents a sweet and gentle nature, often associated with kindness and affection.

Elara
Meaning and Origin: Mortal princess (Greek)
Significance: The association with Greek mythology imbues Elara with a touch of mystery and grandeur.

Eldora
Meaning and Origin: Golden (Spanish)
Significance: Represents someone precious and radiant, often seen as a beacon of light and positivity.

Enya
Meaning and Origin: Grain; kernel (Irish)
Significance: The meaning connects Enya to the natural world and the potential for growth and abundance.

Everly
Meaning and Origin: Boar dwelling (British)
Significance: The most prominent meaning suggests a connection to the natural world, with the image of a wild boar roaming a meadow. The name embodies courage, strength, and peace.

Faelan
Meaning and Origin: Little Wolf (Irish)
Significance: Indicates someone with a strong, independent spirit and a deep connection to nature and instinct.

Fenella
Meaning and Origin: White shoulder (Irish)
Significance: Fenella represents purity and grace, often associated with a delicate and refined personality. The name suggests a person who is elegant and serene, embodying a sense of calm and purity. Fenella evokes images of gentle landscapes and pristine beauty, reflecting a soothing and graceful presence.

Fern
Meaning and Origin: symbol of sincerity (Old English)
Significance: Fern is directly derived from the name of the plant, which is known for its lush green foliage and graceful appearance in woodland settings. Ferns are known for their ability to thrive in various conditions. The name might symbolize resilience and adaptability.

Fioralba
Meaning and Origin: Flower of Dawn (Albanian)
Significance: Reflects a fresh, blossoming presence, often associated with new beginnings and hope.

Flora
Meaning and Origin: Flower (Latin)
Significance: Flora directly translates to "flower," connecting the name to beauty, nature's bounty, and the cycle of growth.

Frieda
Meaning and Origin: Peace, joy (German)
Significance: The primary meaning refers to someone who brings calmness and serenity. It could also represent a desire for peace in the child's life.

Galadriel
Meaning and Origin: Maiden crowned with a radiant garland (Sindarin)
Significance: Galadriel represents light and purity, often linked to wisdom and ethereal beauty. The name carries a sense of mystical and otherworldly charm, suggesting a person of deep insight and spiritual presence. Galadriel is known from Tolkien's Middle-earth legendarium, further adding to its association with grace and leadership.

Galatea
Meaning and Origin: She Who is Milk-White (Greek)
Significance: Symbolizes purity and beauty, often associated with mythological grace and elegance.

Galene
Meaning and Origin: Calm seas (Greek)
Significance: Galene, a minor Greek goddess, personified the calm seas. The name embodies tranquility, peace, and a sense of calmness.

Gloriana
Meaning and Origin: Glorious (Latin)
Significance: Symbolizes honor and magnificence, reflecting a radiant and majestic personality. Gloriana evokes a sense of grandeur and elegance, embodying the essence of glory and splendor.

Hanako
Meaning and Origin: Flower child (Japanese)
Significance: Hanako's meaning evokes images of blooming flowers, symbolizing beauty, innocence, and the delicate nature of life.

Helena
Meaning and Origin: Light; bright (Greek)
Significance: Helena represents illumination and brilliance, often associated with a radiant and intelligent personality. The name suggests a person who is enlightening and inspiring, bringing clarity and insight to those around them. Helena evokes images of classical beauty and wisdom, reflecting a dignified and luminous character.

Hesperia
Meaning and Origin: Evening Star (Greek)
Significance: Reflects a mysterious and enchanting personality, bringing a sense of wonder and allure.

Hestia
Meaning and Origin: Hearth, home (Greek)
Significance: Hestia is often chosen to symbolize the importance of home and family bonds. It reflects a wish for the child to embody qualities of stability, nurturing, and a strong sense of belonging. It also can represent warmth and comfort, often seen as a nurturing and caring presence.

Hyacinth
Meaning and Origin: Blue flower; precious stone (Greek)
Significance: This name signifies beauty and nature, as well as eternal life and something of high value.

Iggy
Meaning and Origin: Like fire; fiery (Spanish)
Significance: This name embodies passion, willpower, and tenacity.

Inara
Meaning and Origin: Ray of light; heaven sent (Arabic)
Significance: Inara embodies someone elegant, radiant, and very beautiful. It is also connected to a positive attitude and refers to someone hopeful.

Isidore
Meaning and Origin: Gift of Isis (Greek)
Significance: Isidore reflects a divine connection and a generous, kind-hearted nature. It is a name that resonates with a deep sense of purpose and divine guidance.

Ivy
Meaning and Origin: Vine (British)
Significance: A vine is a strong yet beautiful part of nature, which signifies a strong bond. This name embodies the everlasting qualities of loyalty, strength, resilience, and evergreen-ness.

Jaiyana
Meaning and Origin: Good; excellent (Arabic)
Significance: This name is given to someone to suggest positive qualities such as excellence and achievement.

Jareth
Meaning and Origin: Descent (English)
Significance: Suggests a grounding presence, someone who brings stability and balance to their surroundings.

Jasmina
Meaning and Origin: Jasmine Flower (Persian)
Significance: Represents beauty and elegance, often associated with grace and charm.

Jena
Meaning and Origin: Small bird (Arabic)
Significance: Symbolizes freedom and grace, reflecting a delicate and agile personality. Jena evokes a sense of lightness and beauty, embodying the essence of a bird in flight and the freedom it represents.

Jocasta
Meaning and Origin: Shining moon (Greek)
Significance: Jocasta represents brilliance and mystery, often associated with a complex and intriguing personality. The name suggests a person who is multifaceted and captivating, embodying a sense of depth and allure. Jocasta evokes images of moonlit nights and mythological tales, reflecting a sense of mystique and enigma.

Josephina
Meaning and Origin: God will add (Hebrew)
Significance: Represents divine blessing and abundance, reflecting a strong and faithful personality. Josephina carries a sense of growth and prosperity, often associated with spiritual and material increase.

Kaida
Meaning and Origin: Little Dragon (Japanese)
Significance: Symbolizes strength and resilience, often associated with a fierce and determined personality.

Kalliope
Meaning and Origin: Beautiful Voice (Greek)
Significance: Kalliope is often chosen to symbolize a love for literature, poetry, and music. It reflects a wish for the child to embody qualities of creativity, intelligence, and a passion for the arts.

Katya
Meaning and Origin: Pure; perfect (Russian)
Significance: Katya is often chosen for its simplicity and elegance. It reflects a wish for the child to embody qualities of grace, honesty, and a straightforward nature.

Katrin
Meaning and Origin: Pure; flawless (Greek)
Significance: The meaning "pure" suggests qualities like innocence, cleanliness, and moral goodness. It also offers a unique way to deviate from traditional names such as Katherine.

Keziah
Meaning and Origin: Cassia Tree (Hebrew)
Significance: Symbolizes strength and resilience, often associated with healing properties and a nurturing spirit.

Lake
Meaning and Origin: A body of water (American)
Significance: The most prominent association with Lake is its connection to nature and bodies of water. It suggests a serene and peaceful quality.

Leocadia
Meaning and Origin: Bright, Clear (Spanish)
Significance: Represents clarity and brightness, bringing a sense of insight and enlightenment.

Liora
Meaning and Origin: Light (Hebrew)
Significance: Reflects a bright, optimistic personality, bringing hope and inspiration to others.

Lysandra
Meaning and Origin: Liberator, one who frees (Greek)
Significance: Lysandra symbolizes freedom and empowerment, often associated with a strong and independent personality. The name suggests a person who is capable of breaking free from constraints and achieving their own destiny. Lysandra evokes images of liberation and strength, reflecting a resilient and empowering character.

Marius
Meaning and Origin: The Sea (Latin)
Significance: Suggests a deep, introspective nature with a strong connection to the ocean and its mysteries.

Melea
Meaning and Origin: Full; filled (Hebrew)
Significance: This name signifies being whole or complete. It is a beautiful name for a last-born child as it signifies the family is complete. It also provides a message of being enough as is.

Meliora
Meaning and Origin: Better (Latin)
Significance: Reflects a striving for improvement and excellence, often associated with ambition and determination.

Melisande
Meaning and Origin: Strong in Work (German)
Significance: Represents diligence and perseverance, often associated with a strong work ethic and determination.

Mina
Meaning and Origin: Determined protector (German)
Significance: This name suggests strength, determination, and a protective nature.

Mirielle
Meaning and Origin: Wonderful; miraculous (Latin)
Significance: This name suggests something exceptional, blessed, or extraordinary.

Morgana
Meaning and Origin: Bright Sea circle (Welsh)
Significance: The meaning "sea-born" or "sea circle" connects Morgana to the ocean's depth and power. It can suggest someone deep and intuitive and possessing hidden potential.

Myrtle
Meaning and Origin: Spring (Greek)
Significance: In Greek mythology, the Myrtle wreath was associated with Aphrodite, the goddess of love and beauty. It also symbolized good luck and prosperity.

Nebula
Meaning and Origin: Mist; cloud (Latin)
Significance: Nebulae are vast clouds of gas and dust in space, often associated with the birth of new stars. The name evokes a sense of mystery, potential, and the vastness of the universe.

Nerida
Meaning and Origin: Sea Nymph (Greek)
Significance: Represents grace and beauty, often associated with a free-spirited and adventurous nature.

Nyssa
Meaning and Origin: Goal (Greek)
Significance: Symbolizes determination and ambition, often seen as a driven and focused personality.

Odessa
Meaning and Origin: Wrathful (Greek)
Significance: Reflects a passionate and determined personality, often associated with strength and resilience.

Onyx
Meaning and Origin: Claw; fingernail (Greek)
Significance: Onyx was believed to offer protection and strength, like a claw or fingernail. The black and white banded variety of onyx is a semi-precious gemstone prized for its beauty and elegance.

Oriana
Meaning and Origin: Golden (Latin)
Significance: Symbolizes radiance and a warm, inviting personality, often seen as a source of joy and positivity.

Peregrine
Meaning and Origin: Traveler (Latin)
Significance: Reflects a wandering spirit and a thirst for adventure, bringing a sense of discovery and exploration.

Petra
Meaning and Origin: Rock (Greek)
Significance: Symbolizes strength and stability, often seen as a steadfast and reliable figure.

Philippa
Meaning and Origin: Lover of horses (Greek)
Significance: Horses were often associated with strength, nobility, and freedom in ancient cultures. This name embodies someone who values all those qualities associated with horses.

Philomena
Meaning and Origin: Lover of strength (Greek)
Significance: Its "lover of strength" meaning refers to someone who values inner strength, determination, and perseverance.

Piper
Meaning and Origin: Flute player (English)
Significance: Piper conveys creativity and skill, while representing musical talent and creativity.

Quinlan
Meaning and Origin: Strong, Fit (Irish)
Significance: Indicates physical and mental resilience, often associated with perseverance and determination.

Quintessa
Meaning and Origin: Essence (Latin)
Significance: Represents purity and a quintessential nature, often associated with a refined and elegant presence.

Racquel
Meaning and Origin: Innocent (Spanish)
Significance: Racquel carries connotations of status and dignity. Racquel also signifies innocence or purity.

Rain
Meaning and Origin: Falling water (British)
Significance: Rain is essential for life and symbolizes growth, renewal, and fertility. The name Rain can evoke a connection to nature's life-giving power.

Rhea
Meaning and Origin: Flowing (Greek)
Significance: Reflects a calm and soothing presence, often associated with grace and tranquility.

Rhiannon
Meaning and Origin: Great Queen (Welsh)
Significance: Symbolizes royalty and grace, often seen as a powerful and influential figure.

Rue
Meaning and Origin: Friend; companion (Hebrew)
Significance: This name embodies the characteristics of a good friend and companion, such as positivity, loyalty, and being a good listener.

Sander
Meaning and Origin: Derived form of Alexander (Dutch)
Significance: This name comes from Alexander, which means "defender of men." It embodies someone who is strong and stands up for what is right.

Serenity
Meaning and Origin: Peaceful (Latin)
Significance: which refers to a state of being calm, peaceful, and untroubled. As a name, Serenity embodies qualities of tranquility, harmony, and inner peace.

Sheba
Meaning and Origin: Oath (Hebrew)
Significance: Sheba's most prominent significance lies in its connection to the Queen of Sheba, a legendary figure from the Hebrew Bible known for her wisdom and riches. This association imbues the name with a sense of mystery, power, and intellect.

Solange
Meaning and Origin: Abundant; flowing (French)
Significance: The name suggests someone with dignity, faith, and a connection to religious traditions. It also embodies wealth and riches.

Soraya
Meaning and Origin: Pleiades (Persian)
Significance: Represents a celestial connection and a mystical presence, often associated with guidance and wisdom.

Sybil
Meaning and Origin: Prophetess (Greek)
Significance: Sybil is directly linked to the sibyls in Greek mythology, who were revered as female oracles and prophets who could foresee the future. The name suggests wisdom, intuition, and a connection to the divine.

Tansy
Meaning and Origin: Yellow flower (British)
Significance: Tansy represents a connection to nature and plants. It also embodies beauty that is natural and bold.

Tanya
Meaning and Origin: Fairy queen; Princess (Russian)
Significance: Tanya is often associated with grace and beauty, embodying elegance and a regal presence. It is a name that suggests charm and a touch of royalty.

Taqueria
Meaning and Origin: Taco shop (Spanish)
Significance: The name Taqueria is a modern, creative name inspired by the Spanish word "taqueria," which means taco shop. While it doesn't have a traditional meaning or origin, it carries a unique and contemporary significance. Taqueria suggests someone who is lively, vibrant, and has a zest for life. It evokes images of flavorful experiences, cultural richness, and a sense of community.

Thalassa
Meaning and Origin: Sea (Greek)
Significance: Reflects a deep, tranquil nature with a strong connection to the ocean and its vastness.

Ulani
Meaning and Origin: Cheerful (Hawaiian)
Significance: Ulani's meaning directly translates to "cheerful," suggesting someone with a positive and optimistic outlook on life.

Ulric
Meaning and Origin: Wolf Power (German)
Significance: Suggests a strong, determined personality with a natural leadership quality and a protective nature.

Undine
Meaning and Origin: Little wave (Latin)
Significance: Undine evokes a strong connection to water, particularly the gentle flow and beauty of waves. It suggests someone with a graceful and adaptable nature.

Vail
Meaning and Origin: Joyful clearing (British)
Significance: Vail could suggest a connection to a joyous place in nature.

Valor
Meaning and Origin: Bravery; worthiness (Latin)
Significance: Valor is a name that evokes images of heroes and warriors, referring to someone brave, determined, and willing to stand up for what they believe in.

Verity
Meaning and Origin: Truth (Latin)
Significance: Verity represents honesty and integrity, often associated with a sincere and trustworthy personality. The name suggests a person who values truth and is committed to upholding ethical principles. Verity evokes images of clarity and transparency, reflecting a character that is both reliable and genuine.

Vespera
Meaning and Origin: Evening (Latin)
Significance: Vespera represents a calm, soothing presence, often associated with peace and tranquility.

Vida
Meaning and Origin: Life (Spanish)
Significance: Vida, based on its most common meaning, is a beautiful celebration of life and all its possibilities. It refers to someone who embraces life's experiences and cherishes its beauty.

Whisper
Meaning and Origin: Soft-spoken (American)
Significance: The act of whispering can create a sense of mystery or intrigue. The name signifies a soft-spoken person who prefers quiet over noise.

Wildad
Meaning and Origin: Affection; friendship (Arabic)
Significance: The name Wildad comes from Arabic origins, meaning "affection" or "friendship." It embodies a sense of warmth, kindness, and a nurturing spirit. This name suggests someone who values close relationships and has a natural ability to form deep, meaningful connections with others

Wilhelmina
Meaning and Origin: Will; desire and protection (German)
Significance: Wilhelmina embodies strength and determination, often linked to a protective and resolute personality. The name is both strong-willed and caring, capable of providing support and security. Wilhelmina evokes images of historical queens and noble figures, reflecting a sense of power and protection.

Wrenley
Meaning and Origin: Small bird (British)
Significance: The wren is a small bird known for its lively spirit and melodic song. It suggests a connection to nature and its beauty.

Xanthe
Meaning and Origin: Golden, Yellow (Greek)
Significance: Symbolizes brightness and warmth, bringing joy and energy to those around them.

Xenia
Meaning and Origin: Guest (Greek)
Significance: Xenia is rooted in the ancient Greek concept of xenia, which emphasized hospitality and generosity toward guests and strangers. The name refers to someone who is welcoming, open-minded, and accepting of others.

Xyla
Meaning and Origin: Forest; wood (Greek)
Significance: Xyla directly translates to "wood" or "forest," suggesting a strong connection to nature and the natural world. It might resonate with parents who appreciate the beauty and serenity of forests.

Yara
Meaning and Origin: Water Lady (Arabic)
Significance: Reflects a fluid, adaptable nature with a deep connection to water and its life-giving properties.

Ysabel
Meaning and Origin: God is my oath (Spanish)
Significance: Ysabel symbolizes faith and devotion, often linked to a pious and committed personality. The name suggests a person who is deeply spiritual and loyal, dedicated to their beliefs and principles. Ysabel evokes images of nobility and grace, reflecting a refined and dignified character.

Yseult
Meaning and Origin: Fair, beautiful (Irish)
Significance: Indicates beauty and grace, often seen as a charming and captivating figure.

Zaina
Meaning and Origin: Beautiful (Arabic)
Significance: Represents beauty and elegance, often associated with grace and dignity.

Zaya
Meaning and Origin: Fate; destiny (Mongolian)
Significance: This name signifies positivity, radiance, and a certain path to a successful future.

Zinnia
Meaning and Origin: Zinn's flower (German)
Significance: Zinnia signifies a direct connection to the beautiful and vibrant zinnia flower, known for its long-lasting blooms and diverse colors. The name represents endurance, resilience, and the ability to flourish in challenging conditions.

While some love unique names, it might not be the route you and your partner want to go. That's totally okay! Up next, we'll explore names that are slightly less unique and common in certain countries. These international names might just be the perfect middle ground you've been looking for.

CHAPTER 6: INTERNATIONAL NAMES

Choosing an international name for your baby can be a wonderful way to celebrate our interconnected world and open doors to future possibilities. Imagine your child feeling a connection to a different culture simply because of their name! International names can also be beautiful and unique, standing out from the crowd. Plus, an international name can be a conversation starter, sparking curiosity about your family's background or your hopes for your child's future as a global citizen. So, if you're looking for a name that's both meaningful and memorable, consider exploring the vast landscape of international names! Here are a few names from around the globe that celebrate cultural richness and diversity.

Boys' Names from Different Cultures

You might be surprised to learn that many of the names that we find common today actually originated in different cultures. Choosing an international name for your baby boy might be a good way to combine familiarity with uniqueness in less obvious ways. Here are some boys' names that honor heritage and tradition, representing diverse cultural backgrounds.

Aarav
Meaning and Origin: Peaceful (Hindi)
Significance: Aarav carries a significance of peace and harmony. It can represent a child who brings calmness and tranquility.

Ahmed
Meaning and Origin: Highly praised; one who constantly thanks God (Arabic)
Significance: Ahmed symbolizes gratitude and excellence. It represents a person who is thankful, virtuous, and highly regarded by others.

Akash
Meaning and Origin: Sky (Sanskrit)
Significance: Akash symbolizes vastness, freedom, and limitless potential. It represents a person who is open-minded, ambitious, and boundless in their aspirations.

Aksel
Meaning and Origin: Father of peace (Scandinavian)
Significance: Aksel signifies harmony and tranquility. It represents a person who brings peace and calmness to their surroundings.

Alexei
Meaning and Origin: Defending me (Russian)
Significance: Alexei is a Russian variation of the Greek Alexander; it is featured in famous literary works such as Anna Karenina by Russian author Leo Tolstoy.

Alvaro
Meaning and Origin: Elf warrior (Spanish)
Significance: Alvaro carries connotations of nobility, protection, and vigilance. it also embodies someone who is watchful of others and makes it their mission to protect their loved ones.

Amadeus
Meaning and Origin: Lover of God (Latin)
Significance: Most notable as the middle name of famous composer Wolfgang Amadeus Mozart, this name signifies a love for music and for a higher power.

Amir
Meaning and Origin: Prince; ruler (Arabic)
Significance: Amir symbolizes leadership and nobility. It represents a person who is destined for greatness and commands respect and authority.

Andrei
Meaning and Origin: Manly (Russian)
Significance: Andrei is the Russian form of Andrew. It signifies strength, courage, and bravery when faced with challenges.

Angus
Meaning and Origin: One strength (Irish)
Significance: The meaning can be interpreted as a symbol of strength and independence, someone who carves their own path. In Irish mythology, Angus Óg was a youthful god associated with love, beauty, and poetic inspiration. This connection adds a touch of magic and wonder to the name.

Aniket
Meaning and Origin: Lord of all (Sanskrit)
Significance: Aniket symbolizes sovereignty and omnipresence. It represents a person who is influential, powerful, and respected.

Anton
Meaning and Origin: Priceless (Latin)
Significance: Anton symbolizes value and uniqueness. It represents a person who is cherished and considered invaluable by those around him.

Antonio
Meaning and Origin: Beyond praise; highly praiseworthy (Latin)
Significance: Antonio carries a sense of strength, worthiness, and a character deserving of praise.

Argyle
Meaning and Origin: An Irishman; from the land of the Gaels (Scottish)
Significance: Argyle holds significance by connecting your child to their ancestral heritage of Scotland. However, Argyle is also a diamond pattern which signifies perfection and beauty.

Armand
Meaning and Origin: Soldier (French)
Significance: Armand symbolizes strength, bravery, and military prowess. It represents a person who is courageous and steadfast in their endeavors.

Artem
Meaning and Origin: Safe; sound (Greek)
Significance: Artem symbolizes health, safety, and well-being. It represents a person who is secure, protected, and brings a sense of
safety to others.

Bastien
Meaning and Origin: Venerable, revered (French)
Significance: Bastien symbolizes respect and honor. It represents a person who is admired and holds a place of high regard in the hearts of others.

Benito
Meaning and Origin: Blessed (Spanish)
Significance: Benito symbolizes divine favor and blessing. It represents a person who is fortunate and brings blessings to those around him.

Bjorn
Meaning and Origin: Bear (Swedish)
Significance: Bears were seen as powerful and majestic creatures in Swedish history. Choosing Bjorn attributes these qualities to your child. Bjorn can also represent hope that your child will be a strong and protective individual.

Bodhi
Meaning and Origin: Awakening; enlightenment (Sanskrit)
Significance: For parents who value spirituality, Bodhi signifies hope that their child will pursue a path of self-discovery and enlightenment.

Bohdan
Meaning and Origin: Given by God (Slavic)
Significance: Bohdan symbolizes divine gift and favor. It represents a person who is considered a precious gift and brings joy to others.

Bruno
Meaning and Origin: Brown (German)
Significance: Brown is often associated with earth, nature, and a sense of strength and stability. Bruno can embody these qualities, representing someone who is grounded and reliable.

Calvin
Meaning and Origin: Bald (Latin)
Significance: Calvin symbolizes simplicity and humility. It represents a person who is modest, down-to-earth, and values authenticity.

Casper
Meaning and Origin: Keeper of treasure (German)
Significance: Its meaning can be interpreted in a literal sense, suggesting someone who cares for valuables. However, it can also hold a more symbolic meaning, implying that the bearer of the name is considered precious or holds great value.

Cassian
Meaning and Origin: Hollow (Latin)
Significance: Cassian symbolizes depth and introspection. It represents a person who is thoughtful, reflective, and possesses profound inner strength.

Cillian
Meaning and Origin: War; strife (Irish)
Significance: Cillian symbolizes resilience and determination in the face of challenges. It represents a person who is strong, courageous, and unyielding.

Conrad
Meaning and Origin: Brave counsel (German)
Significance: The meaning "brave counsel" imbues Conrad with a sense of strength, courage, and the ability to offer advice. It suggests someone who is both a good leader and a thoughtful individual.

Cormac
Meaning and Origin: Charioteer (Irish)
Significance: Cormac boasts a rich history in Ireland. It has been borne by several high kings and legendary figures, imbuing the name with a sense of nobility, strength, and leadership.

Dante
Meaning and Origin: Enduring (Italian)
Significance: Dante symbolizes resilience and strength. It represents a person who is steadfast, determined, and capable of enduring life's challenges.

Dario
Meaning and Origin: Possessor of good (Persian)
Significance: Dario symbolizes wealth and goodness. It represents a person who is generous, kind, and blessed with good fortune.

Dion
Meaning and Origin: Child of heaven and earth (Greek)
Significance: Dion is imbued with a sense of celebration, joy, and the importance of finding pleasure in life.

Eamon
Meaning and Origin: Wealthy protector (Irish)
Significance: Eamon signifies prosperity and guardianship. It represents a person who is both prosperous and protective of their loved ones.

Eduard
Meaning and Origin: Wealthy guardian (German)
Significance: Eduard symbolizes prosperity and protection. It represents a person who is both prosperous and protective of their loved ones.

Eero
Meaning and Origin: Eternal ruler (Finnish)
Significance: Eero symbolizes everlasting leadership and authority. It represents a person who is strong, enduring, and respected as a leader.

Elias
Meaning and Origin: The Lord is my God (Hebrew)
Significance: Elias symbolizes faith and divine connection. It represents a person who is pious, devoted, and guided by their spiritual beliefs.

Elio
Meaning and Origin: Sun (Italian)
Significance: The association with the sun imbues Elio with a sense of brightness, warmth, and positivity. It can represent someone who brings light and joy to others.

Emilio
Meaning and Origin: Rival (Spanish)
Significance: Emilio symbolizes competition and ambition. It represents a person who is driven, determined, and strives for excellence.

Ender
Meaning and Origin: Very rare (Turkish)
Significance: This name holds connotations of strength or resourcefulness.

Enrique
Meaning and Origin: Home ruler (Spanish)
Significance: Enrique symbolizes domestic leadership and strength. It represents a person who is responsible and takes charge of their home and family.

Estienne
Meaning and Origin: Crown (French)
Significance: The meaning "crown" imbues Estienne with a sense of royalty and nobility. In medieval times, crowns symbolized power and authority, so the name carries a historical connotation of high social status.

Fabian
Meaning and Origin: Bean grower (Latin)
Significance: Fabian symbolizes growth and productivity. It represents a person who nurtures and cultivates success and abundance.

Farid
Meaning and Origin: Unique; precious (Arabic)
Significance: Farid symbolizes uniqueness and rarity. It represents a person who is considered exceptional and valuable.

Fausto
Meaning and Origin: Fortunate (Italian)
Significance: Fausto signifies luck and prosperity. It represents a person who is blessed with good fortune and brings positivity to others.

Fedor
Meaning and Origin: Gift of God (Russian)
Significance: Fedor symbolizes divine blessing and favor. It represents a person who is seen as a precious gift and brings joy to those around them.

Finnian
Meaning and Origin: Fair; white (Irish)
Significance: Finnian symbolizes purity and fairness. It represents a person who is just, honorable, and holds high moral standards.

Florian
Meaning and Origin: Flowering (Latin)
Significance: Florian symbolizes growth, beauty, and vitality. It represents a person who brings life and positivity wherever they go.

Gael
Meaning and Origin: Gaelic; stranger (Irish)
Significance: Gael signifies a connection to Gaelic heritage and culture. It represents a person who is proud of their roots and embraces their cultural identity.

Galen
Meaning and Origin: Calm; healer (Greek)
Significance: Galen symbolizes tranquility and healing. It represents a person who is peaceful and brings comfort and healing to others.

Gareth
Meaning and Origin: Gentle (Welsh)
Significance: Gareth symbolizes kindness and nobility. It represents a person who is gentle, courteous, and respected for their noble character.

Gaspard
Meaning and Origin: Treasurer (French)
Significance: Gaspard symbolizes wealth and guardianship. It represents a person who is responsible, trustworthy, and holds valuable knowledge or resources.

Graham
Meaning and Origin: Gravelly homestead (Scottish)
Significance: Graham symbolizes stability and strength. It represents a person who is grounded, reliable, and offers a solid foundation to those around him.

Hamza
Meaning and Origin: Lion (Arabic)
Significance: Hamza symbolizes bravery and strength. It represents a person who is courageous, powerful, and protective of their loved ones.

Hans
Meaning and Origin: God is gracious (German)
Significance: Hans signifies divine grace and favor. It represents a person who is humble, kind, and appreciative of the blessings in their life.

Harlan
Meaning and Origin: Rocky land (English)
Significance: Harlan symbolizes stability and strength. It represents a person who is grounded, reliable, and offers a solid foundation to those around him.

Haruki
Meaning and Origin: Spring child (Japanese)
Significance: The meaning of "springtime" associates Haruki with ideas of new beginnings, growth, and renewal.

Hiro
Meaning and Origin: Abundant; magnificent (Japanese)
Significance: The meaning of Hiro suggests positive qualities like abundance, vastness, magnificence, or heroism.

Hugo
Meaning and Origin: Mind; intellect (German)
Significance: Hugo symbolizes intelligence and thoughtfulness. It represents a person who is wise, insightful, and values knowledge.

Isa
Meaning and Origin: Jesus (Arabic)
Significance: Isa symbolizes spirituality and divine connection. It represents a person who is pious, compassionate, and holds a deep spiritual significance.

Itamar
Meaning and Origin: Island of palms (Hebrew)
Significance: Itamar signifies peace and tranquility. It represents a person who is calm, serene, and brings a sense of peace to their surroundings.

Iker
Meaning and Origin: Visitation (Basque)
Significance: Iker signifies a spiritual or divine encounter. It represents a person who is seen as a messenger or bearer of important news.

Ivo
Meaning and Origin: Yew wood; archer (German)
Significance: The meaning "yew" imbues Ivo with a significance tied to nature and the enduring strength of the yew tree. Yew trees are known for their resilience and ability to survive for centuries.

Jacek
Meaning and Origin: Hyacinth (Polish)
Significance: Jacek symbolizes beauty and elegance. It represents a person who is graceful and admired for their charming personality.

Janus
Meaning and Origin: Gateway (Latin)
Significance: Janus symbolizes new beginnings and transitions. It represents a person who is open to change and embraces new opportunities.

Joaquin
Meaning and Origin: God will judge (Spanish)
Significance: Joaquin signifies divine judgment and justice. It represents a person who values fairness and righteousness.

Jovan
Meaning and Origin: God is gracious (Slavic)
Significance: Jovan symbolizes divine grace and mercy. It represents a person who is kind, compassionate, and grateful for the blessings they receive.

Julian
Meaning and Origin: Youthful; downy (Latin)
Significance: Julian symbolizes youth and vitality. It represents a person who is energetic, lively, and brings a sense of joy and enthusiasm to those around him.

Karim
Meaning and Origin: Generous; noble (Arabic)
Significance: Karim signifies kindness, generosity, and nobility. It represents a person who is compassionate and always willing to help others.

Kato
Meaning and Origin: Second-born twin (African)
Significance: Kato symbolizes the unique bond of twins and signifies companionship and duality. It represents someone who values relationships and close connections.

Keanu
Meaning and Origin: Cool breeze (Hawaiian)
Significance: Keanu symbolizes calmness and serenity. It represents peace and brings a sense of tranquility to their surroundings.

Kenji
Meaning and Origin: Intelligent second son (Japanese)
Significance: Kenji signifies wisdom and intelligence, especially in the context of familial hierarchy. It represents a person who is smart and holds a respected position in the family.

Kieran
Meaning and Origin: Little dark one (Irish)
Significance: (Kieran symbolizes depth and mystery. It represents a person who is intriguing, profound, and holds a unique perspective on life.

Killian
Meaning and Origin: Little church (Irish)
Significance: Killian symbolizes spirituality and devotion. It represents a person who is dedicated, faithful, and connected to their spiritual beliefs.

Lachlan
Meaning and Origin: Land of lakes (Scottish)
Significance: Lachlan signifies a connection to nature, particularly to water bodies. It represents a person who is serene, adaptable, and in tune with their environment.

Lars
Meaning and Origin: Crowned with laurel (Scandinavian)
Significance: Lars symbolizes victory and honor. It represents a person who is accomplished and celebrated for their achievements.

Leif
Meaning and Origin: Heir, descendant (Scandinavian)
Significance: Leif signifies heritage and lineage. It represents a person who values their ancestry and carries forward the legacy of their forebears.

Leonel
Meaning and Origin: Little lion (Spanish)
Significance: Leonel symbolizes courage and strength in a modest form. It represents a person who is brave and determined, yet gentle and caring.

Lorenzo
Meaning and Origin: From Laurentum (Italian)
Significance: Lorenzo symbolizes heritage and nobility. It represents a person who is proud of their roots and embraces their cultural identity.

Luca
Meaning and Origin: Light (Italian)
Significance: Luca symbolizes illumination and enlightenment. It represents a person who brings light, understanding, and positivity to others.

Lucien
Meaning and Origin: Light (French)
Significance: The association with light imbues Lucien with a sense of illumination, knowledge, and the dispelling of darkness. It can represent a child who brings light and understanding to the world.

Marius
Meaning and Origin: Male, virile (Latin)
Significance: Marius symbolizes strength and masculinity. It represents a person who is robust, powerful, and exhibits strong leadership qualities.

Nadir
Meaning and Origin: Rare; precious (Arabic)
Significance: Nadir symbolizes uniqueness and value. It represents a person who is treasured and considered exceptional.

Niko
Meaning and Origin: Victory of the people (Greek)
Significance: Niko is a diminutive of Nikolaos, symbolizing triumph, and success. It represents a person who achieves greatness and brings victories to those around him.

Nikolai
Meaning and Origin: Victory of the people (Russian)
Significance: Nikolai carries the same meaning as Niko, emphasizing leadership and success. It represents a person who leads others to victory and is celebrated for their achievements.

Nasir
Meaning and Origin: Helper, supporter (Arabic)
Significance: Nasir signifies someone who offers assistance and support to others. It represents a person who is dependable and always ready to help.

Omar
Meaning and Origin: Flourishing; Long-lived (Arabic)
Significance: Omar symbolizes prosperity and longevity. It represents a person who is successful, blessed with a long life, and brings abundance to their community.

Otis
Meaning and Origin: Wealth (German)
Significance: Otis signifies prosperity and good fortune. It represents a person who brings abundance and success to their life in the lives of others.

Paolo
Meaning and Origin: Small (Italian)
Significance: Paolo is a variant of Paul, symbolizing humility, and modesty. It represents a person who is humble yet significant in their actions and contributions.

Pascal
Meaning and Origin: Easter (French)
Significance: Easter often coincides with spring, so Pascal can also imply new beginnings and rebirth.

Pasha
Meaning and Origin: Small (Russian)
Significance: Pasha is a diminutive of Pavel, meaning "small." It symbolizes humility and modesty, representing someone who makes a significant impact despite their modest beginnings.

Pavel
Meaning and Origin: Small (Slavic)
Significance: Pavel symbolizes humility and modesty. It represents a person who makes a big impact despite their modest beginnings.

Pedro
Meaning and Origin: Rock; stone (Spanish)
Significance: Pedro signifies strength, stability, and reliability. It represents a person who is dependable and grounded, offering a solid foundation to those around him.

Peregrine
Meaning and Origin: Traveler; Pilgrim (Latin)
Significance: Peregrine symbolizes exploration and adventure. It represents a person who is curious, adventurous, and always seeking new experiences.

Pierre
Meaning and Origin: Rock; stone (French)
Significance: The meaning of "rock" imbues Pierre with a sense of strength, reliability, and dependability. It suggests someone who can be counted on in difficult times.

Quentin
Meaning and Origin: Fifth (Latin)
Significance: Quentin symbolizes order and structure. It represents a person who values organization and plays a significant role in maintaining balance.

Rafael
Meaning and Origin: God has healed (Hebrew)
Significance: Rafael symbolizes healing and divine favor. It represents a person who brings comfort, healing, and positivity to others.

Rafiq
Meaning and Origin: Friend; companion; gentle (Arabic)
Significance: The meaning of "companion" highlights the value Rafiq places on friendship, loyalty, and strong bonds with others. The connotation of "gentle" suggests a nature that is kind, compassionate, and understanding.

Raiden
Meaning and Origin: Thunder and lightning (Japanese)
Significance: Raiden is the name of the Japanese god for hunger and lightning. This name signifies strength and power, as well as an unpredictable nature.

Rasmus
Meaning and Origin: Beloved; desired (Greek)
Significance: Rasmus is a variant of Erasmus, symbolizing love and administration. It signifies a person who is cherished and held in high regard by others.

Reinhard
Meaning and Origin: Brave counsel (German)
Significance: The meaning of Reinhard imbues it with a sense of leadership and the ability to make wise decisions. It refers to someone who is both courageous and strategic.

Renzo
Meaning and Origin: Third link or connection (Italian)
Significance: Renzo is a diminutive of Lorenzo, meaning "from Laurentum." It signifies a person who is part of a larger chain, representing connections, heritage, and community.

Rian
Meaning and Origin: Little King (Irish)
Significance: Rian signifies leadership and nobility in a humble form. It embodies a balance of strength and humility, representing a person who leads with kindness and respect.

Rohan
Meaning and Origin: Ascending (Sanskrit)
Significance: Rohan symbolizes growth, progress, and spiritual elevation. It signifies a person who is continually evolving and striving for higher goals.

Roman
Meaning and Origin: Citizen of Rome (Latin)
Significance: The Roman Empire was renowned for its military prowess, engineering feats, and legal system. Choosing the name Roman can symbolize hope for your child to inherit these qualities of strength, determination, and leadership.

Rune
Meaning and Origin: Secret (Old Norse)
Significance: Rune signifies mystery, wisdom, and ancient knowledge. It represents a person who is insightful and possesses a deep understanding of life's mysteries.

Saif
Meaning: Sword (Arabic)
Significance: Saif symbolizes strength, protection, and valor. It represents a person who is courageous and ready to defend what is right.

Salim
Meaning: Safe; secure (Arabic)
Significance: Salim embodies peace and safety. It signifies a person who is calm, reliable, and brings a sense of security to those around them.

Samir
Meaning: Entertaining companion (Arabic)
Significance: Samir signifies a person who is sociable, pleasant, and enjoys bringing joy to others. It represents someone who is a cherished friend in confidant.

Santiago
Meaning and Origin: Saint James (Spanish)
Significance: Santiago holds a strong religious significance. Saint James is the patron saint of Spain, so the name can also represent a connection to Spanish heritage.

Sava
Meaning and Origin: Old man, sage (Slavic)
Significance: Sava signifies wisdom and experience. It represents a person who is knowledgeable, respected, and valued for his guidance.

Soren
Meaning and Origin: Stern; thunder (Danish)
Significance: Soren carries a sense of strength, determination, and a serious nature.

Sven
Meaning and Origin: Young man; warrior (Scandinavian)
significance: Sven is often associated with strength and youthful vigor. It signifies a person who is brave, strong, ready to face challenges.

Talako
Meaning and Origin: Eagle (Native American)
Significance: This name represents someone who soars above the rest and is very observant. It also embodies great strength and a connection to nature.

Teo
Meaning and Origin: God (Greek)
significant: Teo is a short form of Theodore, meaning "gift of God". It symbolizes divine blessing and the belief in a higher power guiding one's life.

Thiago
Meaning and Origin: May God protect (Portuguese)
Significance: Thiago symbolizes divine protection and care. It represents a person who is blessed and brings a sense of security to those around them.

Tibor
Meaning and Origin: Illustrious; glorious (Hungarian)
Significance: The interpretation of "illustrious" or "glorious" imbues Tibor with a sense of strength, achievement, and potential for greatness.

Timo
Meaning and Origin: Honoring God (Finnish)
Significance: In Finnish, Timo is a shortened version of the name Timotei (Timothy). Timothy comes from the Greek word "Timotheos," which translates to "one who honors God."

Tomas
Meaning and Origin: Twin (Aramaic)
Significance: Tomas represents duality and companionship. It suggests a person who is deeply connected to others and values relationships, embodying loyalty, and unity.

Tygo
Meaning and Origin: Lover of God (Italian)
Significance: Choosing Tygo can hold a religious significance, referencing the meaning "gift of God."

Ulrich
Meaning and Origin: Prosperity; Power (German)
Significance: Ulrich symbolizes strength and wealth. It represents a person who is influential, powerful, and brings prosperity to their community.

Valerio
Meaning and Origin: strong; Healthy (Lane)
Significance: Valerio conveys a sense of vigor and resilience. It signifies a person who is robust, capable, and embodies vitality and strength.

Vasco
Meaning and Origin: Crow (Basque)
Significance: Vasco is historically associated with the famous explorer Vasco da Gama, symbolizing adventure, exploration, and leadership. It also signifies a connection to nature.

Vasily
Meaning and Origin: Royal (Slavic)
Significance: Vasily represents a sense of nobility, strength, and leadership potential.

Vincenzo
Meaning and Origin: Conquering (Italian)
Significance: Vincenzo symbolizes victory and achievement. It represents a person who is determined, successful, and admired for their accomplishments.

Werner
Meaning and Origin: Protecting army; defending warrior (German)
Significance: Werner's represents a sense of strength, bravery, and the willingness to protect others.

Willem
Meaning and Origin: Resolute protector (Dutch)
Significance: The meaning of Willem inherently signifies strength, determination, and a willingness to protect.

Yusuf
Meaning and Origin: God will increase (Arabic)
Significance: Yusuf symbolizes growth and divine favor. It represents a person who is blessed, prosperous, and brings abundance to those around him.

Girls' Names from Different Cultures

Choosing an international name for your daughter can be a delightful adventure! Imagine her name sparking curiosity and becoming a conversation starter wherever she goes. It can be a gateway to exploring different cultures and traditions, fostering a sense of connection to the wider world. The process of choosing can be a fun exploration of different languages and cultural heritages. So, unleash your inner explorer and discover the world of international names for your precious baby girl!

Aisha
Meaning and Origin: Alive; Living (Arabic)
Significance: Aisha is a name of Arabic origin meaning "alive" or "living." It holds significant cultural and historical importance as the name of one of Prophet Muhammad's wives, known for her wisdom and knowledge.

Alta
Meaning and Origin: High; tall (Latin)
Significance: This name signifies someone who is physically tall or possesses a sense of elevated stature, accomplishment, or nobility.

Amelie
Meaning and Origin: Work; striving (French)
Significance: This name implies the value of hard work and dedication. It can be a meaningful choice for parents who want to instill these qualities in their children.

Anastasia
Meaning and Origin: Resurrection (Greek)
Significance: Anastasia carries a profound meaning of resurrection or rebirth, symbolizing new beginnings and hope. It is associated with Saint Anastasia, who is revered in Orthodox Christianity.

Anika
Meaning and Origin: Brilliant; fearless; graceful (Sanskrit)
Significance: Anika's diverse origins allow parents to celebrate their heritage or simply appreciate the beauty of a name that transcends borders. Anika carries positive connotations of grace, strength, sweetness, or intelligence.

Britta
Meaning and Origin: The lofty one; exalted one (Scandinavian)
Significance: The meaning "exalted one" imbues Britta with a sense of strength, nobility, and potentially high aspirations.

Calandra
Meaning and Origin: Lark; songbird (Greek)
Significance: The core meaning of Calandra is "lark" or "songbird." This evokes a sense of beauty, melody, and the joy of song.

Calla
Meaning and Origin: Beautiful (Greek)
Significance: The origin evokes a sense of grace and aesthetics. The association with the Calla Lily adds a touch of nature and purity to the name.

Camille
Meaning and Origin: Perfect; Unblemished (French)
Significance: Camille conveys a sense of perfection and purity. It has been a popular name in French-speaking countries and symbolizes grace and elegance.

Cassandra
Meaning and Origin: She who entangles men (Greek)
Significance: In Greek mythology, Cassandra was gifted with prophecy but cursed so that her predictions were never believed. The name reflects foresight and the struggle to be heard.

Chiara
Meaning and Origin: Light; clear (Italian)
Significance: The core meaning of Chiara imbues it with a sense of light, positivity, and inner radiance. It can represent a child who brings joy and illuminates the lives of those around them.

Elena
Meaning and Origin: Bright; shining light (Greek)
Significance: Elena symbolizes a bright and shining light. It is a name that reflects warmth, intelligence, and compassion.

Elodie
Meaning and Origin: Foreign riches (French)
Significance: This name suggests a connection to wealth, or possessions acquired through one's own efforts or unique qualities. It can represent someone who achieves success through unconventional means.

Esmeralda
Meaning and Origin: Emerald (Spanish)
Significance: Esmeralda is from the Spanish word for emerald, symbolizing beauty, rarity, and preciousness.

Fia
Meaning and Origin: Weaver of wisdom (Portuguese)
Significance: Fia represents someone who is wise and who values justice.

Fleur
Meaning and Origin: Flower (French)
Significance: Fleur inherently signifies a connection to nature, specifically the beauty and delicate charm of flowers. Flowers are often associated with femininity, grace, and delicacy. These qualities are also conveyed through the name Fleur.

Freya
Meaning and Origin: Lady; Noblewoman (Norse)
Significance: Freya is the Norse goddess of love, beauty, and fertility. The name embodies strength, femininity, and leadership.

Gemma
Meaning and Origin: Precious stone; jewel (Italian)
Significance: Choosing the name Gemma signifies that you view your child as a precious gem, someone of great value and worth.

Giulia
Meaning and Origin: Youthful; Downy (Italian)
Significance: Giulia represents youthfulness and freshness. It is a name that exudes vitality and optimism.

Heidi
Meaning and Origin: Noble kind; of good family (German)
Significance: Its primary meaning imbues Heidi with a sense of nobility, kindness, and a gentle spirit.

Inez
Meaning and Origin: Pure; chaste (Spanish)
Significance: The core meaning of Inez suggests qualities of purity and innocence.

Ingrid
Meaning and Origin: Fair; beautiful (Scandinavian)
Significance: The core meaning of Ingrid directly references beauty, making it a lovely choice for parents who want a name that reflects this quality in their child.

Itzel
Meaning and Origin: Rainbow lady (Mayan)
Significance: The meaning of "rainbow woman" imbues Itzel with a connection to nature's beauty and the wonder of rainbows. In Mayan culture, rainbows symbolized pathways between different worlds. By extension, Itzel can represent a connection to the spiritual realm or a bridge between different realities.

Jacqueline
Meaning and Origin: Supplanter (French)
Significance: Jacqueline is the feminine diminutive of Jacques, the French form of James/Jacob. Jacqueline carries a sense of strength and the ability to succeed.

Jasmine
Meaning and Origin: Jasmine flower (Persian)
Significance: Jasmine is named after the fragrant flower, symbolizing grace, elegance, and purity.

Jutta
Meaning and Origin: Woman of Judea; Jewish woman (Hebrew)
Significance: With a historical and cultural connection to Judea or the Jewish faith, Jutta offers a beautiful and feminine name choice.

Kim
Meaning and Origin: Golden; precious (Korean)
Significance: This name signifies someone precious and worthy of favor. It is often interpreted as gold, which is highly valued.

Kira
Meaning and Origin: Beam of light; Sparkle (Russian)
Significance: Kira denotes a beam of light or sparkle, suggesting brightness, clarity, and positivity.

Liesel
Meaning and Origin: God has sworn; God is my oath (German)
Significance: The name signifies a sense of faith, piety, and a strong connection to a higher power.

Maeve
Meaning and Origin: She who intoxicates (Irish)
Significance: Maeve denotes a woman who intoxicates or dazzles, symbolizing allure, power, and sovereignty.

Manon
Meaning and Origin: Bitter; wished for (French)
Significance: This name acknowledges the bitterness and sweetness of life, triumphing in both. It is given to a child who is strong-willed and who embodies beauty and grace.

Marisol
Meaning and Origin: Sea and sun (Spanish)
Significance: Marisol inherently signifies a connection to nature, specifically the beauty and vastness of the sea bathed in sunshine. The imagery of sun and sea evokes a sense of vibrancy, optimism, and positive energy.

Marit
Meaning and Origin: Pearl (Aramaic)
Significance: Marit directly references the sea, imbuing the name with a sense of vastness, mystery, and the power of nature. It also embodies someone rare and precious.

Megumi
Meaning and Origin: Blessing (Japanese)
Significance: The meaning "blessing" imbues Megumi with a sense of hope, optimism, and the belief that the child will have a fortunate life.

Natasha
Meaning and Origin: Birthday of the Lord (Russian)
Significance: The core meaning of Natasha creates a natural association with Christmas and the themes of new beginnings, and joy.

Niamh
Meaning and Origin: Bright (Irish)
Significance: The meaning "bright" imbues Niamh with a sense of optimism, hope, and the potential to illuminate the world around them.

Nisa
Meaning and Origin: Women; dream (Turkish)
Significance: This name represents a woman worthy of your dreams. It embodies elegance, subtle beauty, and luxury.

Ophelia
Meaning and Origin: Help (Greek)
Significance: Ophelia symbolizes help or succor. It is associated with Shakespeare's tragic heroine in "Hamlet," embodying beauty and innocence.

Paloma
Meaning and Origin: Dove (Spanish)
Significance: The association with doves imbues Paloma with a strong sense of peace, tranquility, and calmness.

Pia
Meaning and Origin: From Mount Olympus (Latin)
Significance: Pia represents valuing religious faith and committing to one's beliefs. It also signifies a strong moral compass and a sense of righteousness.

Quinn
Meaning and Origin: Descendant of Conn (Irish)
Significance: Quinn means descendant of Conn, representing wisdom, leadership, and strength.

Rhea
Meaning and Origin: Flowing stream (Greek)
Significance: Rhea symbolizes a flowing stream, representing fertility, abundance, and nurturing qualities.

Saskia
Meaning: Saxon (Dutch)
Significance: Saskia carries a sense of strength and a connection to a rich heritage.

Serena
Meaning and Origin: Serene; Calm (Latin)
Significance: Serena signifies serenity and calmness. It is a name associated with peace and tranquility.

Sora
Meaning and Origin: Sky; conch shell (Japanese)
Significance: This name represents a connection to the sky and the seas. It also represents unity and peace, as well as immense internal power.

Soraya
Meaning and Origin: Star of clusters (Persian)
Significance: This name evokes a sense of wonder, beauty, and destiny. It also represents positive energy, vitality, and leadership.

Tatiana
Meaning and Origin: Fairy queen (Russian)
Significance: Tatiana denotes a fairy queen, symbolizing magic, grace, and enchantment.

Tula
Meaning and Origin: Place of reeds (Mexico)
Significance: This name connects to nature and the plant world. It also carries the significance of power and history.

Uma
Meaning and Origin: Flax; Splendor; Tranquility (Sanskrit)
Significance: Uma carries meanings of flax, splendor, and tranquility. It is associated with the Hindu goddess Parvati.

Valentina
Meaning and Origin: Strength; health (Latin)
Significance: The name Valentina is a powerful choice for parents who wish their children strength, health, and resilience.

Vera
Meaning and Origin: Faith (Russian)
Significance: Vera signifies faith and truthfulness. It is a name that represents reliability and loyalty.

Viveca
Meaning and Origin: Alive; place of refuge (Swedish)
Significance: Viveca signifies someone full of life, energy, and enthusiasm.

Willa
Meaning and Origin: Desire (German)
Significance: Willa, meaning "desire," is deeply rooted in German origin. It symbolizes strength, courage, and determination, embodying the essence of resolute protection.

Ximena
Meaning and Origin: Hearkening (Spanish)
Significance: Ximena signifies hearkening or listening. It is a name that embodies attentiveness and responsiveness.

Zuri
Meaning and Origin: Good; beautiful (Swahili)
Significance: Zuri represents femininity, beauty, and being naturally good. It embodies characteristics worthy of royalty.

If none of these names sparked something inside you, that's totally okay. There are still many other names to explore, and international names aren't for everyone. Up next, let's look to celebrities for some inspiration!

CHAPTER 7: CELEBRITY AND CELEBRITY KID NAMES

Celebrities are constantly in the spotlight. Whether due to their fashion choices, an embarrassing moment, or a new movie being released, they're used to being watched. So, it's no surprise that they often go all-out when it comes to baby names and choose something unique. While that's not everyone's cup of tea, if you're looking for a unique name used by some of your favorite celebrities, this is the chapter for you. While the names are divided into boy and girl names based on the gender of the celebrity's baby, most of these names can be used for the opposite sex as well, so don't get too stuck in one category. If you want to indulge in the glitz and glamour of Hollywood with names inspired by the offspring of the rich and famous, this is the perfect place to start!

Celebrity Names

In an Era where pop culture icons captivate our imagination and set trends across the globe, it's no surprise that many parents look to celebrities for baby name inspiration. This Celebrity and Celebrity Kid name chapter will offer a wide variety of names that will not only inspire you to choose a name for your baby but also draw you to choose something that is timeless and classic.

Adele
Meaning and Origin: Noble; Nobility (English)
Significance: Adele is known for her soulful voice and emotional depth in her music. She has been an advocate for body positivity and has used her platform to support various charitable causes.

Alton
Meaning and Origin: Old Town (British)
Significance: Alton Brown is a chef and television personality known for his scientific approach to cooking and entertaining show formats. He has been influential in culinary education and promoting understanding of food science.

Angelina
Meaning and Origin: Messenger of God; angel (Greek)
Significance: Angelina Jolie is recognized for her acting career, humanitarian efforts, and advocacy for refugee rights and women's health, establishing herself as a prominent figure in both entertainment and philanthropy.

Ariana
Meaning and Origin: Great; large (Italian)
Significance: Ariana Grande is a pop icon known for her vocal range and influential presence in music and fashion. She has been an advocate for mental health awareness and has supported various social causes.

Armando
Meaning: Man of the army (Spanish)
Significance: Pitbull, born Armando Christian Pérez, is an American rapper and entrepreneur known for his energetic performances and global influence. He's been an inspiration for multiculturalism, entrepreneurial success, and philanthropy.

Ashanti
Meaning and Origin: Warlike (African)
Significance: Ashanti, born Ashanti Shequoiya Douglas, is an American singer, songwriter, and actress known for her R&B and hip-hop-influenced music. She has been an inspiration for cultural pride, musical talent, and female empowerment in the music industry.

Ayesha
Meaning and Origin: Alive; living (Arabic)
Significance: Ayesha Curry is a Canadian American actress, celebrity cook, cookbook author, and television personality. She has been an inspiration for culinary innovation, family values, and entrepreneurship, promoting healthy eating and cultural diversity.

Beyoncé
Meaning and Origin: One who surpasses others; beyond others (English)
Significance: Beyoncé is an influential figure in music, known for her powerful voice, impactful performances, and championing of Black culture and female empowerment through her artistry and philanthropy.

Bill
Meaning and Origin: Resolute Protector (English)
Significance: Bill Gates is a business magnate and philanthropist known for co-founding Microsoft and for his contributions to technology and global health through the Bill & Melinda Gates Foundation.

Bobby
Meaning and Origin: Bright; fame (English)
Significance: Bobby Flay is a chef and television personality known for his expertise in grilling and Southwestern cuisine. He has been involved in culinary education and mentoring young chefs.

Brad
Meaning and Origin: Broad; wide (British)
Significance: Brad Pitt is not only for his acting talent but also for his humanitarian work, using his celebrity status to advocate for social causes like housing for the displaced and post-Katrina New Orleans.

Bruce
Meaning and Origin: From the brushwood thicket (English)
Significance: Bruce Springsteen, also known as "The Boss," is a rock legend known for his poetic lyrics and social commentary in his music. He has been an advocate for working-class issues and veterans' rights.

Cara
Meaning and Origin: From the valley (English)
Significance: Cara Delevingne is a model and actress known for her wave in the fashion and entertainment industries. Known for her distinctive eyebrows, edgy style, and versatile talent, Delevingne has redefined beauty standards and brought a unique blend of charisma and authenticity to her work.

Channing
Meaning and Origin: Dried-upriver valley (English)
Significance: Channing Tatum is an actor and dancer known for his roles in films like Magic Mike and Step Up. He has been involved in initiatives supporting veterans and has used his platform to raise awareness about social issues.

Chrissy
Meaning and Origin: Follower of Christ (Greek)
Significance: Chrissy is a short form of Christine. Chrissy Teigen is a model, television personality, and cookbook author known for her wit and outspokenness. She is an advocate for body positivity and has supported various social causes, including women's rights.

Ciara
Meaning and Origin: Dark; black (Irish)
Significance: Ciara Princess Harris, known professionally as Ciara, is an American singer, songwriter, and dancer. She has been an inspiration for female empowerment, resilience, and artistic innovation, with hit songs that have influenced pop and R&B music.

Conan
Meaning and Origin: Little wolf; hound (Irish)
Significance: Conan O'Brien is a comedian and television host known for his late-night talk shows. He has been involved in entertainment and charitable events, supporting causes ranging from education to disaster relief.

Conor
Meaning and Origin: Lover of hounds (Irish)
Significance: Conor McGregor is a mixed martial artist and former UFC champion known for his fighting skills and brash personality. He has been involved in various business ventures and has supported charitable causes in Ireland.

Cornell
Meaning and Origin: Horn; horn-shaped (Latin)
Significance: Nelly, born Cornell Iran Haynes Jr., is an American rapper, singer, and actor known for his hit songs and contributions to hip-hop culture. He has been an inspiration for musical innovation, entrepreneurship, and philanthropy.

Cristiano
Meaning and Origin: Follower of Chris (Portuguese)
Significance: Cristiano Ronaldo is a soccer superstar known for his exceptional skills and goal-scoring abilities. He has been active in philanthropy, supporting causes related to children's healthcare and disaster relief.

Curtis
Meaning and Origin: Someone who lived near a stone or rock (English)
Significance: Curtis Stone is a chef and television personality known for his cooking expertise and entrepreneurial ventures in the culinary world. He's been involved in culinary education and mentoring young chefs.

Dua
Meaning and Origin: Love (Albanian)
Significance: Dua Lipa is a pop sensation known for her powerful vocals and chart-topping hits. She is a vocal advocate for women's empowerment, using her platform to promote inclusivity and self-expression.

Dwayne
Meaning and Origin: Son of John (English)
Significance: Dwayne Johnson, also known as "The Rock," transitioned from a successful wrestling career to become a blockbuster movie star. Beyond entertainment, he promotes positivity and resilience through his personal story and motivational messages.

Ed
Meaning and Origin: Wealthy guard (English)
Significance: Ed Sheeran is a Grammy-winning artist known for his heartfelt songwriting and acoustic sound. He has been involved in charitable efforts, including supporting education and children's hospitals.

Elon
Meaning and Origin: Oak Tree (Hebrew)
Significance: Elon Musk is a business magnate known for founding SpaceX, Tesla, and other innovative ventures. He has been a visionary in advancing technology and advocating for sustainable energy solutions.

Gail
Meaning and Origin: My father is joyful (English)
Significance: Gail Simmons is a food writer and television personality known for her role as a judge on cooking competition shows. She has been influential in culinary education and promoting understanding of diverse cuisines.

Gigi
Meaning and Origin: Farmer (French)
Significance: Gigi Hadid is a supermodel known for her runway success and campaigns with top fashion brands. She has been vocal about her Palestinian heritage and has advocated for diversity in the fashion industry.

Giada
Meaning and Origin: Jewel (Italian)
Significance: Giada De Laurentiis is a chef and television personality known for her Italian cuisine and approachable recipes. She has been influential in culinary education and has inspired many with her cooking shows and books.

Gordon
Meaning and Origin: Spacious; A fort (Scottish)
Significance: Gordon Ramsay is a chef and television personality known for his fiery temperament and culinary expertise. He has been involved in hospitality and entertainment and has supported young chefs through mentorship.

Halle
Meaning and Origin: From the manor house (Old English)
Significance: Halle Berry is an American actress known for her roles in films such as "Monster's Ball" and "X-Men." She has been an inspiration for diversity in Hollywood, breaking barriers as the first African American woman to win an Academy Award for Best Actress.

Heston
Meaning and Origin: Brushwood settlement (German)
Significance: Heston Blumenthal is a chef known for his innovative approach to cooking and molecular gastronomy. He has been influential in culinary arts and has contributed to the evolution of modern cuisine.

Idris
Meaning and Origin: Fiery; impulsive (Welsh)
Significance: Idris Elba is an acclaimed actor and DJ known for his roles in "The Wire" and "Luther." He has been an advocate for diversity in Hollywood and has used his platform to address social issues.

Issa
Meaning and Origin: Salvation (Arabic)
Significance: Issa Rae is a writer, producer, and actress known for her work on the web series "Awkward Black Girl" and the HBO series "Insecure." She has been an inspiration for representation and diversity in television, showcasing authentic stories of Black women.

Jada
Meaning and Origin: Wise; knowing (Hebrew)
Significance: Jada Pinkett Smith is an actress, singer, and businesswoman known for her roles in "The Matrix" and "Gotham." She is also an advocate for mental health awareness and has used her platform to discuss issues related to mental wellness and family dynamics.

Jessica
Meaning and Origin: God beholds (Hebrew)
Significance: Jessica Alba is an actress and businesswoman known for her roles in "Fantastic Four" and "Sin City." She is the co-founder of The Honest Company, which promotes non-toxic household products and has been involved in various charitable efforts.

Justin
Meaning and Origin: Just; righteous (Latin)
Significance: Justin Timberlake is a singer, songwriter, and actor known for his successful music career and acting roles. He has been involved in various charitable efforts and has supported causes related to education and children's health.

Kanye
Meaning and Origin: Let's give; to honor (African)
Significance: Kanye West is a rapper, producer, and fashion designer known for his influential music and bold statements. He has been involved in various philanthropic efforts and has used his platform to address social issues.

Kelly
Meaning and Origin: Warrior (Irish)
Significance: Kelly Clarkson is a singer and television personality known for winning "American Idol" and her subsequent music career. She has been an advocate for mental health awareness and has supported various charitable causes.

Kim
Meaning and Origin: Gold (Korean)
Significance: Kim Kardashian is a reality television star and businesswoman known for her influential presence in media and fashion. She has used her platform to advocate for criminal justice reform and has been involved in various charitable efforts.

Kristen
Meaning and Origin: Follower of Christ (Latin)
Significance: Kristen Bell is an actress known for her roles in "Veronica Mars" and "Frozen." She has been an advocate for mental health awareness and has supported various charitable causes, including animal rights and children's health.

Laila
Meaning and Origin: Night; dark beauty (Arabic)
Significance: Laila Ali is a former professional boxer and television personality known for her undefeated record and advocacy for health and wellness. She has been an inspiration for women in sports and has supported various charitable causes.

Leonardo
Meaning and Origin: Brave as a lion (Italian)
Significance: Leonardo DiCaprio is an actor and environmental activist known for his roles in films like "Titanic" and "The Revenant." He has been an advocate for climate change awareness and has supported various environmental conservation efforts.

Lindsay
Meaning: and Origin From the island of linden trees (English)
Significance: Lindsay Lohan is an actress and singer known for her roles in "Mean Girls" and "The Parent Trap." She has been involved in various charitable efforts and has supported causes related to children's health and education.

Lisa
Meaning and Origin: God is my oath (Hebrew)
Significance: Lisa Kudrow is an actress known for her role as Phoebe Buffay on "Friends." She has been involved in various charitable efforts and has supported causes related to mental health and education.

Madonna
Meaning and Origin: My lady (Italian)
Significance: Madonna is a pop icon known for her influential music career and boundary-pushing performances.

Malala
Meaning and Origin: Grief-stricken (Arabic)
Significance: Malala Yousafzai is an education activist known for her advocacy for girls' education and women's rights. She survived an assassination attempt by the Taliban and has been a global inspiration for her bravery and dedication to education.

Mariah
Meaning and Origin: The Lord is my teacher (Hebrew)
Significance: Mariah Carey is a singer known for her powerful voice and chart-topping hits. She has been involved in various charitable efforts and has supported causes related to children's health and education.

Martin
Meaning and Origin: God of war (Latin)
Significance: Martin Lawrence is a comedian, actor, and producer known for his work in stand-up comedy and his roles in "Martin" and the "Bad Boys" film series. He has been influential in the comedy genre and has supported various charitable efforts, including those related to health and education.

Meryl
Meaning and Origin: Blackbird (English)
Significance: Meryl Streep is an acclaimed actress known for her versatility and numerous awards. She has been involved in various charitable efforts and has supported causes related to the arts and women's rights.

Natalie
Meaning and Origin: Christmas Day (Latin)
Significance: Natalie Portman is an actress known for her roles in "Black Swan" and "V for Vendetta." She has been involved in various charitable efforts and has supported causes related to animal rights and education.

Oprah
Meaning and Origin: Fawn (Hebrew)
Significance: Oprah Winfrey is a media mogul known for her talk show "The Oprah Winfrey Show" and her work in television and film. She has been an inspiration for her philanthropy and advocacy for education and empowerment.

Orlando
Meaning and Origin: Famous throughout the land (Italian)
Significance: Orlando Bloom is an actor known for his roles in "The Lord of the Rings" and "Pirates of the Caribbean." He has been involved in various charitable efforts and has supported causes related to children's health and education.

Rihanna
Meaning and Origin: Sweet basil (Arabic)
Significance: Rihanna is a singer, actress, and businesswoman known for her music and entrepreneurial ventures. She has been involved in various charitable efforts and has supported causes related to education and disaster relief.

Serena
Meaning and Origin: Serene; tranquil (Latin)
Significance: Serena Williams is a tennis champion known for her powerful playing style and numerous Grand Slam titles. She has been an inspiration for women's sports and has supported various charitable efforts related to education and health.

Simone
Meaning and Origin: One who hears (Hebrew)
Significance: Simone Biles is a gymnast known for her record-breaking performances and numerous Olympic medals. She has been an advocate for mental health awareness and has supported various charitable efforts.

Tiger
Meaning and Origin: Powerful; swift (English)
Significance: Tiger Woods is a golfer known for his numerous tournament wins and impact on the sport. He has been involved in various charitable efforts and has supported causes related to children's health and education.

Zendaya
Meaning and Origin: To give thanks (African)
Significance: Zendaya is an actress and singer known for her roles in "Euphoria" and "Spider-Man." She has been an advocate for diversity and representation in the entertainment industry and has supported various charitable efforts.

Boys' Celebrity Kid Names

Celebrities often choose abstract names for their sons that have personal significance. However, if you think it sounds cool, go for it! Here are names chosen by celebrities for their sons, reflecting trends and personal style.

Aaric
Meaning and Origin: Ruler (English)
Significance: Son of Aaron Donald and Erica Jamary, Aaric Donald reflects leadership qualities, symbolizing strength, and authority.

Ace
Meaning and Origin: One, unity (Latin)
Significance: Chosen by Jessica Simpson and Eric Johnson for their son Ace Knute Johnson, representing uniqueness and excellence.

Aire
Meaning and Origin: Lion of God (Hebrew)
Significance: Kylie Jenner and Travis Scott named their son Aire, which means Lion of God. Kylie admitted to wanting a name that sounded cool but also carried special meaning to her and her faith.

Alejandro
Meaning and Origin: Defender of mankind (Spanish)
Significance: Son of Sergio Ramos and Pilar Rubio, Alejandro Ramos symbolized defender of mankind and growth.

Apple
Meaning and Origin: The fruit (American)
Significance: Actor Gwyneth Paltrow and singer Chris Martin named their son Apple. They chose the name because it sounded wholesome and Biblical. Apple also evokes a connection to nature and the abundance of the harvest season.

August
Meaning and Origin: Great, magnificent (Latin)
Significance: Mark Zuckerberg and his wife have chosen this name for their son, possibly to commemorate the month of his birth or to celebrate qualities of greatness and magnificence. The name August also evokes a sense of warmth and harvest, reflecting the fullness and richness of late summer.

Axel
Meaning and Origin: Father of peace (Scandinavian)
Significance: Son of Gareth Bale and Emma Rhys-Jones, symbolizing peace, and purity.

Bear
Meaning and Origin: Strong fire; protective flame (British)
Significance: Kate Winslet and Ned Rocknroll named their son Bear Blaze after a childhood friend who was nicknamed Bear. They also shared that they met in a house fire, which is why they chose Blaze as a second name.

Ben
Meaning and Origin: Son (Hebrew)
Significance: Chosen by Andy Cohen for his son, symbolizing familial connection and heritage.

Braylen
Meaning and Origin: Courageous (Irish)
Significance: Son of Bradley Beal and Kamiah Adams, symbolizing courage, and handsomeness.

Bronny
Meaning and Origin: Derived from LeBron (American)
Significance: Savannah and LeBron James chose this name for their son, reflecting his father's legacy and name.

Bronx
Meaning and Origin: Urban jungle (Dutch)
Significance: Ashely Simpson and Pete Wentz wanted to give their child a name that honored their upbringing in New York, so they chose the first name Bronx. They both share a love for the animated film The Jungle Book and the beloved character Mowgli, which is how they decided on the second name.

Bryce
Meaning and Origin: Bryce: Speckled; freckled (English)
Significance: Savannah and LeBron James chose this name for their son, symbolizing uniqueness.

Buddy
Meaning and Origin: Companion (British)
Significance: Jamie Oliver and Juliette Norton are known to name their children very unique names. Buddy was simply a name they both liked, while Maurice was the name of Juliette's late father. Buddy Bear Maurice creates a unique and playful combination. It emphasizes friendliness, strength, and a touch of sophistication or established heritage.

Camden
Meaning and Origin: From the winding valley (English)
Significance: Kristin Cavallari and Jay Cutler chose the name Camden for their son, reflecting a connection to nature and the picturesque imagery of a winding valley.

Canon
Meaning and Origin: Official; standard (English)
Significance: Steph Curry and Ayesha Curry chose this name, symbolizing precision or authority.

Charlie
Meaning and Origin: Free man (German)
Significance: Zooey Deschanel and Jacob Pechenik named their son Charlie Wolf because they both adore the animal (wolf) and thought Charlie was a cute name to go with it.

Ciro
Meaning and Origin: Ancient Roman magistrate (Italian)
Significance: Son of Lionel Messi and Antonela Roccuzzo, symbolizing ancient authority and divine gift.

Cristiano
Meaning and Origin: Christian (Greek)
Significance: Son of Cristiano Ronaldo and Irina Shayk, symbolizing Christian values and wise counsel.

Curtys
Meaning and Origin: Courteous; polite (French)
Significance: Son of Pierre-Emerick Aubameyang and Alysha Behague, Curtys Aubameyang symbolizes politeness and courtesy.

Davi
Meaning and Origin: Beloved (Hebrew)
Significance: Son of Neymar Jr. and Carolina Dantas, symbolizing being beloved, light, from the forest, and of the saints.

Deuce
Meaning and Origin: Second-born (English)
Significance: Son of Bradley Beal and Kamiah Adams, symbolizing being the second-born and handsome.

Diar
Meaning and Origin: Gift of Go (English)
Significance: Son of DeMar DeRozan and Kiara Morrison, symbolizing blessing from God and the complexities of life.

Draymond
Meaning and Origin: Strong; handsome (English)
Significance: Son of Draymond Green and Jelissa Hardy, symbolizing strength, and beauty.

Egypt
Meaning and Origin: From the country Egypt (Greek)
Significance: Alicia Keys and Swizz Beatz chose this name, reflecting fascination with ancient culture or origins.

Eissa
Meaning and Origin: God is salvation (Arabic)
Significance: Janet Jackson and Wissam Al Mana named their baby boy Eissa. The name stems from the Arabic word for Jesus and has a beautiful meaning that signifies faith.

Future
Meaning and Origin: Time to come; destiny (English)
Significance: Singer Ciara named their son Future to honor the baby's father, rapper Future. The name signifies forward thinking and a positive outlook.

Gavin
Meaning and Origin: White hawk (Welsh)
Significance: Son of Claude Giroux and Ryanne Giroux, symbolizing vigilance and keen vision.

Gene
Meaning and Origin: Noble descent; well-born (English)
Significance: Amy Schumer and Chris Fischer chose this name for their son, reflecting familial pride and heritage.

Genesis
Meaning and Origin: Beginning (Greek)
Significance: Alicia Keys and Swizz Beatz named their son Genesis Ali Dean, representing a new beginning and creativity.

Goncalo
Meaning and Origin: Battle, war (Portuguese)
Significance: Son of Bruno Fernandes and Ana Pinho, Gonçalo Fernandes symbolizes bravery.

Hayes
Meaning and Origin: Enclosure (Scottish)
Significance: Cash Warren and Jessica Alba named their son Hayes, fitting with the names of his two sisters, Haven and Honor.

Hawk
Meaning and Origin: Bird of prey (English)
Significance: Toni Braxton named her son Denim Cole Braxton-Lewis, reflecting a sense of freedom and vision.

Ibrahim
Meaning and Origin: Father of nations (Arabic)
Significance: Son of Karim Benzema and Chloe de Launay, Ibrahim Benzema symbolizes paternal heritage and elevation, embodying dignity, and growth.

Ilya
Meaning and Origin: God is my salvation (Russian)
Significance: Son of Alex Ovechkin and Nastya Ovechkina, Ilya Ovechkin symbolize divine salvation and faith.

Ivano
Meaning and Origin: God is gracious (Slavic)
Significance: Son of Luka Modric and Vanja Bosnic, symbolizing divine grace and blessing.

Jace
Meaning and Origin: Healer (Greek)
Significance: Son of John Tavares and Aryne Fuller, Jace Tavares symbolizes healing and restoration.

Jaxon
Meaning and Origin: Son of Jack (English)
Significance: Chosen by Kristin Cavallari and Jay Cutler for their son, signifies familial ties, emphasizing lineage and the traditional name Jack with a modern twist.

Jayden
Meaning and Origin: God has heard (American)
Significance: Son of James Harden and Nia Long, Jayden James Harden Jr. reflects divine favor and strength, symbolizing answered prayers and resilience.

Jayson
Meaning and Origin: Healer (American)
Significance: Son of Jayson Tatum and Toriah Lachell, symbolizing healing, and divine guidance.

Jet
Meaning and Origin: Black gemstone (British)
Significance: Former Olympian Shawn Johnson East and her retired football player husband, Andrew East, named their second child Jet after her husband's brother as well as her great-great-great-grandmother.

Kayan
Meaning and Origin: Strong (Turkish)
Significance: Son of Mohamed Salah and Magi Salah, Kayan Salah symbolizes strength and determination, embodying resilience, and fortitude.

Kayden
Meaning and Origin: Companion (American)
Significance: The name Kayden, chosen by Kyrie Irving and Andrea Wilson, is noted for its contemporary and friendly sound, reflecting a sense of companionship and modern appeal.

Keyaan
Meaning and Origin: King (Arabic)
Significance: Son of Paul Pogba and Zulay Pogba, Keyaan Pogba symbolizes royalty and stature.

Khari
Meaning and Origin: Kingly (African)
Significance: Son of Kevin Durant and Monica Wright, Khari Durant reflects regal qualities, symbolizing strength, and leadership.

Kian
Meaning and Origin: Ancient (Persian)
Significance: The name Kian Irving, chosen by Kyrie Irving and Andrea Wilson, symbolizes ancient roots and natural beauty, blending historical and environmental significance.

Lautaro
Meaning and Origin: Famous in battle (Spanish)
Significance: Son of Luis Suarez and Sofia Balbi, Lautaro Suarez symbolizes renown and bravery, embodying courage, and determination.

Leevi
Meaning and Origin: Beloved (Finnish)
Significance: Son of Mikko Rantanen and Emmi Kainulainen, symbolizing love and devotion.

Lennox
Meaning and Origin: Lives near the place abounding in elms (Scottish)
Significance: Son of Gabriel Landeskog and Melissa Landeskog, symbolizing strength, and resilience.

Leodis
Meaning and Origin: Lion-like (American)
Significance: Keke Palmer and Darius Jackson have named their son Leodis but call him Leo. The name embodies the strength of a lion, as well as courage and bravery.

Luai
Meaning and Origin: Shiel; protector (Arabic)
Significance: Lindsay Lohan and her husband, Bader Shammas, named their son Luai. They chose the name due to its meaning and origin.

Lucca
Meaning and Origin: Light (Italian)
Significance: Son of John Carlson and Gina Nucci, symbolizing brightness, and familial heritage.

Lukas
Meaning and Origin: Light (German)
Significance: Son of Andrei Vasilevskiy and Kseniya Vasilevskaya, symbolizing brightness and clarity.

Maceo
Meaning and Origin: Gift of God; a variation of Mateo (Spanish)
Significance: Halle Berry and Oliver Martinez named their child Maceo. The name signifies that the child was a blessing and someone to cherish.

MacKenly
Meaning and Origin: Son of the wise ruler (Scottish)
Significance: Son of LeBron James and Savannah James, symbolizing wisdom, and protection.

Manolo
Meaning and Origin: God is with us (Spanish)
Significance: Sofia Vergara and her former husband, Joe Gonzalez, gave their boy the name Manolo, the Spanish variant of Manuel meaning God is with us. They chose the name because it symbolizes divine presence and protection.

Marco
Meaning and Origin : Warlike (Latin)
Significance: Son of Sergio Ramos and Pilar Rubio, Marco Ramos symbolizes strength, and growth.

Mason Dash
Meaning and Origin: Stone worker; bricklayer (Armenian)
Significance: Kourtney Kardashian and Scott Disick named their son Mason because it shared meaning with Kourtney's name in Armenian, both signifying stone workers. They also added Dash as a second name to honor Kourtney's late father whose nickname was Dash.

Mateo
Meaning and Origin: Gift of God (Hebrew)
Significance: Son of Cristiano Ronaldo and Georgina Rodriguez, symbolizing being a divine gift and wise counsel.

Max
Meaning and Origin: Greatest (Latin)
Significance: Jennifer Lopez and Marc Anthony had twins, and they were named Emme and Max. The name signifies greatness and strength.

Moroccan
Meaning and Origin: Relating to Morocco (Spanish)
Significance: Mariah Carey and Nick Cannon had twins who they named Moroccan and Monroe. They chose the name Moroccan because Cannon proposed to Carey in a Morocco-inspired room.

Nakoa-Wolf
Meaning and Origin: Spiritual warrior of the sea (Hawaiian)
Significance: Lisa Bonet and Jason Momoa named their son Nakoa-Wolf Manakauapo Namakaeha. While Wolf isn't that unique in Hollywood circles, the other names hold very special meanings. Nakoa, meaning warrior in Hawaiian, celebrates heritage and strength. Manakauapo combines three Hawaiian words that mean spiritual power. Finally, Kaua means rain, and the baby was born during a storm.

Neza
Meaning and Origin: Boy (Slovenian)
Significance: Son of Anze Kopitar and Ines Kopitar, symbolizing youth, and vitality.

Nikita
Meaning and Origin : Unconquerable (Russian)
Significance: Son of Nikita Kucherov and Anastasiya Kucherova, symbolizing strength and resilience.

Palmer
Meaning and Origin: Pilgrim (English)
Significance: Son of Claude Giroux and Ryanne Giroux, symbolizing a journey and faith.

Pilot
Meaning and Origin: Vehicle operator
Origin: American
Significance: Beth Riesgraf and Jason Lee named their child Pilot based on the opening track of Grandaddy's album, titled *He's Simple, He's Dumb, He's the Pilot*. A pilot can represent someone who excels at navigating challenges and guiding others.

Psalm
Meaning and Origin: Song (Hebrew)
Significance: Kim Kardashian and Kanye West named their son Psalm, but it was Kim's mother, Kris Jenner, who championed the name. Psalm's primary meaning of "song" suggests a connection to music and creativity.

Reign
Meaning and Origin: Rule; sovereign (British)
Significance: Reign is another son of Kourtney Kardashian and Scott Disick. The name was selected because it was a name they both liked and contemplated for their older two children as well.

Remington
Meaning and Origin: Settlement by the riverbank (English)
Significance: Kelly Clarkson and Brandon Blackstock named their son Remington Alexander. The raven symbolizes wisdom, mystery, and prophecy.

Rio
Meaning and Origin: River (Portuguese)
Significance: Son of Victor Hedman and Sanna Grundberg, Rio Hedman symbolizes flow and continuity.

Riot
Meaning and Origin: Dispute (French)
Significance: Rihanna and A$AP Rocky's second child was named Riot, following the tradition of names starting with "R" in the family. As a name, Riot embodies a break from tradition and a strong rebellious spirit. It suggests someone who isn't afraid to challenge the status quo and express themselves freely.

River
Meaning and Origin: Power; ambition; field near water (German)
Significance: Jamie Olivier and Juliette Norton created this name for their son. River Rocket Blue Dallas is significant to them as the name of Oliver's first restaurant, which launched his career.

Rocket
Meaning and Origin: Missile (English)
Significance: Pharrell Williams named his son Rocket Ayer Williams, symbolizing aspiration and innovation.

Rocky
Meaning and Origin: Stony (English)
Significance: The name Rocky, chosen by Sarah Michelle Gellar and Freddie Prinze Jr., represents strength and resilience, evoking the solid and enduring qualities of stone.

Rome
Meaning and Origin: From Rome (Latin)
Significance: Son of Kevin De Bruyne and Michele Lacroix, Rome De Bruyne symbolizes heritage and simplicity, embodying resilience and warmth.

Ronnie
Meaning and Origin: Ronnie: Counselor, advisor (English)
Significance: Son of Phil Foden and Rebecca Cooke, symbolizing guidance and wisdom.

Saint
Meaning and Origin: Holy; sacred (Latin)
Significance: Kim chose Saint for their son as a tribute to Kanye's roots. This is a title usually used for people recognized for exceptional holiness or piety by the church.

Sergei
Meaning and Origin: Servant (Russian)
Significance: Sergi is the son of Alex Ovechkin and Anastasia Shubskaya, symbolizing service and paternal heritage.

Shakur
Meaning and Origin: Thankful (Arabic)
Significance: Son of Paul Pogba and Zulay Pogba, Shakur Pogba symbolizes gratitude and stature.

Sparrow
Meaning and Origin: Small; chirpy (English)
Significance: Nicole Richie and Joel Madden named their son Sparrow James Midnight. Overall, it is a very descriptive and unique name. Sparrow connects nature and possibly masculinity, James provides a biblical connection, and Midnight adds a touch of mystery and uniqueness.

Trey
Meaning and Origin: Three, Third (Old French)
Significance: Trey Smith, whose full name is Willard Carroll "Trey" Smith III, is the eldest son of Will Smith and his first wife, Sheree Zampino. The name "Trey" signifies that he is the third Willard Carroll Smith in the family lineage, highlighting the continuation of the family name and legacy.

Tydus
Meaning and Origin: Heart (Greek)
Significance: Tydus is the son of Trae Young and Shelby Miller, symbolizing bravery, and sovereignty.

Win
Meaning and Origin: Blessed; fair (Welsh)
Significance: A name Ciara and now husband Russel Wilson chose for one of their boys is win. Win signifies a victorious spirit. The name suggests someone with qualities of fairness, purity, and blessings.

Yannis
Meaning and Origin: God is gracious (Greek)
Significance: Son of Eden Hazard and Natacha Van Honacker, symbolizing divine grace and blessing.

Zack
Meaning and Origin: Blessed (Hebrew)
Significance: Son of Patrice Bergeron and Stephanie Bergeron, symbolizing divine favor and grace.

Girls' Celebrity Kid Names

Up next, it's time to explore some of the names celebrities give their baby girls. Some of my favorite names from the entire book are in this section, so if you're looking for something exuding strength, sophistication, and elegance, this is the section to be in!

Alayah
Meaning and Origin: Exalted (Arabic)
Significance: Daughter of Andrew Wiggins and Mychal Johnson, symbolizing being highly cherished and beloved.

Alba
Meaning and Origin: White; dawn (Spanish)
Significance: Daughter of Gareth Bale and Emma Rhys-Jones, Alba Violet Bale symbolizes purity and beauty, embodying innocence, and charm.

Ariah
Meaning and Origin: Lion (Hebrew)
Significance: Daughter of Mike Evans and Ashli Evans, Ariah Lynn Evans symbolizes courage and tranquility, embodying strength, and peace.

Audrielle
Meaning and Origin: Noble strength (English)
Significance: Daughter of Khris Middleton and Samantha Dutton, symbolizing strength and nobility.

Aurelia
Meaning and Origin: The golden one (Latin)
Significance: Mark Zuckerberg proudly announced his baby girl's name on Instagram, calling her his little blessing. The name, meaning golden, embodies a sense of preciousness and value, suggesting that someone is highly cherished.

Azurie
Meaning and Origin: Sky blue (French)
Significance: The name Azurie Elizabeth, chosen by Kyrie Irving and Andrea Wilson, symbolizes divine promise and peace, blending the serene qualities of the sky with a profound spiritual commitment.

Bianka
Meaning and Origin: White; pure (Italian)
Significance: The name Bianka Bella, chosen by Kobe Bryant and Vanessa Bryant, reflects purity and beauty, capturing the essence
of grace and elegance.

Bluebell Madonna
Meaning and Origin: Bluebell flower (English)
Significance: Bluebell Madonna is the daughter of Geri Halliwell, symbolizing beauty and nature.

Blue Ivy
Meaning and Origin: Blue; ivy Plant (English)
Significance: Daughter of Beyoncé and Jay-Z, symbolizing growth, beauty, and uniqueness.

Bree
Meaning and Origin: Strength (Irish)
Significance: Daughter of Jalen Ramsey and Monica Giavanna, symbolizing strength, and connection to nature.

Camryn
Meaning and Origin: Bent nose (Scottish)
Significance: The name Camryn Alexis, chosen by Chris Paul and Jada Crawley, may reflect family heritage and qualities of protection and defense.

Chicago
Meaning and Origin : Striped skunk (French)
Significance: Kim Kardashian and Kanye West named their second daughter Chicago to pay homage to Kanye's roots.

Coco
Meaning and Origin: Help (French)
Significance: Daughter of Courteney Cox and David Arquette, symbolizing sweetness and charm.

Daisy Boo
Meaning and Origin: Day's eye; term of endearment (English)
Significance: Jamie Oliver and Juliette Norton named one of their children Daisy Boo Pamela. The name symbolizes purity, innocence, new beginnings, and sweetness.

Daisy Dove
Meaning and Origin: Day's eye; peace, gentleness (English)
Significance: Orlando Bloom and Katy Perry named their daughter Daisy Dove because it reminded them of purity and joy, which is what their little one meant to them.

Delfina
Meaning and Origin: Dolphin (Italian)
Significance: Daughter of Luis Suarez and Sofia Balbi, symbolizing intelligence, and playfulness.

Delta Bell
Meaning and Origin: Mouth of a river; Beautiful (Greek and English)
Significance: Daughter of Kristen Bell and Dax Shepard, symbolizing change and beauty.

Dezia
Meaning and Origin: Flowering (Hebrew)
Significance: Daughter of Davante Adams and Devanne Villarreal, Dezia Adams symbolizes beauty and brightness, embodying elegance and grace.

Elsie Otter
Meaning and Origin: Pledged to God (Scottish)
Significance: Zooey Deschanel and Jacob Pechenik named their little girl Elsie Otter because they both love the adorable creature (otter) but also wanted to give her a name that was slightly more common (Elsie).

Faith
Meaning and Origin: Trust, belief, devotion (English)
Significance: Nicole Kidman and Keith Urban named their second daughter Faith Margaret. Faith embodies someone hopeful and trustworthy, while Margaret signifies something of value and innocence.

Frances
Meaning and Origin: Free one (Latin)
Significance: Jimmy Fallon, host of *The Tonight Show*, and his wife, Nancy Juvonen, named their youngest daughter Frances. The name embodies the characteristics of a free spirit and someone independent by nature.

Frankie
Meaning and Origin: Free (American)
Significance: Drew Barrymore and her ex-husband, Will Kopelman, named their second child Frankie because they both really liked the name. Will came up with the name a few months before her birth, and they both liked it for their little girl.

Grace
Meaning and Origin: Favored fighter (Latin)
Significance: Steve Irwin's daughter, Bindi Irwin, named her little girl Grace Warrior as a tribute to her father's legacy as a wildlife warrior. The name embodies someone strong and courageous yet just and gracious.

Haven
Meaning and Origin: Safe place; refuge (British)
Significance: Born in her amniotic sac, Jessica Alba decided to name her baby girl Haven, as she was born in her safe haven. The name represents someone who provides a sense of security or someone who feels safe and secure themselves.

Honor
Meaning and Origin: Integrity (French)
Significance: Older sister to Haven, Honor is the eldest daughter of Jessica Alba and Cash Warren. The name symbolizes someone who is connected to moral values and is trustworthy and respected.

Ivalyn
Meaning and Origin: Desired (American)
Significance: Daughter of Giannis Antetokounmpo and Mariah Riddle sprigger, symbolizing longing and strength.

Jada
Meaning and Origin: Jade stone (English)
Significance: Daughter of Bradley Beal and Kamiah Adams, Jada Beal symbolizes strength and beauty, reflecting resilience and elegance.

Jaeda
Meaning and Origin: Thankful (American)
Significance: Daughter of Aaron Donald and Erica Jamary, Jaeda Donald reflects gratitude and appreciation, symbolizing a thankful and gracious spirit.

Jayla
Meaning and Origin: Jay bird (American)
Significance: Daughter of Kevin Durant and Monica Wright, Jayla Durant symbolizes freedom and endurance, embodying resilience and lasting qualities.

Juno
Meaning and Origin: Queen of the heavens (Latin)
Significance: Daughter of Will Kopelman and Drew Barrymore, symbolizing leadership and divine protection.

Kaari
Meaning and Origin: Pure (Finnish)
Significance: Daughter of Ja Morant and KK Dixon, Kaari symbolizes purity, and divine hearing.

Kaia
Meaning and Origin: Sea (Hawaiian)
Significance: Kaia Jordan is the daughter of Cindy Crawford and Rande Gerber, symbolizing the earth and legacy.

Kalii
Meaning and Origin: The flower (Hawaiian)
Significance: Daughter of Damian Lillard and Kay'La Hanson, symbolizing beauty, and strength in battle.

Khai
Meaning and Origin: Ocean (Hawaiian)
Significance: Gigi Hadid and Zayn Malik named their daughter Khai, representing Hawaiian waters and someone who has a deep connection to peace.

Klara
Meaning and Origin: Bright; Clear (Latin)
Significance: Daughter of Robert Lewandowski and Anna Lewandowska, symbolizing brightness, and lion-like strength.

Kulture
Meaning and Origin: Culture (English)
Significance: Kulture is the daughter of Cardi B and Offset, symbolizing heritage and uniqueness.

Kyla
Meaning and Origin: Beautiful; victorious (Gaelic)
Significance: Daughter of Draymond Green and Jelissa Hardy, symbolizing beauty, triumph, and strength.

Lina
Meaning and Origin: Tender; Delicate (Arabic)
Significance: Daughter of Joshua Kimmich and Lina Meyer, Lina Kimmich symbolizes tenderness, and delicacy.

Linnea
Meaning and Origin: Lime; Linden tree (Swedish)
Significance: Daughter of Gabriel Landeskog and Melissa Landeskog, symbolizing vitality, and renewal.

Lola
Meaning and Origin: Sorrows (Spanish)
Significance: Chosen by Lisa Bonet and Jason Momoa for their daughter, reflecting a sense of melancholy or beauty.

Lyra
Meaning and Origin: Harp; opposite to the Arctic (Greek)
Significance: Famous singer Ed Sheeran and his wife Cherry Seaborn named their first child Lyra Antarctica. Sheeran wanted a unique name for his baby and chose Lyra, while the second name came from a memorable voyage the couple made earlier in their relationship.

Makka
Meaning and Origin: Pilgrimage place (Arabic)
Significance: Daughter of Mohamed Salah and Magi Salah, Makka Salah symbolizes religious significance and virtue, embodying spirituality, and integrity.

Malti
Meaning and Origin: Small flower (Indian)
Significance: Nick Jonas and Priyanka Chopra named their little daughter Malti in honor of Priyanka's Indian roots. The primary meaning of "small, fragrant flower" suggests beauty and a delicate nature.

Mari
Meaning and Origin: Sea (Welsh)
Significance: Daughter of DeMar DeRozan and Kiara Morrison, symbolizing strength, and resilience amidst life's bitterness.

Maven
Meaning and Origin: Expert (Hebrew)
Significance: Maven is the daughter of Stacey Keibler and Jared Pobre, symbolizing knowledge and skill.

Melia
Meaning and Origin: Sweetness (Greek)
Significance: Daughter of Karim Benzema and Chloe de Launay, Melia Benzema symbolizes beauty and elevation.

Melody
Meaning and Origin: Music (English)
Significance: Daughter of Raheem Sterling and Paige Milian, symbolizing harmony, and excellence.

Milan
Meaning and Origin: Beloved; gracious (Slavic)
Significance: Daughter of Darius Leonard and Kayla Leonard, symbolizing being beloved and strong like a lion.

Monroe
Meaning and Origin: From the hill (Scottish)
Significance: Mariah Carey and Nick Cannon named their daughter Monroe after the late actress Marilyn Monroe. Carey wanted to celebrate her love for the iconic Marilyn Monroe by giving her last name to their baby girl. The name carries a significance tied to nature, specifically hills, and a sense of strength.

Mya
Meaning and Origin: Emerald (Greek)
Significance: Daughter of James Harden and Arabella Roby, Mya Harden reflects courage and preciousness, symbolizing strength, and beauty.

Nahla
Meaning and Origin: First drink of water (Arabic)
Significance: Halle Berry and Gabriel Aubry chose this name for their daughter, symbolizing purity, and new beginnings.

Nala
Meaning and Origin: Gift (African)
Significance: The name Nala, chosen by Anthony Davis and Marlen P, symbolizes a precious gift, representing the joy and value brought into their lives.

Natalia
Meaning and Origin: Birthday; born on or around Christmas Day (Latin)
Significance: Daughter of Nikola Jokic and Natalija Macesic, symbolizing birth, and divine establishment.

Nava
Meaning and Origin: Beautiful (Hebrew)
Significance: Daughter of Gareth Bale and Emma Rhys-Jones, Nava Valentina Bale symbolizes beauty and strength, embodying resilience, and vitality.

Nia
Meaning and Origin: Brightness (Welsh)
Significance: Daughter of Anthony Davis and Marlen P, Nia Davis reflects illumination and clarity, symbolizing brightness, and positivity.

Nila
Meaning and Origin: Blue; sapphire (Sanskrit)
Significance: Daughter of Virgil van Dijk and Rike Nooitgedagt, symbolizing blue and connection to the dike.

North
Meaning and Origin: Northerly direction (British)
Significance: The eldest daughter of Kim Kardashian and Kanye West was named North. Originally, the name was brought up as a joke by Jay Leno, but the couple loved it so much that they decided to stick with it. North can symbolize moving forward, progress, or aiming high.

Ognjena
Meaning and Origin: Fiery (Serbian)
Significance: The name Ognjena, chosen by Nikola Jokic and Natalija Macesic, reflects strength and passion, evoking a sense of fiery determination and energy.

Olive
Meaning and Origin: Olive tree (Latin)
Significance: Drew Barrymore and ex-husband Will Kopelman named their eldest daughter Olive after reading a maternity book where the baby's size was compared to an olive. Drew immediately fell in love with the name, and they never looked back. The name can inherently carry a significance tied to nature, as the olive tree symbolizes wisdom, peace, and abundance.

Olympia
Meaning and Origin: Connected to Mount Olympus (Greek)
Significance: Serena Williams and husband, Alexis Ohanian, named their daughter Alexis Olympia, but she goes by her second name. Serena chose this name to embody her athletic spirit and because she wanted the baby's initials to match the Australian Open, which she won while pregnant with her daughter.

Onyx
Meaning and Origin: Precious gem (Greek)
Significance: Onyx Solace is the daughter of Alanis Morissette and Mario Treadway, symbolizing strength and peace.

Penelope
Meaning and Origin: Weaver (Greek)
Significance: The oldest daughter of Kourtney Kardashian and Scott Disick was named Penelope. The name embodies a patient nature combined with loyalty and perseverance.

Poppy Honey
Meaning and Origin: Red flower (British)
Significance: Jamie Oliver and Juliette Norton named their eldest daughter Poppy Honey Rosie. The name signifies beauty, sweetness, love, and peace.

Rainbow
Meaning: Colorful arc (English)
Significance: Rainbow Aurora is the daughter of Holly Madison, symbolizing hope and new beginnings.

River
Meaning: Flowing water (British)
Significance: River Rose is the first daughter of Kelly Clarkson and ex-husband Brandon Blackstock. The name connects to nature, symbolizing a constant flow of love and peace.

Sasha
Meaning: Defender of mankind (Greek)
Significance: Daughter of Paul George and Daniela Rajic, Sasha George symbolizes protection and strength, embodying resilience, and courage.

Seraphina
Meaning and Origin: Fiery one (Hebrew)
Significance: Ben Affleck and Jennifer Garner named their little girl Seraphina. The name embodies a fiery spirit and someone passionate, burning with love and enthusiasm.

Sofia
Meaning and Origin: Wisdom (Greek)
Significance: Daughter of Luka Modric and Vanja Bosnic, Sofia Modric symbolizes wisdom, and knowledge.

Stormi
Meaning and Origin: Impetuous (American)
Significance: Kylie Jenner and Travis Scott named their eldest baby Stormi. The name is associated with strength, power, and the ability to weather challenges.

Sunday
Meaning and Origin: Born on a Sunday (Latin)
Significance: Nicole Kidman and Keith Urban named their first daughter Sunday Rose. This name represents hope and beauty.

Sunny
Meaning and Origin: Bright; cheerful (English)
Significance: Daughter of Adam Sandler and Jackie Sandler, symbolizing happiness and warmth

Suri
Meaning and Origin: Princess (Sanskrit)
Significance: Daughter of Kevin De Bruyne and Michele Lacroix, Suri De Bruyne symbolizes royalty and simplicity, embodying grace, and warmth.

Tallulah
Meaning and Origin: Leaping water (Native American)
Significance: Daughter of Bruce Willis and Demi Moore, symbolizing nature and energy.

Tennessee James
Meaning and Origin: Gathering place (Native American)
Significance: Son of Reese Witherspoon and Jim Toth, representing heritage and community.

Trixie
Meaning and Origin: Bringer of joy (Latin)
Significance: Daughter of Ellen Pompeo and Chris Ivery, symbolizing happiness and delight.

True
Meaning and Origin: Real, genuine, loyal (English)
Significance: Chloe Kardashian and Tristan Thompson ended up choosing the name True for their baby. While Chloe was still pregnant, this name stuck with her and the only way she could get it out of her head was if she named her baby True, which eventually led to True Thompson. This was also a family tradition and was a name that her great grandfather and grandfather had previously in their names.

Ulla Jones
Meaning and Origin: Wealthy (German)
Significance: Daughter of Grace Jones. The name Ulla signifies prosperity and abundance, reflecting a sense of richness and success.

Ursie
Meaning and Origin: Little bear (Latin)
Significance: Daughter of Karen Elson and Jack White. Ursie is a diminutive of Ursula, symbolizing strength and a protective nature, akin to a bear's qualities.

Violet
Meaning and Origin: Purple; flower (Latin)
Significance: Another name that Jennifer Garner and Ben Affleck chose is Violet. The name is a symbol of faith and someone who is delicately beautiful.

Vivian
Meaning and Origin: Full of life; bright (Latin)
Significance: Tom Brady and Gisele Bündchen named their daughter Vivian. Vivian is a charming name that signifies optimism, vibrancy, and a zest for life.

Vivienne
Meaning and Origin: Alive (French)
Significance: Daughter of Harry Kane and Katie Goodland, Vivienne Jane Kane symbolizes vitality and divine favor, embodying energy, and compassion.

Winnie
Meaning and Origin: Blessed (Welsh)
Significance: Jimmy Fallon and Nancy Juvonen named their eldest daughter Winnie because she is a "win" for them. Winnie signifies a beautiful, blessed, and full-of-life person.

Xochitl
Meaning and Origin: Flower (Nahuatl)
Significance: Daughter of Alondra and Ralph Lazo, representing beauty and nature.

Zada
Meaning and Origin: Prosperous (Arabic)
Significance: Daughter of Anthony Davis and Marlen P, symbolizing prosperity, and lineage.

Zahara
Meaning and Origin: Flowering (Swahili)
Significance: Zahara Marley is the daughter of Angelina Jolie and Brad Pitt, symbolizing beauty and music.

Ziggy
Meaning and Origin: Victory (German)
Significance: Ziggy Blu is the daughter of Fantasia Barrino and Kendall Taylor, symbolizing success and tranquility.

Zola
Meaning and Origin: Piece of earth (African)
Significance: Zola Ivy is the daughter of Eddie Murphy and Nicole Mitchell, symbolizing peace and growth.

These celebrity names might be a little too adventurous, but perhaps they can spark a name that your heart will love! In the next chapter, we'll explore some of the best fictional names from movies, books, and shows. So, if you're looking for something fun with a nod to your favorite movie, the next one is for you!

CHAPTER 8: FICTIONAL NAMES

Unleash your inner storyteller and consider the magic of a fictional name for your baby! Imagine a name that sparks curiosity and wonder, a conversation starter that hints at fantastical worlds and epic adventures. Fictional names can be brimming with creativity and chosen for their sound, meaning, or connection to a beloved book or character. They offer a chance to celebrate your love for literature and weave a touch of whimsy into your child's identity. While some fictional names might be a bit out there, others hold surprising beauty and strength waiting to be discovered. So, delve into the enchanting realm of fiction and find a name that perfectly embodies the unique spirit you imagine for your child.

While many of these names have more traditional meanings, you're interested in them because of the characters they represent. So, to help you make the right choice regarding significance, we're focusing on what their character(s) represented.

Aang
Meaning and Origin: Peaceful soaring (Chinese)
Significance: Represents the *Avatar*, bringing balance and harmony to the world. In the series: Aang is the *last Airbender* and the Avatar, destined to bring peace to the Four Nations by mastering all elements.

Agatha
Meaning and Origin: Good; honorable (Greek)
Significance: Agatha Bridgerton is one of the Bridgerton siblings in "*Bridgerton*." Known for her warmth, loyalty, and protective nature towards her family, Agatha embodies themes of sibling camaraderie, familial duty, and the enduring bonds forged through shared experiences and unconditional love. Her character explores the complexities of sibling dynamics, the joys and challenges of family life, and the resilience found in unity amidst the trials and triumphs of Regency-era aristocracy.

Ahsoka
Meaning and Origin: Without sorrow; without grief (Sanskrit)
Significance: Known for independence and compassion, Ahsoka is a well-known *Star Wars* character. The name carries the resilience of the fan-favorite character, as well as her wisdom and passion.

Alaric
Meaning and Origin: Ruler of all; noble leader (German)
Significance: Alaric Saltzman is a vampire hunter, history teacher, and surrogate father figure in "*The Vampire Diaries*." Known for his intellect, protective nature, and tragic past, Alaric embodies themes of mentorship, redemption, and the quest for justice in a world where the line between good and evil is often blurred. His character explores the complexities of grief, resilience, and the pursuit of knowledge amidst ongoing supernatural conflicts.

Albus
Meaning and Origin: Bright; white (Latin)
Significance: Most famous as the first name of the headmaster of Hogwarts, Albus carries a sense of wisdom and illumination.

Alec
Meaning and Origin: Defender of the people (Greek)
Significance: Alec is a member of the Volturi guard and Jane's twin brother. Alec supports Jane in enforcing Volturi's laws and maintaining order among vampires in the Twilight series.

Alicia
Meaning and Origin: Noble; honorable (Old German)
Significance: Alicia Spinnet is a Gryffindor student known for her talent as a Chaser on the Quidditch team and her role in Dumbledore's Army. As a determined and loyal friend, Alicia embodies themes of teamwork, perseverance, and the bonds formed through shared goals and experiences at Hogwarts.

Amun
Meaning and Origin: The hidden one; the mysterious one (Egyptian)
Significance: Amun is the leader of the Egyptian coven and a skilled creator of vampire hybrids. Known for his ancient wisdom, ambition, and desire to maintain the status quo, Amun's character represents a formidable figure in the Twilight series, influencing vampire politics and alliances.

Anakin
Meaning and Origin: Warrior, soldier (English)
Significance: Anakin Skywalker, later known as Darth Vader, is one of the central characters in the *Star Wars* saga. His journey from a promising Jedi Knight to the Sith Lord Darth Vader is a pivotal storyline, exploring themes of redemption, power, and destiny.

Angel
Meaning and Origin: Purity; divine connection (English)
Significance: Angel, or Warren Worthington III, has white-feathered wings that grant him flight. His character explores themes of identity, privilege, and the complexities of being a mutant with a striking physical mutation, navigating between heroism and personal challenges within the *X-Men* universe.

Appa
Meaning and Origin: Father (Turkish)
Significance: Represents a protective and nurturing figure, Aang's loyal sky bison. Appa is Aang's flying bison and constant companion, in *Avatar The Last Airbender* aiding in travel and battles.

Aragorn
Meaning and Origin: Revered king (Sindarin)
Significance: The rightful heir to the throne of Gondor and a pivotal leader in the fight against Sauron.

Arwen
Meaning and Origin: Very fair; great beauty (Welsh)
Significance: While instantly recognizable to any *Lord of the Rings* fan, Arwen is still an uncommon name. As such, it carries a rarity, along with its more obvious connotations of beauty, nobility, and grace.

Arya
Meaning and Origin: Noble, honorable (Sanskrit)
Significance: Synonymous with *Game of Thrones*, Arya is strong and resilient while maintaining a noble and gracious nature.

Azula
Meaning and Origin: Blue (Spanish)
Significance: Reflects her fierce and powerful personality as a firebender. Azula is Zuko's sister, in *Avatar The Last Airbender* a prodigiously talented firebender with a ruthless and cunning nature.

Balin
Meaning and Origin: Gentle (Old Norse)
Significance: A dwarf who is part of Thorin's company in "The Hobbit" and later attempts to reclaim Moria.

Balon Greyjoy
Meaning and Origin: Warrior or Soldier (Old Norse)
Significance: The head of House Greyjoy, Lord of the Iron Islands, and father of Theon and Yara Greyjoy. He leads a failed rebellion against the Iron Throne.

Barristan Selmy
Meaning and Origin: From Barr's Town (English)
Significance: A legendary knight of the Kings guard, known for his honor and skill in combat, serving several kings loyally.

Benjen
Meaning and Origin: Son of Ben (Hebrew)
Significance: Eddard Stark's younger brother, Benjen Stark is a First Ranger of the Night's Watch who mysteriously disappears beyond the Wall.

Beren
Meaning and Origin: Bold (Sindarin)
Significance: A mortal man whose love for the elf Lúthien led to epic quests and legendary tales.

Binx
Meaning and Origin: Searching for meaning (American)
Significance: Originally from the classic novel *The Moviegoer*, Binx represents a need to experience the most out of life. Binx is also the name of the cat in *Hocus Pocus*, which adds a little magical flair to the name.

Bishop
Meaning and Origin: High-ranking clergyman, often entrusted with spiritual leadership (English)
Significance: Bishop, or Lucas Bishop, is a mutant with the ability to absorb and redirect energy. Hailing from a dystopian future, Bishop's character explores themes of survival, justice, and the consequences of altering the timeline, adding depth to the *X-Men's* narrative through his moral struggles and determination.

Blaise
Meaning and Origin: Lisping, stuttering (Latin)
Significance: Blaise Zabini is a Slytherin student known for his elegance, intelligence, and mysterious background. As a member of Draco Malfoy's inner circle, Blaise embodies themes of sophistication, ambition, and the pursuit of power and influence in the competitive environment of Hogwarts.

Blob
Meaning and Origin: Shapeless mass (English)
Significance: Blob, or Frederick J. Dukes, possesses superhuman strength and durability, along with an impenetrable layer of fat. His character challenges conventional superhero aesthetics and explores themes of body image, self-acceptance, and societal perceptions of strength within the *X-Men* universe.

Boromir
Meaning and Origin: Jeweled hand (Sindarin)
Significance: A brave warrior from Gondor who initially seeks to use the Ring but redeems himself through sacrifice.

Bran
Meaning and Origin: Raven (Welsh)
Significance: Bran Stark's name reflects his mystical connection to ravens and his abilities as the Three-Eyed Raven in *Game of Thrones*. Ravens are symbols of prophecy and insight in various mythologies.

Brienne
Meaning and Origin: Noble, high (Celtic)
Significance: Brienne of Tarth is a female knight known for her loyalty, strength, and combat skills, dedicated to protecting the Stark family.

Brom
Meaning and Origin: Someone who works the land (Dutch)
Significance: One of the main characters in the *Eragon* book series, Brom is a wise, if slightly irritable, man who guides the series' hero. Possessing his own strength and heroic past, Brom combines the sometimes-opposing characteristics of wisdom and action.

Brynden Tully
Meaning and Origin: Hill, mound (Welsh)
Significance: Known as the Blackfish, he is a seasoned warrior and the uncle of Catelyn Stark, a loyal member of House Tully.

Caius
Meaning and Origin: Blind; concealed (Latin)
Significance: Caius is a member of the Volturi and one of its leaders. Known for his ruthlessness and commitment to vampire laws, Caius is a formidable adversary and enforcer of the Volturi's authority in the *Twilight series*.

Carlisle
Meaning and Origin: Wise; protective (English)
Significance: Carlisle Cullen is the patriarch of the Cullen vampire family. Known for his compassion, medical expertise, and ethical behavior as a vampire, Carlisle is a central figure in guiding his family and maintaining peace between vampires and humans.

Carmen
Meaning and Origin: Song; poem (Spanish)
Significance: Carmen is a member of the Denali coven known for her compassion and intuitive nature. Her role in supporting her family and her relationships with other vampires reflect her deep empathy and understanding in the *Twilight series*.

Catelyn
Meaning and Origin: Pure (Greek)
Significance: Catelyn Stark is known for her loyalty and dedication to her family. Her name signifies her purity of heart and her protective nature.

Cedric
Meaning and Origin: Kindly; loved (English)
Significance: Cedric Diggory is the talented and honorable Hufflepuff Seeker and Triwizard Tournament champion. Known for his fair play, integrity, and bravery, Cedric embodies themes of sportsmanship, loyalty, and the recognition of innate goodness. His character explores the values of fair competition, moral integrity, and the tragic consequences of being in the wrong place at the wrong time amidst larger conflicts.

Celeborn
Meaning and Origin: Silver tree (Sindarin)
Significance: The husband of Galadriel and co-ruler of Lothlórien, known for his wisdom and leadership.

Celebrian
Meaning and Origin: Silver queen (Sindarin)
Significance: The wife of Elrond and mother of Arwen, known for her tragic capture and departure to Valinor.

Cersei
Meaning and Origin: bird (Greek)
Significance: Cersei Lannister is a complex character known for her cunning and ambition. Cersei derives from Circe which means bird. This name also evokes the mythical enchantress Circe, known for her manipulation and power.

Chani
Meaning and Origin: Grace; favor (Hebrew)
Significance: A fan-favorite in *Dune*, especially since the release of the Denis Villeneuve movies, Chani is a resourceful, strong, and independent woman who is also the love interest of the book's main character and hero.

Cho
Meaning and Origin: Beautiful; fine (Korean)
Significance: Cho Chang is a Ravenclaw student and Harry's first love interest at Hogwarts. Known for her intelligence, athleticism, and emotional depth, Cho embodies themes of love, loss, and the complexities of teenage relationships. Her character explores themes of grief, resilience, and the power of emotional connections amidst the backdrop of magical education and growing up in a world filled with both wonder and danger.

Circe
Meaning and Origin: Bird (Greek)
Significance: A powerful enchantress who turned Odysseus's men into swine, Circe symbolizes transformation, magic, and the duality
of nature.

Cirilla
Meaning and Origin: Masterful; lordly (Greek)
Significance: A powerful princess from *The Witcher*, Cirilla, had an adventurous childhood. She is intelligent and brave and carries a sense of destiny and purpose.

Clark
Meaning and Origin: Wise; intelligent scholar (Latin)
Significance: From the hit series *the 100*, Clark is known as a very resourceful, caring girl. She is intelligent and leads with her heart. However, she often gets in trouble for making decisions that others don't agree with due to her ability to see the bigger picture.

Cobb
Meaning and Origin: Lump; large (British)
Significance: A resourceful character from *The Mandalorian*, Cobb has historically been used to describe those with larger physiques. However, a large personality would be just as fitting.

Colin
Meaning and Origin: Victory of the people (Scottish)
Significance: As one of the Bridgerton siblings in the book series, *Bridgerton*, Colin is a calm and soft-spoken man who pays attention to detail. He is kind and caring and has a good relationship with his siblings. He is also a hopeless romantic who enjoys writing.

Colossus
Meaning and Origin: Massive; monumental (Latin)
Significance: Colossus, or Piotr Rasputin, can transform his body into organic steel, granting him immense strength and durability. His gentle nature, unwavering loyalty, and artistic talent contrast with his imposing mutant abilities, making him a beloved member of the *X-Men* known for his courage and selflessness.

Cosette
Meaning and Origin: Little thing (French)
Significance: Famous from *Les Misérables*, Cosette represents the hope of a better future. The name also carries a sense of innocence and resilience.

Cressida
Meaning and Origin: Gold; golden (Greek)
Significance: Cressida Cowper is a wealthy socialite in "*Bridgerton*." Known for her beauty, social standing, and competitive nature, Cressida embodies themes of ambition, rivalry, and the quest for status amidst the elite circles of Regency-era London. Her character explores the complexities of social climbing, the pressures of maintaining appearances, and the lengths one will go to secure a coveted place in high society.

Cyclops
Meaning and Origin: Focused vision; a powerful gaze (Greek mythology)
Significance: Cyclops, or Scott Summers, emits powerful optic blasts from his eyes, which he must control with special glasses or visors. As a leader of the *X-Men*, Cyclops embodies discipline, strategy, and the burden of leadership.

Cypher
Meaning and Origin: A secret code (English)
Significance: Represents betrayal and the desire to return to ignorance. In the *Matrix* Cypher is a crew member who betrays Neo and the others to return to the Matrix and live a life of comfort.

Daario Naharis
Meaning and Origin: Wealthy or Possessor (Persian)
Significance: A flamboyant and deadly sellsword who becomes a loyal follower and lover of Daenerys Targaryen.

Daedalus
Meaning and Origin: Skilled worker (Greek)
Significance: A master craftsman and inventor who created the Labyrinth, Daedalus symbolizes ingenuity, creativity, and the consequences of hubris.

Daenerys
Meaning and Origin: Lady of light; lady of hope (Welsh)
Significance: Carrying hope and optimism as well as strength, bravery, and intelligence, Daenerys has since become a household name since the release of *Game of Thrones*.

Damon
Meaning and Origin: One who tames; subdues (Greek)
Significance: As one of the iconic brothers in *The Vampire Diaries*, Damon is known for his charm, good looks, and passion. Even though he is very misunderstood in the series, he loves deeply and always does his best to help those he loves.

Danbury
Meaning: Stronghold of the family (English)
Significance: Lady Danbury is a prominent and influential figure in London's social scene in "*Bridgerton*." Known for her sharp wit, wisdom, and no-nonsense attitude, Lady Danbury embodies themes of societal norms, female empowerment, and the complexities of navigating high society. Her character explores the nuances of friendship, mentorship, and the impact of personal choices on one's reputation and legacy in Regency-era England.

Davos Seaworth
Meaning and Origin: Beloved (Hebrew)
Significance: Known as the Onion Knight, he is a smuggler turned loyal advisor to Stannis Baratheon and later to Jon Snow.

Dazzler
Meaning and Origin: Brightness; brilliance (English)
Significance: Dazzler, or Alison Blaire, can convert sound vibrations into light and energy beams. Her character's career as a singer and mutant superhero reflects themes of celebrity, identity, and the intersection of artistry with super heroics within the *X-Men* series, adding a unique dimension to mutant representation.

Demetri
Meaning and Origin: Follower of Demeter, the goddess of agriculture (Greek)
Significance: Demetri is a member of the Volturi guard known for his exceptional tracking abilities. His talent in finding individuals makes him an asset to the Volturi's efforts in enforcing vampire laws and dealing with potential threats in the Twilight series.

Denethor
Meaning and Origin: Lithe; lank (Sindarin)
Significance: The Steward of Gondor, who succumbs to despair and madness during the war.

Dolores
Meaning and Origin: Sorrows; pains (Latin)
Significance: Dolores Umbridge is the sadistic and authoritarian Senior Undersecretary to the Minister for Magic and later Hogwarts High Inquisitor. Known for her pink attire and love of kittens, Umbridge embodies themes of oppression, abuse of power, and the dangers of bureaucratic tyranny. Her character explores the darker aspects of authority, conformity, and the abuse of magical and political influence.

Dorian
Meaning and Origin: Gift (Greek)
Significance: Dorian is one of the many characters in the *Throne of Glass* book series that we immediately fall in love with. At first, he seems juvenile, charming his way through life, but we quickly learn there is more to him. Dorian is known for his intelligence, caring heart, and bravery to stand up for what's right.

Earendil
Meaning and Origin: Sea lover (Quenya)
Significance: A mariner who became a star, playing a crucial role in the history of Middle-earth.

Echo
Meaning and Origin: Sound (Greek)
Significance: A nymph who was cursed to only repeat the words of others, Echo symbolizes unrequited love, reflection, and the consequences of deceit.

Eddard
Meaning and Origin: Wealthy Guard (Old English)
Significance: Eddard Stark, also known as Ned, is a symbol of honor and loyalty. His name reflects his role as a protector of his family and his people.

Edwina
Meaning and Origin: Rich friend; blessed friend (English)
Significance: Edwina Sharma is Kate Sharma's younger sister in "*Bridgerton*." Known for her beauty, kindness, and gentle nature, Edwina embodies themes of sisterly love, romantic aspirations, and the pursuit of happiness amidst the competitive world of Regency-era courtship. Her character explores the dynamics of sibling rivalry, the complexities of sisterly bonds, and the transformative power
of love in a society where marriage can secure both social status and personal fulfillment.

Eldarion
Meaning and Origin: Son of the Eldar (Sindarin)
Significance: The son of Aragorn and Arwen, future king of Gondor and Arnor.

Eleazar
Meaning and Origin: God has helped; God is my help (Hebrew)
Significance: Eleazar is a member of the Denali coven with the ability to discern the special talents of other vampires. His loyalty to his family and his insightful nature contribute to the Denali coven's dynamics and their interactions with other vampire covens in the *Twilight series*.

Elrond
Meaning and Origin: Star-dome (Sindarin)
Significance: The lord of Rivendell, an elf who provides refuge and counsel to the Fellowship.

Embry
Meaning and Origin: Work in the fields (English)
Significance: Embry Call is a member of the Quileute werewolf pack. Known for his athleticism, curiosity, and close friendship with Jacob Black, Embry navigates the complexities of werewolf life and the challenges posed by vampire adversaries in the *Twilight series*.

Erestor
Meaning and Origin: Heir (Sindarin)
Significance: A chief counsellor to Elrond in Rivendell, known for his wisdom and strategic mind.

Ernie
Meaning and Origin: Serious (English)
Significance: Ernie Macmillan is a Hufflepuff student known for his loyalty, bravery, and strong sense of justice. As a member of Dumbledore's Army and a leader within his house, Ernie embodies themes of loyalty, fairness, and the importance of standing up for one's principles.

Euron Greyjoy
Meaning and Origin: Warrior, Soldier (Old Norse)
Significance: A ruthless and ambitious pirate who seeks to dominate the seas and claim the Iron Throne.

Faramir
Meaning: Sufficient jewel (Sindarin)
Significance: The younger brother of Boromir, known for his wisdom and integrity.

Feanor
Meaning and Origin: Spirit of fire (Quenya)
Significance: The greatest of the Noldor, creator of the Silmarils, whose actions led to much of the turmoil in Middle earth.

Feyre
Meaning and Origin: Fair; beautiful; light-haired (French)
Significance: Feyre is the brave, loyal, and brilliant heroine of the *A Court of Thorns and Roses* book series. Never backing down from who she is or from what is right, Feyre is a powerful name for an independent daughter.

Filius
Meaning and Origin: Son (Latin)
Significance: Filius Flitwick is the cheerful Charms professor at Hogwarts known for his small stature and expertise in magic. As head of Ravenclaw House, Flitwick embodies intelligence, creativity, and the joy of learning. His character highlight's themes of academic excellence, individuality, and the power of perseverance in mastering magical skills.

Finrod
Meaning and Origin: Hair of gold (Sindarin)
Significance: Finrod Felagund is an ancient elf lord who founded the kingdom of Nargothrond and sacrificed himself for a friend.

Fleur
Meaning and Origin: Flower; Beauty, grace (French)
Significance: Fleur Delacour is a talented Beaux batons student and Triwizard Tournament champion known for her elegance, bravery, and Veela heritage. As a member of the Order of the Phoenix and wife to Bill Weasley, Fleur embodies themes of courage, resilience, and the celebration of diverse magical traditions.

Forge
Meaning and Origin: A skilled craftsman; Creator (English)
Significance: Forge is a mutant with an intuitive genius for invention, specializing in creating advanced technology. His character explores themes of innovation, responsibility, and the impact of technology on society within the *X-Men* universe, providing crucial support to the team with his inventions and strategic insights.

Frances
Meaning and Origin: From France; Free one (Latin)
Significance: Frances Bridgerton is one of the Bridgerton siblings in "*Bridgerton*." Known for her intelligence, grace, and compassionate nature, Frances embodies themes of familial love, personal integrity, and the pursuit of happiness amidst the glittering world of Regency-era London society.

Frodo
Meaning and Origin: Wise; sagacious (British)
Significance: The kind, courageous, and persevering hero of *The Lord of the Rings*, Frodo possesses a simple wisdom and enduring spirit that allows him to overcome any challenge.

Gambit
Meaning and Origin: Risky action taken with the expectation of a favorable outcome. (French)
Significance: Gambit, or Remy LeBeau, possesses the ability to kinetically charge objects, turning them into explosive projectiles. Known for his charm, wit, and Cajun background, Gambit's character adds a dynamic mix of romance, adventure, and moral ambiguity to the *X-Men* team.

Gandalf
Meaning and Origin: Elf of the wand (Old Norse)
Significance: A powerful wizard and key member of the Fellowship of the Ring, guiding and protecting Frodo on his quest.

Garrett
Meaning and Origin: Spear Ruler (English)
Significance: Garrett is a nomadic vampire who becomes a member of the Denali coven after falling in love with Kate. Known for his independent spirit, loyalty to his beliefs, and prowess in combat, Garrett's character evolves from a lone wanderer to a valued ally of the Cullen family in the *Twilight series*.

Gellert
Meaning and Origin: Brave with the spear (German)
Significance: Gellert Grindelwald is a dark wizard and former friend of Albus Dumbledore known for his quest to establish wizarding dominance over Muggles. As a charismatic and manipulative figure, Grindelwald embodies themes of power, ideology, and the dangers of unchecked ambition.

Geralt
Meaning and Origin: Spear ruler (German)
Significance: The mysterious and often misunderstood hero of *The Witcher*, Geralt is a kind and compassionate warrior who uses his strength to defend those who can't defend themselves.

Gilly
Meaning and Origin: Joy; Delight (Old English)
Significance: A wildling woman who escapes from Craster's Keep and forms a bond with Samwell Tarly.

Gimli
Meaning: and Origin Listener (Old Norse)
Significance: A dwarf warrior and member of the Fellowship, known for his strength and loyalty.

Ginny
Meaning and Origin: Pure; chaste (Latin)
Significance: Ginny Weasley is the youngest child in the Weasley family and a fiercely independent Gryffindor student. Known for her fiery personality, athletic prowess, and magical abilities, Ginny evolves from Ron's little sister to Harry's confident and supportive girlfriend.

Glorfindel
Meaning and Origin: Golden hair (Sindarin)
Significance: A powerful elf lord who aids Frodo in his journey to Rivendell.

Gregor
Meaning and Origin: Watchful (Greek)
Significance: Gregor Clegane Known as the Mountain, a fearsome and brutal knight serving House Lannister, infamous for his immense size and cruelty.

Hakoda
Meaning and Origin: To listen (Japanese)
Significance: Reflects leadership and wisdom as the leader of the Southern Water Tribe. Hakoda is the father of Katara and Sokka, in *Avatar The Last Airbender* leading the Southern Water Tribe warriors in the war.

Haldir
Meaning and Origin: Hidden hero (Sindarin)
Significance: An elf warden of Lothlórien who helps guide and protect the Fellowship.

Hamlet
Meaning and Origin: Trickster (Danish)
Significance: The titular character in *Hamlet*. This name brings with it a sense of history and culture, as well as its own flavor of mischief.

Han
Meaning and Origin: Gift of God (Hebrew)
Significance: Han Solo is a charismatic smuggler and pilot in *Star Wars* who becomes a hero of the Rebel Alliance. Known for his wit, bravery, and loyalty to his friends, Han Solo embodies the archetype of the roguish hero.

Havok
Meaning and Origin: Chaos; destructive force (English)
Significance: Havok, or Alex Summers, generates powerful plasma blasts that he struggles to control. As the younger brother of Cyclops, Havok's character explores themes of sibling rivalry, identity, and the burden of expectations, adding depth to the *X-Men's* exploration of mutant powers and their consequences.

Hermione
Meaning and Origin: Messenger (Greek)
Significance: No character in the *Harry Potter* series is more connected with being smart than Hermione. Dedicated to her studies, loyal to her friends, and dangerous to her enemies, she is easy to classify as a top-level heroine.

Hester
Meaning and Origin: Star (Persian)
Significance: A strong and independent woman, Hester is the main character in *The Scarlet Letter*. Though initially shamed, her kindness and ability to help others show who she really is and change the false assumptions of those around her.

Horace
Meaning and Origin: Man of time; hourly (Latin)
Significance: Horace Slughorn is the former Potions professor at Hogwarts known for his connections to influential witches and wizards. As head of Slytherin House, Slughorn embodies ambition, networking, and the desire for recognition. His character explores themes of mentorship, ambition, and the ethical dilemmas surrounding power and influence in the wizarding world.

Ichabod
Meaning and Origin: Where is the glory? (Hebrew)
Significance: From *The Legend of Sleepy Hollow*, Ichabod carries a sense of mystery and suspense.

Ignatius
Meaning and Origin: Fiery; ardent (Latin)
Significance: Used in *A Confederacy of Dunces*, Ignatius is a strong name with connotations of passion, determination, and leadership ability.

Igor
Meaning and Origin: Warrior; heroic (Old Norse)
Significance: Igor Karkaroff is the headmaster of Durmstrang Institute and a former Death Eater who betrayed Voldemort's followers to avoid Azkaban. As a cunning and self-serving figure, Karkaroff embodies themes of survival, betrayal, and the moral complexities of seeking redemption amidst dark times. His character explores the consequences of past actions, the pursuit of personal safety, and the ambiguous nature of loyalty in the wizarding world.

Irina
Meaning and Origin: Peace (Russian)
Significance: Irina is a member of the Denali coven and the original source of the misunderstanding that leads to a conflict between the Cullens and the Volturi in Breaking Dawn. Her character reflects loyalty to her family and the consequences of her actions in the *Twilight series*.

Iroh
Meaning and Origin: Peaceful (Japanese)
Significance: Symbolizes wisdom, peace, and guidance Iroh is Zuko's uncle, in *Avatar The Last Airbender* a wise and kind-hearted former general who provides guidance and support.

Jaqen
Meaning and Origin: To hunt (German)
Significance: Jaqen H'ghar is a mysterious assassin of the Faceless Men who helps Arya Stark on her journey.

Jeremy
Meaning and Origin: Appointed by God; God will raise up (Hebrew)
Significance: Jeremy Gilbert is Elena Gilbert's younger brother in "The Vampire Diaries." Known for his artistic talent, emotional sensitivity, and resilience in the face of loss, Jeremy embodies themes of adolescence, growth, and the search for identity amidst supernatural upheaval. His character explores themes of grief, redemption, and the complexities of navigating teenage life while uncovering family secrets and supernatural legacies.

Jenna
Meaning and Origin: White wave; Fair one (English)
Significance: Jenna Sommers is Elena and Jeremy Gilbert's aunt and legal guardian in "The Vampire Diaries." Known for her warmth, independence, and protective nature, Jenna embodies themes of family, sacrifice, and the challenges of parenting in the face of supernatural dangers. Her character explores the bonds of kinship, the impact of loss, and the resilience needed to protect loved ones amidst escalating supernatural conflicts.

Jo
Meaning and Origin: Jehovah is God (Hebrew)
Significance: Jo Laughlin is a witch, Alaric Saltzman's fiancée, and a central figure in "The Vampire Diaries" later seasons. Known for her bravery, magical prowess, and resilience in the face of supernatural threats, Jo embodies themes of love, sacrifice, and the pursuit of happiness amidst the dangers of Mystic Falls. Her character explores the complexities of romantic relationships, the challenges of blending magical and human lives, and the strength found in embracing one's true nature amidst ever-present dangers.

Jorah
Meaning and Origin: Early Rain (Hebrew)
Significance: Jorah Mormont is a loyal and dedicated follower of Daenerys Targaryen. His name signifies renewal and devotion.

Jory Cassel
Meaning and Origin: God will Uplift (Hebrew)
Significance: Captain of the guard at Winterfell, loyal to Eddard Stark, and tragically killed in King's Landing.

Josette
Meaning and Origin: Jehovah increases; May Jehovah add (Hebrew)
Significance: Josette Saltzman, also known as "Josie," is Alaric Saltzman and Jo Laughlin's twin daughter in "*The Vampire Diaries*" and "Legacies." Known for her magical abilities, compassion, and determination, Josie embodies themes of family legacy, individual identity, and the balance between light and darkness within oneself.

Jubilee
Meaning and Origin: Time of celebration and joy (English)
Significance: Jubilee, or Jubilation Lee, generates explosive energy plasmoids that resemble fireworks. Her youthful exuberance, humor, and resilience resonate with audiences, reflecting themes of adolescent growth and finding one's place in a world that fears and misunderstands mutants.

Kali
Meaning and Origin: Time; the divine mother (Sanskrit)
Significance: An aptly named character in *Stranger Things*, Kali is strong and independent with a desire to right the wrongs of the past and punish evil doers. The name also originally comes from the name of the Hindu goddess.

Katara
Meaning and Origin: From the word "Katara" meaning water droplet in Arabic (Arabic)
Significance: Reflects her abilities as a water bender and her nurturing personality. Katara is a skilled water bender in *Avatar The Last Airbender* who plays a crucial role in Aang's journey and the fight against the Fire Nation.

Katniss
Meaning and Origin: Aquatic plant (Greek)
Significance: As the main character in The Hunger Games, Katniss is known for being smart, strong, and protective. Her story starts when she volunteers in her sister's place as tribute. Along the way, she finds ways to survive, even though she allies herself with weaker tributes. She cares more about the heart than brute strength.

Klaus
Meaning and Origin: Victory of the people (German)
Significance: Klaus Mikaelson is one of the original vampires and a central antagonist/anti-hero in "The Vampire Diaries." Known for his charisma, complexity, and ruthless pursuit of power, Klaus embodies themes of family legacy, redemption, and the search for identity across centuries. His character explores the consequences of immortality, the complexities of familial bonds, and the relentless pursuit of personal ambition amidst a backdrop of supernatural intrigue.

Kol
Meaning and Origin: Coal; dark (Old Norse)
Significance: Kol Mikaelson is one of the original vampires and Klaus Mikaelson's younger brother in "*The Vampire Diaries*." Known for his wit, impulsiveness, and penchant for chaos, Kol embodies themes of unpredictability, sibling rivalry, and the quest for freedom amidst the constraints of family loyalty.

Lee
Meaning and Origin: Clearing; meadow (Old English)
Significance: Lee Jordan is a Gryffindor student known for his mischievous nature and talent as a Quidditch commentator. As a close friend of the Weasley siblings and a member of Dumbledore's Army, Lee embodies themes of humor, loyalty, and the camaraderie found in shared experiences at Hogwarts.

Legion
Meaning and Origin: A large group or assembly; a powerful force (Latin)
Significance: Legion, or David Haller, is a mutant with multiple personalities, each possessing different mutant powers. His character's struggle with mental illness, identity, and the immense potential for both good and evil within him explores themes of psychological complexity, personal growth, and the impact of mental health on superhuman abilities.

Legolas
Meaning and Origin: Green leaf (Sindarin)
Significance: An elf prince from the Woodland Realm, known for his archery skills and member of the Fellowship.

Leia
Meaning and Origin: Weary, tired (Hebrew)
Significance: A brave and intelligent princess in *Star Wars*, it is Leia's integrity that has often left fans most inspired. Her ability to remain true to what is right has helped many viewers keep the dark side at bay.

Liv
Meaning and Origin: Life (English)
Significance: Liv Parker is a witch and Kai Parker's younger sister in "The Vampire Diaries." Known for her compassion, determination, and magical abilities, Liv embodies themes of sibling loyalty, self-discovery, and the pursuit of justice amidst escalating supernatural conflicts.

Liz
Meaning and Origin: God is my oath (Hebrew)
Significance: Liz Forbes is Caroline Forbes' mother and the sheriff of Mystic Falls in "The Vampire Diaries." Known for her integrity, dedication to justice, and evolving understanding of supernatural realities, Liz embodies themes of law enforcement, parental love, and the challenges of maintaining order in a town plagued by supernatural occurrences.

Loras Tyrell
Meaning and Origin: From the Laurel Tree (Latin)
Significance: Known as the Knight of Flowers, a skilled and charismatic knight with a secret romantic relationship with Renly Baratheon.

Ludo
Meaning and Origin: Playing, Game, Gambling (Latin)
Significance: Ludo Bagman is a former Quidditch player and Ministry of Magic official known for his charm, recklessness, and gambling habits. As a figure of light-heartedness and occasional incompetence, Bagman embodies themes of risk-taking, redemption, and the consequences of living in the shadow of past mistakes.

Luthien
Meaning and Origin: Daughter of flowers (Sindarin)
Significance: An elf maiden whose love for the mortal Beren led to legendary deeds and sacrifices.

Lyanna
Meaning and Origin: Derived from Lee and Anna (English)
Significance: Lyanna Stark is the sister of Eddard Stark, whose abduction by Prince Rhaegar Targaryen sparked Robert's Rebellion.

Mace
Meaning and Origin: Gift of God (English)
Significance: Mace Windu is a powerful Jedi Master known for his mastery of the lightsaber combat form Vaapad and his leadership as a member of the Jedi High Council. His character explores themes of justice, inner balance, and the consequences of wielding great power.

Magik
Meaning and Origin: A mystical or supernatural connection (English)
Significance: Magik, or Illyana Rasputin, is a mutant with teleportation powers and magical abilities derived from the dimension known as Limbo.

Magneto
Meaning and Origin: A powerful force (English)
Significance: Magneto, also known as Erik Lehnsherr, is a mutant with the ability to manipulate magnetic fields. His character is complex, often portrayed as an antagonist due to his belief in mutant superiority and conflict with Professor X's vision of peaceful coexistence between mutants and humans.

Mai
Meaning and Origin: Dance (Chinese)
Significance: Reflects grace and precision, reflecting her skills as a fighter. Mai is a skilled and stoic warrior, in *Avatar The Last Airbender* and Zuko's love interest, known for her proficiency with throwing weapons.

Margaery Tyrell
Meaning and Origin: Pearl (Greek)
Significance: Margaery Tyrell is known for her beauty and political acumen. Her name reflects her valuable and multifaceted nature.

Marietta
Meaning and Origin: Bitter; beloved (Hebrew)
Significance: Marietta Edgecombe is a Ravenclaw student and member of Dumbledore's Army who betrays the group to Umbridge. Her character represents themes of loyalty, betrayal, and the consequences of choices made under duress. Marietta's role in the series highlights the complexities of peer pressure, the search for personal integrity, and the moral dilemmas faced by young witches and wizards amidst growing tensions in the wizarding world.

Marina
Meaning and Origin: Marine; The sea (Latin)
Significance: Marina Thompson is a cousin of the Featherington family in "*Bridgerton*." Known for her beauty, charm, and mysterious background, Marina embodies themes of secrets, scandal, and the consequences of impulsive choices amidst the rigid social expectations of Regency-era England.

Marrow
Meaning and Origin: Refers to bone; resilience or inner strength (English)
Significance: Marrow, or Sarah, can project and control bone growth from her body. Her character's struggles with identity, trauma, and acceptance within the Morlocks community and later with the *X-Men* highlight themes of physical mutation, survival, and finding strength in adversity.

Meera Reed
Meaning and Origin: Prosperous; Happy (Sanskrit)
Significance: A fierce and loyal companion to Bran Stark, known for her bravery and survival skills.

Megan
Meaning and Origin: Pearl; child of light (Welsh)
Significance: Megan King is a minor character in "*The Vampire Diaries*." Known for her brief involvement with the supernatural world of Mystic Fall.

Melian
Meaning and Origin: Dear gift (Quenya)
Significance: A Maia who became queen of Doriath, mother of Lúthien, and a powerful enchantress.

Meriadoc
Meaning and Origin: Great lord (Celtic)
Significance: Meriadoc Brandybuck is a hobbit and member of the Fellowship, known for his courage and resourcefulness.

Millicent
Meaning and Origin: Hardworking (Old German)
Significance: Millicent Bulstrode is a Slytherin student known for her physical strength and loyalty to Draco Malfoy and the Death Eaters. As a member of the Inquisitorial Squad, Millicent embodies themes of loyalty, discipline, and the willingness to enforce authority in the face of opposition.

Milo
Meaning and Origin: Soldier; merciful (German)
Significance: Aligning with the name's original meaning, Milo in *Catch-22* was a soldier, although he may have spent more time trying to make extra money for his company. Therefore, Milo has both strong and entrepreneurial qualities.

Minerva
Meaning and Origin: The goddess of wisdom and strategic warfare
 (Latin)
Significance: Minerva McGonagall is the strict but fair Deputy Headmistress of Hogwarts and head of Gryffindor House. Known for her intelligence, unwavering principles, and powerful magical abilities, McGonagall symbolizes wisdom, discipline, and the importance of education. Her character embodies themes of mentorship, resilience, and the pursuit of justice in times of adversity.

Moira
Meaning and Origin: Great; noble (Gaelic)
Significance: Moira MacTaggert is a geneticist and ally of the *X-Men*, known for her expertise in mutant genetics and her role in understanding and advancing mutant kind. Her character's dedication to scientific inquiry, ethics, and advocacy for mutant rights contributes to the X-Men's ongoing battles for acceptance and equality.

Mustapha
Meaning and Origin: The chosen one (Arabic)
Significance: A mysterious-sounding name, Mustapha appears as a leader of great power in Aldous Huxley's *A Brave New World*. This pairs well with its meaning, giving the name strong leadership and authoritative qualities.

Mystique
Meaning and Origin: Mystique suggests an air of mystery (English)
Significance: Mystique, or Raven Darkhölme, is a shape-shifting mutant known for her cunning intellect and skill in espionage. Her fluid identity, both literally and figuratively, challenges conventional notions of appearance and morality within the *X-Men* series, making her a complex and formidable antagonist.

Narcissa
Meaning and Origin: The Narcissus Flower (Greek)
Significance: Narcissa Malfoy is the mother of Draco Malfoy and wife of Lucius Malfoy. Despite her allegiance to the Death Eaters, Narcissa is defined by her fierce love for her family and her willingness to protect them at all costs. Her character embodies themes of maternal instinct, sacrifice, and the complexities of morality in a world torn by conflict.

Nemo
Meaning and Origin: No one (Latin)
Significance: Whether you're a fan of Charles Dickens, Jules Verne, or Pixar films, there's a Nemo for you. The name, often used by characters who want to stay anonymous, has taken on an unbreakable link to the sea and the importance of family.

Neville
Meaning and Origin: New town or village (French)
Significance: Neville Longbottom is a courageous Gryffindor student known for his initially timid nature that blossoms into bravery and leadership. As a member of Dumbledore's Army and a key figure in the fight against Voldemort, Neville symbolizes themes of resilience, inner strength, and the importance of standing up for what is right.

Nicholas
Meaning and Origin: Victory of the people (Greek)
Significance: Nicholas Flamel is a legendary alchemist and creator of the Philosopher's Stone, capable of granting immortality. As a figure of mystery and fascination, Flamel embodies themes of discovery, immortality, and the pursuit of knowledge beyond mortal limits. His character explores the allure of alchemical secrets, the ethical implications of eternal life, and the quest for ultimate power in the wizarding world.

Nori
Meaning and Origin: Sun-star; luminous; the other Aenor (French)
Significance: A cute nickname for Elanor that has come alive since the release of *The Lord of the Rings: The Rings of Power*. Norri is curious and adventurous while still being responsible and caring.

Norm
Meaning and Origin: From the north (Scandinavian)
Significance: Represents a bridge between human and Na'vi cultures through science. Norm Spellman is a scientist and Avatar driver in *Avatar Movie Series* who supports Jake and helps the Na'vi understand human technology and tactics.

NorthStar
Meaning and Origin: A guiding light or beacon (English)
Significance: NorthStar, or Jean-Paul Beaubier, possesses superhuman speed and flight abilities. His character is notable in mainstream comics, exploring themes of identity, acceptance, and the pursuit of justice within the *X-Men* series.

Oberyn Martell
Meaning and Origin: Bear (German)
Significance: Known as the Red Viper, a charismatic and deadly warrior seeking vengeance for his sister's death.

Olenna Tyrell
Meaning and Origin: Light (Greek)
Significance: The sharp-witted and politically savvy matriarch of House Tyrell, known for her cunning and influence.

Osha
Meaning and Origin: Bear (Old English)
Significance: A wildling woman who becomes a protector and guide to the Stark children.

Otto Hightower
Meaning and Origin: Wealth; prosperity (German)
Significance: A wise and cautious counselor from *The House of the Dragon*, Otto also has a long and proud heritage in the real world.

Ozai
Meaning and Origin: Power (Chinese)
Significance: Symbolizes authoritarian power and control as the Fire Lord. Ozai is the main antagonist, in *Avatar The Last Airbender* the tyrannical ruler of the Fire Nation seeking world domination.

Pansy
Meaning: and Origin Thoughtfulness; remembrance (English)
Significance: Pansy Parkinson is a Slytherin student known for her beauty, ambition, and allegiance to Draco Malfoy and the Death Eaters. As a figure of cunning and manipulation, Pansy embodies themes of ambition, peer pressure, and the desire for social status in the competitive environment of Hogwarts.

Peregrin
Meaning and Origin: Traveler (Latin)
Significance: Peregrin Took is a hobbit and member of the Fellowship, known for his curiosity and bravery.

Peta
Meaning and Origin: Rock (Hebrew)
Significance: From the very popular book series and movie adaptations, *The Hunger Games*, Peta is the main love interest of the lead character, Katniss. Even though Peta is incredibly strong physically, he is loved for his soft-spoken manner and his caring heart, always putting the needs of others above his own.

Petyr Baelish
Meaning and Origin: Rock, Stone (Greek)
Significance: Known as Littlefinger, a cunning and ambitious manipulator who plays a key role in the political intrigues of Westeros.

Phileas
Meaning and Origin: Loving, affectionate; dear (Greek)
Significance: The eccentric hero of *Around the World in Eighty Days*, Phileas carries tender and caring characteristics combined with an intense curiosity and love of exploration.

Pi
Meaning and Origin: The ratio of a circle's radius to its circumference (Greek)
Significance: A great name for both readers and mathematicians, Pi is the titular character in *Life of Pi*. Charming and creative, the name Pi brings a sense of reliability and imagination.

Pierce
Meaning and Origin: Force a way through; penetrate (Latin)
Significance: The instigator of all the mystery and intrigue in *The Crying of Lot 49*, Pierce carries connotations of breaking through barriers and getting to the truth no matter what.

Pippi
Meaning and Origin: Lover of horses (Scandinavian)
Significance: The titular character of *Pippi Longstocking*, Pippi brings an unmistakable innocence and a sense of fun, as well as a unique way of thinking.

Podrick Payne
Meaning and Origin: Warrior (Welsh)
Significance: A loyal squire who serves Tyrion Lannister and later Brienne of Tarth, known for his bravery and modesty.

Polaris
Meaning and Origin: Connection to magnetism or polarity (Latin)
Significance: Polaris, or Lorna Dane, can manipulate magnetic fields, like Magneto. Her character's journey explores themes of identity, mental health, and finding purpose within the mutant community, contributing to the diversity of experiences among *X-Men* characters.

Pomona
Meaning and Origin: The goddess of fruitful abundance (Latin)
Significance: Pomona Sprout is the herbology professor at Hogwarts known for her green thumb and nurturing nature. As head of Hufflepuff House, Sprout embodies patience, kindness, and a deep connection to the natural world.

Portia
Meaning and Origin: Pig (Latin)
Significance: Portia Featherington is the matriarch of the Featherington family in "*Bridgerton*." Known for her social ambition, determination, and protective nature towards her daughters, Portia embodies themes of maternal influence, societal expectations, and the lengths a mother will go to secure advantageous matches for her children.

Prudence
Meaning and Origin: Caution; foresight (Latin)
Significance: Prudence Featherington is the eldest daughter of the Featherington family in "*Bridgerton*." Known for her adherence to social etiquette, loyalty to her family, and desire to fulfill her role as an elder sister, Prudence embodies themes of duty, tradition, and the pressures of conforming to societal norms. Her character explores the challenges of sibling rivalry, the complexities of sisterhood, and the personal sacrifices made in the pursuit of familial harmony and societal acceptance during the Regency era.

Pyro
Meaning and Origin: Fire; heat (Greek)
Significance: Pyro, or St. John Allerdyce, can manipulate flame. His character explores themes of power, addiction, and moral choice as he navigates between heroism and villainy within the mutant world, offering insights into the complexities of mutant powers and their impact on personal identity.

Ramsay Bolton
Meaning and Origin: Wild Garlic (Old English)
Significance: A sadistic and ruthless nobleman who becomes Warden of the North, infamous for his cruelty and manipulative nature.

Remus
Meaning and Origin: Legendary founder of Rome raised by wolves (Latin)
Significance: Remus Lupin is a werewolf and a former Hogwarts professor known for his intelligence, kindness, and struggles with his lycanthropy. As a member of the Marauders and Harry's mentor, Lupin represents themes of acceptance, prejudice, and the power of compassion. His character explores the challenges of living with a hidden identity and the resilience needed to overcome adversity.

Renee
Meaning and Origin: Born again (French)
Significance: Renee Dwyer is Bella Swan's mother. Known for her free-spirited personality and unconventional lifestyle, Renee contrasts with the more grounded presence of Bella's father, Charlie Swan, in the *Twilight series*.

Renesmee
Meaning and Origin: Reborn; loved (French)
Significance: Renesmee's significance is entirely tied to her role as a character in the *Twilight* saga. She is a half-vampire, half-human child born to Bella Swan and Edward Cullen. She is kind and overwhelmingly intelligent, as well as fun and loving.

Rey
Meaning and Origin: King; queen (English)
Significance: Rey is the central protagonist in the *Star Wars* sequel trilogy. Initially a scavenger on the desert planet Jakku, Rey discovers her connection to the Force and becomes a key figure in the Resistance's struggle against the First Order. Her journey is one of self-discovery, resilience, and hope.

Rickon
Meaning and Origin: Strong ; Brave Ruler (Old English)
Significance: The youngest son of Eddard Stark, who becomes separated from his family and faces a tragic fate.

Robb
Meaning and Origin: Bright Fame (Old English)
Significance: The eldest son of Eddard Stark, who becomes King in the North and leads a rebellion against the Iron Throne.

Robinson
Meaning and Origin: Son of Robin (British)
Significance: An adventurer and survivor, the hero of *Robinson Crusoe* went through many trials and always came out on top. This name carries a strong adventuring spirit and the strength and ingenuity to see the journey through.

Rogue
Meaning and Origin: Dishonest, Savage, Unpredictable (English)
Significance: Rogue, or Anna Marie, can absorb powers and memories from others through physical touch. Her struggle with her powers, which make physical contact dangerous, and her journey from villain to hero in the *X-Men* series highlight themes of identity, acceptance, and redemption.

Rohan
Meaning and Origin: Red; red-haired (Irish)
Significance: Not a character but a place in *The Lord of the Rings*, Rohan is the bastion against evil in the world of Middle-earth and represents all that is good about mankind. The name conjures images of bravery, integrity, and strength.

Ron
Meaning and Origin: Ruler's counselor; wise advisor (German)
Significance: Best friend to Harry Potter, Ron is reliable, trustworthy, and more capable than many give him credit for.

Roose Bolton
Meaning and Origin: Rose (Old English)
Significance: The cold and calculating Lord of the Dreadfort, known for his betrayal of the Stark family.

Rosalie
Meaning: Variant of the flower name Rose; Beauty; Grace (English)
Significance: Rosalie Hale is a member of the Cullen vampire family known for her stunning beauty and protective nature towards her family. Her character evolves from a tragic past to finding purpose and love within the Cullen clan.

Rubeus
Meaning and Origin: I am red; Ruddy (Latin)
Significance: Rubeus Hagrid is the gentle giant and Hogwarts gamekeeper known for his love of magical creatures and loyalty to Harry and his friends. Despite his intimidating appearance, Hagrid embodies kindness, innocence, and a deep-seated belief in the goodness of others.

Rufus
Meaning and Origin: Red-haired (Latin)
Significance: Rufus Scrimgeour is the Minister for Magic during the Second Wizarding War, known for his tough stance against Voldemort and his Death Eaters. As a figurehead of authority, Scrimgeour embodies themes of leadership, sacrifice, and the challenges of maintaining order and hope during times of crisis.

Samneric
Meaning and Origin: Sam and Eric (British)
Significance: An interesting duo in *Lord of the Flies*, Samneric represents the average person trying to get by in a tough world. The name evokes a sense of playing by the rules and trying to make sure that others are looked after and happy.

Samwell Tarly
Meaning and Origin: God Heard (Hebrew)
Significance: A member of the Night's Watch known for his intellect, loyalty, and courage, close friend of Jon Snow.

Samwise Gamgee
Meaning and Origin: Half-wise (Old English)
Significance: Frodo's loyal companion and friend, known for his unwavering loyalty and bravery.

Sandor Clegane
Meaning and Origin: Defender of Men (Greek)
Significance: Known as the Hound, a fearsome warrior with a troubled past, who develops a complex relationship with Arya Stark.

Sansa
Meaning and Origin: Praise; charm (Sanskrit)
Significance: In the hit series *Game of Thrones*, Sansa starts out as a slightly spoiled and naive girl. Yet, as the story progresses, Sansa grows into a powerful leader who shows a lot of resilience and restraint and eventually becomes queen. She loves her family dearly and has a good heart.

Saruman
Meaning and Origin: Man of skill (Old English)
Significance: A wizard who turns to evil and seeks the power of the One Ring.

Sati
Meaning and Origin: Truth (Sanskrit)
Significance: Symbolizes purity and potential within the Matrix. Sati is a young program created without a purpose, representing hope and the possibility of change in the *Matrix*.

Sauron
Meaning and Origin: The abhorred (Quenya)
Significance: The primary antagonist, the dark lord who created the One Ring to dominate Middle earth.

Seline
Meaning and Origin: Moon goddess (Greek)
Significance: Seline is a former nanny and a powerful siren in "The Vampire Diaries." Known for her protective nature, maternal instincts, and tragic history with Sybil, Seline embodies themes of sacrifice, redemption, and the enduring bond between surrogate mothers and their charges.

Seraph
Meaning and Origin: Angel (Hebrew)
Significance: Represents purity and protection, serving as a guardian within the Matrix. In the *Matrix* Seraph is a guardian of the Oracle who tests Neo's resolve and loyalty.

Severus
Meaning and Origin: Stern, serious; strict (Latin)
Significance: One of the most hated, and possibly misunderstood, characters in *Harry Potter*, Severus' name is a giveaway as to what we can expect from the character for most of the series. However, the name also carries self-sacrificial and protective elements.

Sherlock
Meaning and Origin: Fair-haired (British)
Significance: The brilliant, if quirky, detective from the *Sherlock Holmes* series brings an air of genius to the name.

Sokka
Meaning and Origin: Stubborn (Japanese)
Significance: Represents a strong-willed and resourceful warrior. Sokka is Katara's brother, in *Avatar The Last Airbender* known for his strategic mind and non-bending combat skills, often providing comic relief.

Stefan
Meaning and Origin: Crown; Garland (Greek)
Significance: Stefan Salvatore is one of the Salvatore brothers and a protagonist in "The Vampire Diaries." Known for his brooding demeanor and conflicted nature as a vampire, Stefan embodies themes of redemption, love, and the struggle between darkness and humanity. His character explores the complexities of immortality, the consequences of personal choices, and the enduring power of love amidst supernatural conflicts.

Stryker
Meaning and Origin: A military or authoritarian figure (English)
Significance: William Stryker is a fanatical anti-mutant crusader who sees mutants as a threat to humanity. His character embodies themes of prejudice, extremism, and the dangers of fear-driven ideologies within the *X-Men* series, serving as a recurring antagonist who tests the X-Men's resolve and moral convictions.

Suki
Meaning and Origin: Beloved (Japanese)
Significance: Represents loyalty and love, reflecting her role as a warrior and leader. Suki is the leader of the Kyoshi Warriors and Sokka's love interest, in *Avatar The Last Airbender* known for her combat skills and bravery.

Theoden
Meaning: and Origin King (Old English)
Significance: The King of Rohan who is initially under Saruman's spell but later becomes a key ally in the war against Sauron.

Thorin
Meaning and Origin: Little Thor; thunder (Norse)
Significance: Leader of his people living in foreign lands after being chased from their home, Thorin is one of the main characters in Tolkien's *The Hobbit*. The name implies an all-or-nothing approach to life and leadership, as well as the willingness to do whatever is necessary to protect one's loved ones.

Thranduil
Meaning: Vigorous spring (Sindarin)
Significance: The Elvenking of Mirkwood and father of Legolas, known for his kingdom's isolation and wealth.

Tommen Baratheon
Meaning and Origin: Twin (German)
Significance: The youngest son of Cersei and Robert Baratheon, who becomes king after the death of his brother Joffrey.

Toph
Meaning and Origin: Tough (English)
Significance: Reflects her strength and resilience as an earthbender. Toph Beifong is a blind earthbending master in *Avatar The Last Airbender* who becomes Aang's teacher, known for her innovative metalbending.

Tormund Giantsbane
Meaning and Origin: Derived from Thor (Old Norse)
Significance: A wildling leader known for his bravery, strength, and loyalty to Jon Snow.

Trudy
Meaning and Origin: Spear of strength (German)
Significance: Represents bravery and loyalty, reflecting Trudy's fearless nature. Trudy Chacón is a combat pilot in *Avatar Movie Series* who defies orders to support Jake and the Na'vi, sacrificing herself in the battle.

Tulkas
Meaning and Origin: Strong (Quenya)
Significance: A Vala known for his strength and good spirits, who aided in the battles against Melkor.

Tyrion Lannister
Meaning and Origin: Lordly (Greek)
Significance: The intelligent and witty youngest son of Tywin Lannister, known for his sharp mind, strategic thinking, and love for wine and books.

Tywin Lannister
Meaning and Origin: War Leader (Old English)
Significance: The powerful and ruthless head of House Lannister, known for his strategic mind and iron-fisted rule.

Valerie
Meaning and Origin: Strong; valiant (Latin)
Significance: Valerie Tulle is a vampire and former lover of Stefan Salvatore in "*The Vampire Diaries*." Known for her resilience, magical talents, and tragic past as a member of the Heretics, Valerie embodies themes of love, redemption, and the quest for acceptance amidst a life marked by betrayal and loss.

Vicki
Meaning and Origin: Victory; conqueror (Latin)
Significance: Vicki Donovan is Matt Donovan's troubled older sister in "The Vampire Diaries." Known for her rebellious spirit, vulnerability, and struggles with addiction, Vicki embodies themes of adolescence, trauma, and the search for identity amidst personal turmoil and supernatural encounters.

Viktor
Meaning and Origin: Conqueror; victor (Latin)
Significance: Viktor Krum is a renowned Seeker for the Bulgarian Quidditch team and a Triwizard Tournament champion. Known for his skill in Quidditch and his stoic demeanor, Krum embodies themes of sportsmanship, determination, and the pursuit of excellence.

Voldemort
Meaning and Origin: Theft of death (French)
Significance: Voldemort, originally known as Tom Riddle, is the primary antagonist in the series. He represents the embodiment of evil, obsession with power, and the quest for immortality through dark magic. Voldemort's character explores themes of fear, prejudice, and the consequences of choices, highlighting the destructive nature of unchecked ambition and the resilience needed to confront darkness.

Walder Frey
Meaning and Origin: Ruler or Power (Old German)
Significance: The head of House Frey, known for his treacherous actions during the Red Wedding.

Wanda
Meaning and Origin: Shepherdess; wanderer (Polish)
Significance: One of the main characters in the Marvel Cinematic Universe, Wanda is an incredibly strong and resourceful character known for her resilience and immense power. This name embodies strength that is both internal and external.

Watson
Meaning and Origin: Son of water (Scottish)
Significance: Watson is known as the helper and best friend of *Sherlock Homes*. He is incredibly intelligent and kind and often keeps the peace between Sherlock and others. He has a high emotional intelligence, which makes him the perfect friend and partner.

Yue
Meaning and Origin: Moon (Chinese)
Significance: Represents her connection to the Moon Spirit and sacrifice for her people. Yue is the princess of the Northern Water Tribe who sacrifices herself to become the Moon Spirit in *Avatar The Last Airbender*.

Zaphod
Meaning and Origin: Clever; president of the galaxy (British)
Significance: One of the main characters in *The Hitchhiker's Guide to the Universe*, Zaphod is the eccentric President of the Universe. While the name is most definitely made up, it does carry a certain sense of adventure, creativity, and whimsy.

Zuko
Meaning and Origin: Glory (Japanese)
Significance: Represents his journey from seeking glory through anger to finding inner peace. Zuko is the exiled prince of the Fire Nation, in *Avatar The Last Airbender* whose complex character arc leads him from antagonist to ally.

These fictional names are a fun way to create meaning for your child's name and pay tribute to your favorite characters. However, if that's not what you're looking for, stick around. In the next chapter, we'll explore old-fashioned names that will never go out of style.

CHAPTER 9: OLD-FASHIONED NAMES

There's a certain magic to choosing an old-fashioned or vintage name for your baby. These names, steeped in history and tradition, offer a timeless elegance that won't go out of style. Imagine your child carrying a name that whispers of a bygone era yet feels fresh and unique in today's world. Vintage names often boast rich meanings and connections to literature or mythology, adding a layer of depth and intrigue. Plus, choosing a less common name can help your child stand out from the crowd. So, embrace the charm of the past and consider a captivating vintage name that will perfectly complement your little one's individuality and become a treasured part of their story. Let's explore vintage boy and girl names that are ripe for a revival in today's modern world.

Vintage Boys' Names

A vintage name doesn't automatically mean something boring or something that sounds old. You don't want your baby to sound like a grandpa, but vintage names can evoke a sense of nostalgia and character, which modern names can't. Here are some retro choices for your baby boy that will evoke class and character.

Abner
Meaning and Origin: Father of light (Hebrew)
Significance: Represents wisdom and enlightenment, reflecting a guiding and knowledgeable personality.

Albert
Meaning and Origin: Noble; bright (German)
Significance: Albert is a name that symbolizes nobility and brilliance. It is often associated with Albert Einstein, one of the most influential physicists.

Alfie
Meaning and Origin: Wise counselor (British)
Significance: Alfie evokes a sense of charm and friendliness. It has a vintage feel due to its use as a nickname for a longer name.

Alfred
Meaning and Origin: Elf Counsel (Old English)
Significance: Alfred means wise or supernatural counsel. It is often associated with Alfred the Great, the legendary king of Wessex who defended England against Viking invasions.

Archie
Meaning and Origin: Genuine; bold (German)
Significance: Archie has a classic, strong feel. The name refers to someone with a genuine and courageous personality.

Amos
Meaning and Origin: Carried by God (Hebrew)
Significance: Amos is a biblical name, associated with a prophet who authored the Book of Amos, emphasizing justice and moral righteousness.

Andrew
Meaning and Origin: Manly, Brave (Greek)
Significance: Andrew is one of the twelve apostles in the New Testament, known for his evangelistic zeal.

Ansel
Meaning and Origin: Divine protection (German)
Significance: Symbolizes safety and guardianship, reflecting a protective and caring personality.

Archibald
Meaning and Origin: Genuine; Bold, Brave (German)
Significance: Archibald signifies true and bold courage. It's a name often associated with Scottish nobility.

Arthur
Meaning and Origin: Bear (Celtic)
Significance: Arthur is famously associated with King Arthur of the Round Table, symbolizing chivalry and heroism.

Augustus
Meaning and Origin: Great, venerable (Latin)
Significance: Augustus was the title given to the first Roman emperor, Octavian. It signifies grandeur and respect.

Barnabas
Meaning and Origin: Son of Encouragement (Aramaic)
Significance Barnabas is a biblical figure known for his role in the early Christian church, supporting Paul the Apostle.

Barnabee
Meaning and Origin: Son of Encouragement (Greek)
Significance: Barnabee carries the meaning of encouragement forward, making it a name associated with being supportive and uplifting.

Benedict
Meaning and Origin: Blessed (Latin)
Significance: Benedict carries a strong religious connotation, representing someone favored by God. It can also be interpreted in a more general sense as someone fortunate or happy.

Bernard
Meaning and Origin: Brave as a Bear (German)
Significance: Bernard signifies strength and courage, often associated with Saint Bernard of Clairvaux.

Bertram
Meaning and Origin: Bright raven (German)
Significance: Represents intelligence and foresight, reflecting a clever and perceptive personality.

Byron
Meaning and Origin: Farm building; near cattle (British)
Significance: It gained popularity as a first name due to the influence of the famous 19th-century poet Lord Byron, known for his romantic and rebellious personality.

Cecil
Meaning and Origin: Blind (Roman)
Significance: Traditionally, a name associated with nobility and aristocracy due to its Roman origins. It can also evoke a sense of sophistication and elegance.

Charles
Meaning and Origin: Free Man (German)
Significance: Charles is a name linked to many kings and emperors, symbolizing nobility, and leadership.

Chester
Meaning and Origin: Camp by the fort (British)
Significance: Chester evokes a sense of history and tradition. It suggests a place with a long and rich past, often associated with Roman settlements in Britain.

Clarence
Meaning and Origin: Bright, clear (Latin)
Significance: Clarence signifies clarity and brightness, often associated with British nobility.

Claude
Meaning and Origin: Strong Willed (Latin)
Significance: Claude is a name often associated with Claude Monet, a founder of French Impressionist painting.

Clayton
Meaning and Origin: Place with soil (British)
Significance: A descriptive name indicating someone who lived in an area with clay-rich soil. Surnames became first names in the 19th century, giving Clayton a vintage feel with a down-to-earth meaning.

Clement
Meaning and Origin: Merciful (Latin)
Significance: Symbolizes kindness and compassion, reflecting a gentle and forgiving personality.

Clyde
Meaning and Origin: Muddy (British)
Significance: While the meaning "muddy" might not be the most glamorous, Clyde has a short, strong sound and Celtic roots, making it a unique vintage choice.

Cornelius
Meaning and Origin: Horn (Latin)
Significance: Cornelius is a name that appears in the New Testament as a Roman centurion who was the first Gentile convert to Christianity.

Crosby
Meaning and Origin: Cross-shaped clearing (British)
Significance: Crosby implies a connection to nature and possibly a religious significance with the presence of a cross. It could also refer to a place where paths intersect.

Desmond
Meaning and Origin: From the South (Irish)
Significance: Desmond evokes a sense of history and heritage, particularly Irish heritage. It can also suggest qualities like independence, strength, and protectiveness.

Dexter
Meaning and Origin: Right-handed; skilled (Latin)
Significance: Dexter suggests dexterity and skill, often associated with competence and capability.

Donald
Meaning and Origin: Ruler of the World (Scottish Gaelic)
Significance: Donald is a name of Scottish origin, often linked to clan leaders and royalty.

Douglas
Meaning and Origin: Dark Stream (Scottish Gaelic)
Significance: Douglas is a prominent Scottish surname, associated with nobility and leadership.

Earl
Meaning and Origin: Noblemen; aristocrat (British)
Significance: Earl is a name steeped in nobility and social status. It refers to someone of high rank, leadership, and power. In some cases, it might also suggest a chivalrous or courtly demeanor.

Edmund
Meaning and Origin: Wealthy protector (British)
Significance: The meaning is significant because it conveys a sense of both material security and the ability to defend oneself or others.

Edson
Meaning and Origin: Guardian of wealth (British)
Significance: Edson's significance lies in its connection to the virtues of protection and prosperity.

Edwin
Meaning and Origin: Wealthy friend (British)
Significance: A name with positive connotations, suggesting prosperity and strong friendships. Popular among royalty in medieval England.

Elmer
Meaning and Origin: Noble, Famous (Old English)
Significance: Elmer is a name that signifies nobility and fame, often associated with admirable qualities.

Ernest
Meaning and Origin: Serious; resolute (German)
Significance: This name conveys a sense of seriousness, determination, and strength. It gained popularity in the 19th century, possibly influenced by German Romanticism.

Eugene
Meaning and Origin: Well-born; noble (Greek)
Significance: Eugene signifies noble birth, often associated with intellectual and cultural refinement.

Ferdinand
Meaning and Origin: Bold voyager (German)
Significance: Symbolizes courage and exploration, reflecting a daring and adventurous personality.

Fitzgerald
Meaning and Origin: Son of Gerald; spear (Irish)
Significance: A well-established Irish surname with a long history. It can evoke images of strong family lineage and leadership and could be a nod to the powerful Fitzgerald dynasty in Ireland.

Flynn
Meaning and Origin: Descendant of the fair one (Irish)
Significance: An Irish surname with a positive connotation of fairness or being descended from a notable person named Flann.

Gary
Meaning and Origin: Spearman (German)
Significance: This name evokes a sense of strength and masculinity.

Gerald
Meaning and Origin: Power of the spear (German)
Significance: Gerald's most common meaning is "power of the spear." This builds upon the concept of strength associated with "spear" and adds a layer of leadership or dominance.

Giles
Meaning and Origin: Young goat (Greek)
Significance: Represents agility and playfulness, reflecting a lively and spirited personality.

Grover
Meaning and Origin: From the Grove (English)
Significance: Grover is associated with nature and tranquility, famously linked to President Grover Cleveland.

Hampton
Meaning and Origin: A home settlement (British)
Significance: Hampton conveys a sense of history and stability, a nod to a long-established settlement. It can also suggest a connection to nature, depending on the specific meaning.

Harlow
Meaning and Origin: Rock hill; army hill (British)
Significance: While Harlow has been around for centuries, it wasn't widely used as a first name until the 19th and 20th centuries. This makes it a vintage choice for parents seeking a name with history.

Harold
Meaning and Origin: Army Ruler (Old English)
Significance: Harold signifies leadership and military strength, famously associated with King Harold II of England.

Harry
Meaning and Origin: Home ruler (German)
Significance: Harry can represent ideas of domesticity, leadership, and strength.

Heine
Meaning and Origin: Noble hedge (German)
Significance: This name represents ideas of protection, nobility, or being unique.

Herbert
Meaning and Origin: Bright Army (German)
Significance: Herbert signifies a strong and bright military force, often associated with intellectual and literary figures like Herbert Hoover.

Homer
Meaning and Origin: Security, Pledge (Greek)
Significance: Homer is famously associated with the ancient Greek poet, author of the Iliad and the Odyssey.

Howard
Meaning and Origin: Brave Heart; high Guardian (German)
Significance: Howard signifies bravery and guardianship, often associated with nobility and leadership.

Hubert
Meaning and Origin: Bright Mind (German)
Significance: Hubert signifies a bright and intelligent mind, often associated with Saint Hubert, the patron saint of hunters.

Hugh
Meaning and Origin: Heart; mind; spirit (German)
Significance: Hugh signifies intellect and spirit, often associated with notable historical figures and leaders.

Hulbert
Meaning and Origin: Bright; gracious (German)
Significance: Hulbert is a vintage name with a somewhat regal feel due to its German origins. It's not as common as some other surnames, which can lend it a bit of uniqueness.

Irving
Meaning and Origin: Green Water (Scottish)
Significance: Irving evokes imagery of nature and tranquility, often associated with literary figures like Washington Irving.

Jerome
Meaning and Origin: Sacred Name (Greek)
Significance: Jerome is associated with Saint Jerome, a notable Christian scholar who translated the Bible into Latin.

Jonathan
Meaning and Origin: Yahweh has Given (Hebrew)
Significance: Jonathan is a biblical name, known for his friendship with David and his loyalty.

Julius
Meaning and Origin: Youthful; Downy (Latin)
Significance: Julius is famously associated with Julius Caesar, the Roman general, and states man.

Lancelot
Meaning and Origin: Servant (French)
Significance: Symbolizes loyalty and bravery, reflecting a devoted and courageous personality.

Lawrence
Meaning and Origin: From Laurentum (Latin)
Significance: Lawrence signifies honor and valor, often associated with Saint Lawrence, a Christian martyr.

Leopold
Meaning and Origin: Bold People (German)
Significance: Leopold signifies bravery and leadership, often associated with royalty and nobility.

Lionel
Meaning and Origin: Young Lion (Latin)
Significance: Lionel evokes the imagery of a young lion, symbolizing strength, and courage.

Lloyd
Meaning and Origin: Grey (Welsh)
Significance: Lloyd signifies wisdom and maturity, often associated with influential leaders and scholars.

Marcus
Meaning and Origin: Warlike (Latin)
Significance: Marcus is associated with Mars, the Roman god of war, symbolizing strength, and bravery.

Marvin
Meaning and Origin: Sea Friend (Welsh)
Significance: Marvin signifies friendship and loyalty, often associated with American cultural figures.

Maurice
Meaning and Origin: Dark-skinned (Latin)
Significance: Maurice signifies a dark-skinned person, often associated with Saint Maurice, the patron saint of soldiers.

Melvin
Meaning and Origin: Gentle chieftain (Irish)
Significance: Melvin is a classic name with a rich history tied to Irish heritage. It evokes a sense of nobility and strength.

Merrick
Meaning and Origin: Dark-skinned (Welsh)
Significance: The Welsh meaning suggests a connection to ancestry or potentially dark hair or complexion.

Michael
Meaning and Origin: Who is Like God; Gift from God (Hebrew)
Significance: Michael is a biblical archangel, symbolizing divine protection and strength.

Montgomery
Meaning: Hill of the goat's pasture (French)
Significance: This name describes the geographical location where the family originated, possibly near a hill with goats. It can also represent resourcefulness and living off the land.

Norman
Meaning: Northman; Viking (Old English)
Significance: Norman signifies a person from the north, often associated with the Norman Conquest of England.

Otto
Meaning and Origin: Wealth; Prosperity (German)
Significance: Otto signifies wealth and fortune, often associated with royalty and leadership.

Pearson
Meaning and Origin: Son of Peter (British)
Significance: Pearson is a patronymic surname, meaning it was given to someone based on their father's name. In this case, it signifies someone whose father was named Peter or a variant.

Percival
Meaning and Origin: Pierces the Valley (Old French)
Significance: Percival is one of the Knights of the Round Table, symbolizing chivalry, and the quest for the Holy Grail.

Percy
Meaning and Origin: Pierces the Valley (Old French)
Significance: Percy is a diminutive of Percival, often associated with nobility and the Arthurian legends.

Phineas
Meaning and Origin: Oracle (Hebrew)
Significance: Phineas is a biblical name, known for his zeal and righteous actions.

Ralph
Meaning and Origin: Wolf Counsel (Old Norse)
Significance: Ralph signifies wise counsel and strength, often associated with literary and historical figures.

Raymond
Meaning and Origin: Wise Protector (German)
Significance: Raymond signifies wisdom and protection, often associated with saints and leaders.

Reginald
Meaning and Origin: Counsel Power (German)
Significance: Reginald signifies powerful counsel, often associated with nobility and leadership.

Ritchie
Meaning and Origin: Powerful leader (Scottish)
Significance: This name evokes a sense of leadership and refers to someone strong both physically and mentally.

Roland
Meaning and Origin: Famous throughout the land; Renowned land (German)
Significance: Roland is a name steeped in history and legend. It was borne by a famous medieval knight, Roland, who was celebrated for his bravery and chivalry in epic poems and songs. The name itself evokes a sense of nobility, strength, and heroism.

Rupert
Meaning and Origin: Bright Fame (German)
Significance: Rupert is a variant of Robert, symbolizing bright fame and often associated with historical leaders.

Sergio
Meaning and Origin: To guard; to save (Latin)
Significance: Sergio has a sophisticated and elegant feel. The name evokes a sense of strength and dependability.

Solomon
Meaning and Origin: Peace (Hebrew)
Significance: Solomon is a biblical king known for his wisdom and peaceful reign, symbolizing wisdom and prosperity.

Stanley
Meaning and Origin: Stone Clearing (Old English)
Significance: Stanley signifies strength and stability, often associated with notable figures in literature and history.

Teddy
Meaning and Origin: Gift from above (German)
Significance: Teddy evokes a sense of cuddliness and innocence due to its connection with teddy bears. It also carries a touch of vintage charm due to its peak popularity in the early 20th century.

Thaddeus
Meaning and Origin: Courageous Heart (Aramaic)
Significance: Thaddeus is a biblical name, associated with one of Jesus' twelve apostles, symbolizing courage, and faith.

Thatcher
Meaning and Origin: Someone who thatched roofs (British)
Significance: Thatcher has a strong connection to history and tradition. It evokes a sense of craftsmanship and practicality. It can also be associated with a specific family history if used as a surname.

Thomas
Meaning and Origin: Twin (Aramaic)
Significance: Thomas is a biblical apostle, known for his doubts about Jesus' resurrection, symbolizing skepticism and faith.

Ulysses
Meaning and Origin: Wrathful (Greek)
Significance: Ulysses is the Roman form of Odysseus, the hero of Homer's epic, symbolizing endurance and cunning.

Victor
Meaning and Origin: Conqueror (Latin)
Significance: Victor signifies victory and triumph, often associated with saints and leaders.

Wilbur
Meaning and Origin: Resolute; brilliant; bright will (German)
Significance: Wilbur carries a connotation of determination, intelligence, and a strong spirit.

Wilfred
Meaning and Origin: Desired Peace (German)
Significance: Wilfred signifies a longing for peace, often associated with saints and historical figures.

Willmar
Meaning and Origin: Famous will; great desire (German)
Significance: Willmar is a name that combines elements of willpower and aspiration, making it a meaningful choice for those seeking a name with a sense of strength or ambition.

Yorick
Meaning and Origin: Farmer (Old English)
Significance: Evokes a sense of hard work and practicality, with literary associations.

Zebulon
Meaning and Origin: To honor; To exalt (Hebrew)
Significance: Zebulon is a name that carries biblical and historical significance. Zebulon can symbolize honor, exaltation, and prosperity.

Vintage Girls' Names

Choosing a vintage name for your little princess is a great way of elevating style and elegance. A vintage name carries a timelessness that few modern names can replicate without being so unique that it opens the door to misunderstanding. Out of all the vintage names to choose from, these are my absolute favorites. So, if you're looking for a fun way to make your baby sound like she comes from old money, this is the category for you.

Ada
Meaning and Origin: Noble; happy (German)
Significance: Ada signifies nobility and cheerfulness, often associated with Ada Lovelace, a pioneer in computer science.

Adelaide
Meaning and Origin: Nobility of kind (German)
Significance: Adelaide carries a legacy of piety, patience, and virtue. This name is classic and sounds elegant with its noble connotations.

Agnes
Meaning and Origin: Pure; virginal (Greek)
Significance: Agnes is associated with purity, innocence, and unwavering faith. This beautiful name evokes a natural beauty and softness.

Agnus
Meaning and Origin: Lamb (Latin)
Significance: Agnus symbolizes purity and innocence, often associated with the Agnus Dei in Christian liturgy.

Alma
Meaning and Origin: Nourishing; kind (Latin)
Significance: Alma signifies nurturing and kindness, often associated with alma maters, symbolizing one's educational roots.

Ambrose
Meaning and Origin: Immortal; divine (Greek)
Significance: Due to its meaning, Ambrose has connotations of immortality, godliness, and possibly even blessedness.

Annabelle
Meaning and Origin: Gracious; beautiful (French)
Significance: Annabelle signifies grace and beauty, often associated with elegance and charm.

Annette
Meaning and Origin: Grace (French)
Significance: Annette signifies gracefulness and elegance, often associated with refinement and poise.

Antonia
Meaning and Origin: Priceless, Inestimable (Latin)
Significance: Antonia signifies high value and worth, often associated with nobility and elegance.

Arabella
Meaning and Origin: Prayerful; yielding to prayer (Latin)
Significance: Arabella conveys a sense of devotion and is a product of prayers. This name sounds very elegant and royal.

Augusta
Meaning and Origin: Great; Venerable (Latin)
Significance: Augusta signifies grandeur and respect, often associated with royalty and nobility.

Bessie
Meaning and Origin: God is My Oath (Hebrew)
Significance: Bessie is a diminutive of Elizabeth, symbolizing devotion, and faithfulness.

Betty
Meaning and Origin: God is my oath (Hebrew)
Significance: Betty gained popularity as a nickname in the medieval period and eventually became a standalone name. With its classic sound and beautiful meaning, it's a timeless choice for your little one.

Beulah
Meaning and Origin: Married (Hebrew)
Significance: Beulah signifies marital happiness and loyalty, often associated with the biblical term for a promised land.

Birdie
Meaning and Origin: Bird (British)
Significance: This name evokes a sense of sweet and charming characteristics. The name also carries the connotation of being cheerful, free-spirited, and full of life.

Blanche
Meaning and Origin: White; pure (French)
Significance: Blanche is a classic feminine name with a timeless elegance. Its meaning evokes innocence, purity, and a bright disposition. Historically, it might have been used as a nickname for someone with fair hair or light skin.

Bridgette
Meaning and Origin: Exalted one; strength (Irish)
Significance: Bridgette is a beautiful name with a strong connotation of power and nobility. Its roots in Irish culture suggest a connection to a rich heritage.

Cassandra
Meaning and Origin: Shining upon man (Greek)
Significance: Cassandra is a name steeped in Greek mythology. She was a Trojan princess gifted with prophecy by the god Apollo. This is a classic name that evokes wisdom.

Cheryl
Meaning and Origin: A combination of Cherie and Beryl (English)
Significance: Cheryl is often considered a combination of "Cherie" (French for "dear one") and "Beryl" (a precious stone). This name became popular in the mid-20th century and is often associated with warmth and affection, reflecting a sense of endearment and value.

Clementine
Meaning and Origin: Mild; merciful; gentle
Origin: Latin
Significance: Clementine is a beautiful name with a positive connotation. It evokes ideas of kindness, understanding, and clemency.

Cora
Meaning and Origin: Maiden; daughter (Greek)
Significance: In Greek mythology, Cora is another name for Persephone, the daughter of Zeus and Demeter. The name carries connotations of innocence, purity, and connection to nature.

Cordelia
Meaning and Origin: Heart; jewel of the sea (Latin)
Significance: The name Cordelia evokes a sense of loyalty, love, and strength. It's also associated with the sea, suggesting a connection to mystery, depth, and vastness.

Cornelia
Meaning and Origin: Horn (Latin)
Significance: Cornelia signifies strength and steadfastness, often associated with the noble Roman family.

Delia
Meaning and Origin: From Delos (Greek)
Significance: Delia signifies connection to the Greek island of Delos, often associated with Artemis, the goddess of the hunt.

Dora
Meaning and Origin: Gift (Greek)
Significance: Dora signifies a divine gift, often associated with charm and simplicity.

Dorothea
Meaning and Origin: Gift of God (Greek)
Significance: Dorothea is a beautiful name with a strong meaning. It conveys a sense of being blessed and cherished.

Dorothy
Meaning and Origin: Gift of God (Greek)
Significance: Dorothy signifies divine blessing, famously associated with the character in "The Wizard of Oz."

Edith
Meaning and Origin: Warlike maiden; rich spear-wielder (British)
Significance: Edith is a name with a strong and independent connotation. It evokes a sense of bravery and nobility.

Edna
Meaning and Origin: Pleasure, delight (Hebrew)
Significance: Edna signifies joy and pleasure, often associated with idyllic beauty and happiness.

Effie
Meaning and Origin: Well-spoken (Greek)
Significance: Effie signifies eloquence and charm, often associated with kindness and grace.

Eleanor
Meaning and Origin: Light; Shining brightly (French)
Significance: Eleanor is a name rich in history, borne by many powerful and influential women throughout European royalty and nobility. The name evokes a sense of elegance, strength, and intelligence.

Eleanora
Meaning and Origin: Light-hearted; shining One (Greek)
Significance: Eleanora is a variant of Eleanor, symbolizing brilliance, and grace.

Elise
Meaning and Origin: Pledge to God (French)
Significance: Elise signifies devotion and faithfulness, often associated with elegance and charm.

Eliza
Meaning and Origin: God is My Oath (Hebrew)
Significance: Eliza is a diminutive of Elizabeth, symbolizing devotion, and grace.

Ella
Meaning and Origin: Fairy Maiden (German)
Significance: Ella signifies beauty and enchantment, often associated with lightness and grace.

Emmeline
Meaning and Origin: Industrious protector; noble defender (German)
Significance: Emmeline is a less common but beautiful vintage name with a strong and virtuous connotation. It refers to someone hardworking, dependable, and willing to stand up for their beliefs.

Esme
Meaning and Origin: Esteemed; beloved (French)
Significance: Esme is a vintage name that has seen a resurgence in popularity in recent years. It has a charming and elegant feel, and its meaning of "esteemed" or "beloved" makes it a lovely choice for a child.

Estelle
Meaning and Origin: Star (French)
Significance: Estelle is a classic French name with a timeless elegance. Its meaning of "star" evokes a sense of brightness, ambition, and destiny and refers to someone destined for great things.

Ethel
Meaning and Origin: Noble (Old English)
Significance: Ethel signifies nobility and honor, often associated with integrity and virtue.

Eudora
Meaning and Origin: Good Gift (Greek)
Significance Eudora signifies a divine blessing, often associated with charm and kindness.

Eugenia
Meaning and Origin: Noble (Greek)
Significance: Eugenia signifies nobility and elegance, often associated with refinement and virtue.

Eva
Meaning and Origin: Life (Hebrew)
Significance: Eva signifies life and vitality, often associated with the first woman in the Bible, Eve.

Evangeline
Meaning and Origin: Good news; bearer of good news (Greek)
Significance: Evangeline name carries connotations of positivity, hope, and joy.

Fannie
Meaning and Origin: Free (Latin)
Significance: Fannie signifies freedom and independence, often associated with liveliness and charm.

Genevieve
Meaning and Origin: Woman of the race; tribe (French)
Significance: A classic and elegant name with a rich history. Genevieve evokes ideas of strength, purity, and family.

Gertrude
Meaning and Origin: Spear of Strength (German)
Significance: Gertrude signifies strength and courage, often associated with notable literary figures.

Gladys
Meaning and Origin: Land; Nation (Welsh)
Significance: Gladys signifies homeland and heritage, often associated with strength and resilience.

Gloria
Meaning and Origin: Glory (Latin)
Significance: Gloria signifies honor and praise, often associated with brightness and magnificence.

Gwendolyn
Meaning and Origin: Blessed Ring (Welsh)
Significance: Gwendolyn signifies blessedness and enchantment, often associated with beauty and charm.

Harriet
Meaning and Origin: Ruler of the home (German)
Significance: Historically, it signified a woman who managed the household. Today, it retains a sense of strength, independence, and domestic responsibility.

Henrietta
Meaning and Origin: Ruler of the Home (German)
Significance: Henrietta signifies leadership and domestic strength, often associated with royalty and nobility.

Imogen
Meaning and Origin: Innocent maiden (Irish)
Significance: A unique and literary name with a touch of mystery that is associated with nobility, purity, and strength.

Isabelle
Meaning and Origin: God is My Oath (Hebrew)
Significance: Isabelle is a variant of Isabel, symbolizing faith and devotion.

Johanna
Meaning and Origin: God is Gracious (Hebrew)
Significance: Johanna signifies divine grace, often associated with kindness and virtue.

Josephine
Meaning and Origin: God will increase (Hebrew)
Significance: Josephine is a classic and elegant name with religious connotations. The name evokes a sense of sophistication and refinement but also has cute nicknames like Josie or Jojo.

Lavinia
Meaning and Origin: Purity (Latin)
Significance: Lavinia signifies purity and beauty, often associated with classical elegance.

Leona
Meaning and Origin: Lioness (Latin)
Significance: Leona signifies strength and courage, often associated with nobility and leadership.

Lilly
Meaning and Origin: Lily (Latin)
Significance: Lilly is a diminutive of Lillian, symbolizing purity and beauty.

Lottie
Meaning and Origin: Little man (German)
Significance: Lottie is a playful and friendly nickname for a more formal name like Charlotte. It gained popularity in the Victorian era and evokes a sense of innocence and charm.

Louise
Meaning and Origin: Famous warrior; loud warrior (German)
Significance: Louise embodies a sense of elegance and grace with a hint of hidden strength. It was a popular name throughout Europe and has remained a classic choice for generations.

Lucille
Meaning and Origin: Light (Latin)
Significance: Lucille signifies brightness and clarity, often associated with elegance and grace.

Mabel
Meaning and Origin: Worthy; loveable (Latin)
Significance: Mabel conveys a sense of sweetness and charm. It was particularly popular in the late 19th and early 20th centuries and is experiencing a resurgence as a vintage name choice.

Madeline
Meaning and Origin: Woman from Magdala (Hebrew)
Significance: Madeline signifies strength and faith, often associated with Mary Magdalene from the New Testament.

Maisie
Meaning and Origin: Pearl (Scottish)
Significance: Maisie has been used in Scotland since around the 16th century. It's a shorter, more informal version of Margaret. While vintage, it has seen a rise in popularity in recent years, offering a timeless yet fresh feel.

Marcella
Meaning and Origin: Warlike (Latin)
Significance: Marcella signifies strength and bravery, often associated with resilience and courage.

Margot
Meaning and Origin: Pearl (French)
Significance: Margot evokes a sense of elegance and sophistication due to its French roots. The meaning of "pearl" adds a touch of preciousness and beauty.

Marguerite
Meaning and Origin: Daisy Pearl (French)
Significance: Marguerite signifies beauty and refinement, often associated with the flower and symbolizing purity.

Maria
Meaning and Origin: Bitter; beloved (Hebrew)
Significance: Maria signifies deep emotion and devotion, often associated with the Virgin Mary, symbolizing purity and faith.

Marjorie
Meaning and Origin: Valuable sea stone (British)
Significance: Marjorie was particularly popular among royalty in medieval times and remained a favorite in the early 20th century. It evokes a sense of elegance and tradition.

Martha
Meaning and Origin: Lady; mistress (Aramaic)
Significance: Martha signifies hospitality and diligence, often associated with the biblical figure known for her domestic virtues.

Matilda
Meaning and Origin: Mighty in battle; strength (German)
Significance: Matilda carries a surprising strength in its meaning. While it might sound sweet and innocent, it holds a powerful message of courage and determination. This creates an interesting contrast that can be appealing.

Maude
Meaning and Origin: Powerful Battler (German)
Significance: Maude signifies strength and resilience, often associated with historical figures of nobility.

Mildred
Meaning and Origin: Gentle Strength (Old English)
Significance: Mildred signifies mildness and strength, often associated with kindness and perseverance.

Minnie
Meaning and Origin: Intellect (German)
Significance: Minnie signifies intelligence and thoughtfulness, often associated with charm and simplicity.

Molly
Meaning and Origin: Star of the sea; beloved (British)
Significance: Molly was originally just a nickname for Mary but has become a popular name since the 1700s. It evokes a sense of love and refers to someone unique.

Myra
Meaning and Origin: Myrrh (Greek)
Significance: Myra signifies preciousness and value, often associated with sweetness and charm.

Nellie
Meaning and Origin: Light (Greek)
Significance: Nellie is a diminutive of Eleanor, symbolizing brightness, and cheerfulness.

Opal
Meaning and Origin: Gem (Sanskrit)
Significance: Opal signifies preciousness and beauty, often associated with the gemstone and symbolizing hope.

Ophelia
Meaning and Origin: Helpfulness (Greek)
Significance: Ophelia's name is significant because of its association with Shakespeare's play. It evokes a sense of beauty, fragility, and, ultimately, tragedy.

Pearl
Meaning and Origin: Precious Gem (Latin)
Significance: Pearl signifies purity and value, often associated with elegance and simplicity.

Priscilla
Meaning and Origin: Ancient (Latin)
Significance: Priscilla signifies antiquity and respect, often associated with early Christian figures.

Rose
Meaning and Origin: Rose (Latin)
Significance: Rose signifies beauty and love, often associated with the flower and symbolizing elegance.

Rosetta
Meaning and Origin: Little Rose (Italian)
Significance: Rosetta signifies beauty and charm, often associated with the flower and symbolizing delicacy.

Sophie
Meaning and Origin: Wisdom (French)
Significance: Sophie carries the weight of a long history associated with knowledge and intelligence. In ancient Greece, philosophers like Socrates and Plato valued wisdom highly, making names like Sophia and Sophie even more meaningful.

Susan
Meaning and Origin: Lily (Hebrew)
Significance: Susan signifies purity and beauty, often associated with the flower and symbolizing innocence.

Sylvia
Meaning and Origin: Forest (Latin)
Significance: Sylvia evokes a connection with nature and the beauty of the woods. In Roman mythology, Silvia was the name of a mythical she-wolf who nursed Romulus and Remus, the founders of Rome. This association imbues the name with a sense of nurturing and wildness.

Tabitha
Meaning and Origin: Gazelle (Aramaic)
Significance: Tabitha signifies beauty and grace, famously associated with the biblical figure known for her good works.

Thea
Meaning and Origin: Goddess (Greek)
Significance: The name evokes a sense of strength, beauty, and divinity.

Theodora
Meaning and Origin: Gift of God (Greek)
Significance: Theodora signifies divine blessing, often associated with nobility and historical figures.

Theresa
Meaning and Origin: Harvester (Greek)
Significance: Theresa signifies diligence and care, often associated with Saint Teresa, symbolizing compassion and devotion.

Victoria
Meaning and Origin: Victory (Latin)
Significance: Victoria is steeped in Roman history. It refers to the Roman goddess Victoria, who personified victory and triumph. The name carries connotations of success, achievement, and the ability to overcome challenges.

Viola
Meaning and Origin: Violet (Latin)
Significance: Viola signifies beauty and charm, often associated with the flower and symbolizing modesty.

Virginia
Meaning and Origin: Pure; virginal (Latin)
Significance: Virginia signifies purity and innocence, often associated with the U.S. state and historical figures.

Zella
Meaning and Origin: Blessed; beautiful (Yiddish)
Significance: Zella signifies blessing and beauty, often associated with charm and grace.

As we reach the end of our vintage names, I'm sure you've already shortlisted some for your little one.
However, don't pick a name (or names) just yet. In the next chapter, we're going to look at Modern names. So, if you want a name that is inspired by current trends, popular culture and freshness be sure to stick around for the next chapter.

CHAPTER 10: MODERN NAMES

There is an undeniable attraction to selecting a modern name for your baby. These contemporary names, often inspired by current trends and popular culture, bring a sense of freshness and relevance that resonates with today's world. Imagine your child carrying a name that reflects the spirit of the times while still retaining a unique and distinctive touch. Modern names often embody innovation and creativity, offering a glimpse into the future and the potential that lies ahead. Choosing a name that is both current and distinctive can help your child stand out and make a memorable impression. So, dive into the exciting world of modern names and find the perfect one that will not only define your child's identity but also set them apart in a vibrant and ever-evolving world. Let us explore contemporary boy and girl names that are perfect for today's generation.

Contemporary Boys' Names

A modern name doesn't automatically mean something trendy or fleeting. You don't want your baby to have a name that feels too common or lacks substance, but modern names can offer a sense of freshness and individuality that vintage names can't. Here are some contemporary choices for your baby boy that will evoke a sense of style and originality.

Aden
Meaning and origin: Attractive or handsome, pleasure given (Hebrew)
Significance: A biblical exile who returned to Israel from Babylon. Aden often is associated with qualities like sensitivity, strength, or fire.

Archer
Meaning and origin: bowman (Latin)
Significance: One who excels at archery. Archer is a name that signifies skill, precision, and possibly a connection to the outdoors and traditional archery.

Atticus
Meaning and origin: From attica or from Athens (Latin)
Significance: Attica was an ancient region in Greece that was known for its strong and noble people.

Bennett
Meaning and origin: Blessed (Latin)
Significance: Reflects gratitude and favor, often associated with a fortunate and contented personality.

Blaine
Meaning and origin: Thin or lean (Scottish)
Significance: Symbolizes agility and grace, reflecting a nimble and adaptable personality.

Brantley
Meaning and origin: A person who lived near a forest fire (German)
Significance: Inspiring to be a beacon of light within your family life, or to be a driven individual who's not afraid to take risks.

Braxton
Meaning and origin: Brock's Town (English)
Significance: Represents strength and leadership, often associated with a commanding and authoritative nature.

Bridger
Meaning and origin: Dweller by the bridge (English)
Significance: Symbolizes connection and support, reflecting a helpful and reliable nature.

Cade
Meaning and origin: Round, barrel (English)
Significance: Represents stability and strength, often associated with a solid and reliable nature.

Cairo
Meaning and origin: Victorious (Arabic)
Significance: Represents success and achievement, often associated with a triumphant and ambitious nature.

Callen
Meaning and origin: Rock (Irish)
Significance: Symbolizes strength and stability, often associated with a steadfast and reliable personality.

Cannon
Meaning and origin: Official of the church (English)
Significance: Symbolizes authority and leadership, reflecting a commanding and influential nature.

Cassius
Meaning and origin: Hollow (Latin)
Significance: Symbolizes depth and complexity, reflecting a thoughtful and introspective personality.

Cayson
Meaning and origin: Rejoice (English)
Significance: Reflects joy and positivity, often associated with a cheerful and uplifting personality.

Cohen
Meaning and origin: Priest (Hebrew)
Significance: Symbolizes spirituality and guidance, often associated with a wise and supportive nature.

Colt
Meaning and origin: Young horse or foal (England)
Significance: Linked to swift-footed horses, emphasizing traits such as speed and vitality.

Benson
Meaning and origin: Son of Ben (English)
Significance: Benson is a name that represents heritage and family, often associated with a respectful and honorable nature.

Corbin
Meaning and origin: Raven (Latin)
Significance: Corbin Represents intelligence and mystery, often associated with a curious and insightful personality.

Dawson
Meaning and origin: Son of David (English)
Significance: Dawson is associated with beloved and cherished, reflecting a loving and affectionate nature.

Dax
Meaning and origin: Leader (Modern)
Significance: Symbolizes strength and leadership, reflecting a powerful and commanding presence. Often associated with determination and ambition.

Decker
Meaning and origin: Ditch Digger (German)
Significance: Symbolizes hard work and determination, reflecting a resilient and industrious personality. Often associated with strength and perseverance.

Declan
Meaning and origin: Full of Goodness (Irish)
Significance: Represents virtue and kindness, reflecting a generous and compassionate personality. Often associated with a sense of integrity and honor.

Deegan
Meaning and origin: Black-haired (Irish)
Significance: Embodies the resilience and spirit of the Irish people, who have faced numerous challenges throughout history.

Drake
Meaning and origin: Dragon (English)
Significance: Represents strength and power, reflecting a fierce and formidable personality. Often associated with courage and leadership.

Edison
Meaning and origin: Son of Edward (English)
Significance: Represents innovation and creativity, often associated with a bright and inventive nature.

Ellis
Meaning and origin: The Lord is my God (Hebrew)
Significance: Ellis symbolizes faith and devotion, reflecting a spiritual and sincere personality.

Finnegan
Meaning and origin: Fair, fair-haired (Irish)
Significance: This name refers to Fionn mac Cumhaill, an Irish mythological hero renowned for his strength and wisdom.

Ford
Meaning and origin: River crossing (English)
Significance: Symbolizes transition and journey, reflecting an adventurous and exploratory nature.

Gage
Meaning and origin: Pledge (French)
Significance: Represents loyalty and commitment, reflecting a trustworthy and dependable personality. Often associated with honor and integrity.

Giovanni
Meaning and origin: God is gracious (Italian)
Significance: The name holds meaning as it translates to God is Gracious in English. In ancient history, Giovanni appears in religious text and religious figures. For instance, the name is linked with Saint John the Baptist in the Bible.

Graysen
Meaning and origin: Son of a steward (Old English)
Significance: Refer to the "son of a gray-haired man", often associated with wisdom, strength and loyalty.

Huxl
Meaning and origin: Inhospitable place (English)
Significance: Habitual in nature, referring to the original family's estate in Cheshire.

Ivan
Meaning and origin: God is gracious (Russian)
Significance: Ivan carries associations of divine favor, strength, and blessing. This name also represents gratitude, reflecting a kind and thankful personality.

Jair
Meaning and origin: He shines, he Enlightened (Hebrew)
Significance: This name is mentioned in the Old Testament of the Bibe, where Jair is identified as a son of Manasseh and also one of the ruling judges of the Israelites.

Jonas
Meaning and origin: Dove (Greek)
Significance: Jonas is a name that symbolizes peace and innocence. This name also represents peace and harmony, reflecting a calm and gentle personality.

Kaiser
Meaning and origin: Emperor (German)
Significance: Represents authority and leadership, often associated with a commanding and powerful nature.

Kenzo
Meaning and origin: Wise; Strong (Japanese)
Significance: In various aspects of Japanese society, the name has been bestowed upon individuals renowned for their wisdom, such as scholars, philosophers, and esteemed leaders.

Kingston
Meaning and origin: King's Town (English)
Significance: Symbolizes royalty and nobility, reflecting a commanding and dignified personality. Often associated with leadership and authority.

Landry
Meaning and origin: Ruler (French)
Significance: Represents leadership and authority, often associated with a commanding and influential nature.

Leighton
Meaning and origin: Meadow; leek (English)
Significance: The name evokes images of rolling green fields and peaceful gardens, which is a lovely association for a name. The name is also associated with nature, growth, and nourishment.

Maddox
Meaning and origin: Son of good; fortunate (Welsh)
Significance: According to Welsh, Modoc was a legendary Welsh prince who sailed to New World three hundred years before Christopher Columbus.

Porter
Meaning and origin: Gatekeeper (English)
Significance: Symbolizes responsibility and vigilance, reflecting a watchful and reliable personality.

Reed
Meaning and origin: Red-haired (English)
Significance: Symbolizes vibrancy and energy, reflecting a lively and spirited personality.

Rhett
Meaning and origin: Enthusiastic (Dutch)
Significance: Represents passion and zest, often associated with a dynamic and energetic personality.

Ronan
Meaning and origin: Little seal (Irish)
Significance: Symbolizes nature and resilience, reflecting a strong and spirited personality.

Stan
Meaning and origin: Derived from Stanley or Stanton (English)
Significance: Stan has gained popularity as a given name, inspired by its use in popular culture and its straightforward, friendly sound.

Stellan
Meaning and origin: Calm (Swedish)
Significance: Symbolizes tranquility and serenity, reflecting a personality that is peaceful and composed.

Talon
Meaning and origin: Claw (French)
Significance: Symbolizes strength and power, reflecting a fierce and formidable nature.

Thorne
Meaning and origin: Thorn Bush (English)
Significance: Represents resilience and protection, reflecting a strong and determined personality. Often associated with a deep connection to nature.

Trace
Meaning and origin: Brave, Fiercer (English and Irish)
Significance: Refers to a mark or sign left behind by someone or something. This is fitting for a name that represents strength and resilience, as if the person with this name leaves an indelible mark on the world around them.

Ty
Meaning and origin: Rock; sharp (Hebrew)
Significance: In various cultures the name signifies strength, resilience and a connection to nature.

Van
Meaning and origin: Of, from (Dutch)
Significance: Associated with marshland, as it is often used to indicate a person's place of origin. For example, if someone's last name is "Van der Meer", it means they are from near the sea.

Wade
Meaning and origin: To Go (English)
Significance: Represents determination and progress, reflecting a forward-thinking and motivated personality. Often associated with a sense of adventure and exploration.

Weston
Meaning and origin: From the Western Town (English)
Significance: Reflects a pioneering and adventurous spirit, often associated with exploration and discovery. Symbolizes a strong connection to heritage and tradition.

Wilder
Meaning and origin: Untamed (English)
Significance: Symbolizes freedom and adventure, reflecting a bold and fearless personality. Often associated with a love for the outdoors and a strong sense of independence.

Zaid
Meaning and origin: To increase or growth (Arabic)
Significance: Zaid is a name that carries a sense of optimism and strength. This name also reflects positivity and progress.

Zain
Meaning and origin: Beauty; grace (Arabic)
Significance: Derived from and is the transcription of the seventh letter of the Hebrew alphabet.

Zayden
Meaning and origin: Increase; Abundance (Modern)
Significance: Symbolizes prosperity and growth, reflecting a dynamic and thriving personality. Often associated with a positive and optimistic outlook on life.

Contemporary Girls' Names

A modern name doesn't have to mean something overly trendy or fleeting. You want your baby girl to have a name that feels fresh and unique without sacrificing depth or meaning. Modern names can offer a sense of elegance and innovation that vintage names sometimes lack. Here are some contemporary choices for your baby girl that will evoke a sense of charm and individuality.

Addilyn
Meaning and origin: Noble (Old German)
Significance: Symbolizes nobility and grace, reflecting a refined and dignified personality.

Adley
Meaning and origin: Honest (Hebrew)
Significance: Symbolizes God's justice or simply a name that reflects your love for the ethereal heather blooms.

Alina
Meaning and origin: Bright, beautiful (Slavic)
Significance: Represents light and beauty, reflecting a radiant and attractive personality.

Aluma
Meaning and origin: Maiden, Sheaf (Hebrew)
Significance: Represents purity and abundance, symbolizing a youthful and nurturing personality. Often associated with growth and fertility, reflecting a connection to nature and life cycles.

Alyse
Meaning and origin: Noble (German)
Significance: Symbolizes nobility and grace, reflecting a refined and dignified personality.

Amaya
Meaning and origin: Night rain (Japanese)
Significance: Represents tranquility and beauty, reflecting a calm and soothing personality.

Amora
Meaning and origin: Love (Spanish)
Significance: Symbolizes deep affection and passion, reflecting a warm and loving personality. Amora evokes a sense of romance and emotional connection, embodying the essence of love and devotion.

Aspen
Meaning and origin: Shaking Tree (Old English)
Significance: Symbolizes resilience and adaptability, reflecting a dynamic and flexible personality. Often associated with nature and the ability to thrive in various environments.

Blakely
Meaning and origin: Dark meadow (English)
Significance: Symbolizes mystery and strength, reflecting a deep and powerful personality.

Briella
Meaning and origin: God is My Strength (Italian)
Significance: Reflects a divine connection and inner strength, often associated with resilience and faith.

Cadenza
Meaning and origin: Rhythmic (Italian)
Significance: Evokes a sense of musicality and creativity, symbolizing a unique and artistic personality.

Candela
Meaning and origin: Candle (Spanish)
Significance: Represents light and warmth, symbolizing guidance and hope.

Caia
Meaning and origin: Rejoice (Latin)
Significance: Represents joy and happiness, embodying a cheerful and positive disposition.

Calista
Meaning and origin: Most beautiful (Greek)
Significance: Represents beauty and elegance, reflecting a graceful and charming personality.

Daleyza
Meaning and origin: Delightful (Spanish)
Significance: Reflects joy and charm, often associated with a cheerful and enchanting personality.

Dara
Meaning and origin: Pearl of Wisdom (Hebrew)
Significance: Reflects intelligence and insight, symbolizing a wise and thoughtful personality. Often associated with clarity and the ability to provide valuable advice.

Davina
Meaning and origin: Beloved (English)
Significance: Davina symbolizes love and affection, reflecting a warm and caring personality.

Emilia
Meaning and origin: Rival (Latin)
Significance: Represents competition and ambition, reflecting a determined and driven personality.

Esti
Meaning and origin: Little star (Latin)
Significance: Carries significant cultural weight, particularly in the Biblical context. The book of Esther in the Old Testament tells the captivating story of Queen Esther, the Jewish wife of the King of Persia.

Haylee
Meaning and origin: Hayfield (English)
Significance: Represents a connection to nature and open spaces, symbolizing a free-spirited and grounded personality. Often associated with simplicity, warmth, and a down-to-earth approach to life.

India
Meaning and origin: From India (Hindi)
Significance: Represents cultural richness and diversity, symbolizing a person with a broad perspective and deep understanding of different traditions and histories.

Jovie
Meaning and origin: Joyful (American)
Significance: Symbolizes happiness and positivity, reflecting a cheerful and uplifting personality.

Juniper
Meaning and origin: Young (Latin)
Significance: Symbolizes youth and vitality, reflecting a fresh and energetic personality. Often associated with rejuvenation and the ability to bring new ideas and perspectives.

Kaylee
Meaning and origin: Keeper (American)
Significance: Represents a protective and nurturing personality, symbolizing someone who is reliable and trustworthy. Often associated with guardianship and a strong sense of responsibility, Kaylee reflects a caring nature and a dedication to looking after others.

Lila
Meaning and origin: Dark, Born in the Night (Arabic)
Significance: Reflects mystery and depth, symbolizing a person with a rich inner life and a strong sense of intuition. Often associated with beauty and the ability to navigate through life's challenges.

Livia
Meaning and origin: Olive (Latin)
Significance: Livia Represents peace and tranquility, reflecting a calm and harmonious personality.

London
Meaning and origin: Name of a city (Modern)
Significance: Represents a blend of historical depth and modern vibrancy, symbolizing a person who is cultured, dynamic, and adaptable. Often associated with a cosmopolitan outlook and a strong sense of identity, the name London reflects a connection to heritage while embracing the future.

Luna
Meaning and origin: Moon (Latin)
Significance: Symbolizes tranquility and illumination, reflecting a serene and calming personality. Often associated with the night and the ability to bring light to dark situations.

Mabeline
Meaning and origin: Lovable (English)
Significance: Symbolizes affection and charm, reflecting a warm and endearing personality. Often associated with kindness and a nurturing nature.

Maeva
Meaning and origin: Welcome (Polynesian)
Significance: Represents hospitality and friendliness, reflecting an inviting and gracious personality. Often associated with warmth and generosity.

Maelynn
Meaning and origin: Beautiful May (Modern)
Significance: Symbolizes beauty and renewal, reflecting a fresh and vibrant personality. Often associated with a love for nature and a positive outlook.

Marlowe
Meaning and origin: Driftwood (English)
Significance: Represents adaptability and resilience, reflecting a flexible and strong personality.

Mireya
Meaning and origin: Admirable (Spanish)
Significance: Symbolizes beauty and grace, reflecting an elegant and charming personality. Often associated with a sense of admiration and respect.

Navi
Meaning and origin: Kind to People (Hebrew)
Significance: Symbolizes kindness and compassion, reflecting a warm and caring personality. Often associated with empathy and a generous spirit.

Noemi
Meaning and origin: Pleasantness (Hebrew)
Significance: Symbolizes joy and charm, reflecting a delightful and cheerful personality. Often associated with a positive and uplifting presence.

Nyla
Meaning and origin: Winner or one who achieves (Arabic)
Significance: Embodies the admirable qualities of a champion; one who engages in fierce battles and emerges victorious.

Olesia
Meaning and origin: A Girl from the Forest (Slavic)
Significance: Represents a strong connection to nature and a sense of independence, symbolizing a person who is grounded and self-reliant. Often associated with resilience and the ability to thrive in natural surroundings.

Paris
Meaning and origin: Name of a city (Modern)
Significance: Symbolizes beauty, elegance, and a romantic spirit. Associated with creativity and artistic expression, the name Paris reflects a sophisticated and charismatic personality. It evokes a sense of wonder and enchantment, often seen as someone who inspires others through their refined tastes and charm.

Raelynn
Meaning and origin: Beam of light (English)
Significance: Represents brightness and positivity, reflecting a cheerful and optimistic personality.

Remi
Meaning and origin: From Rheims (French)
Significance: Reflects a refined and cultured personality, symbolizing a connection to history and tradition. Often associated with elegance and a sophisticated outlook on life.

Sable
Meaning and origin: Black (English)
Significance: Represents elegance and mystery, reflecting a sophisticated and enigmatic personality.

Shakti
Meaning and origin: Power (Hindi)
Significance: Symbolizes strength and energy, reflecting a dynamic and powerful personality. Often associated with the ability to inspire and lead others.

Sky
Meaning and origin: Sky; Sheltering (English)
Significance: Represents a sense of freedom and expansiveness, symbolizing a person with a broad and open-minded perspective. Often associated with protection and the ability to provide a sense of security to others.

Summer
Meaning and origin: Warm (English)
Significance: Summer is a straightforward name reflecting the warmth and joy of the season, summer name evokes positive feelings of sunshine, warmth, fun and carefree days—perfect for summer babies.

Sylvie
Meaning and origin: Spirit of the wood (Latin)
Significance: The mythological god of the forest was associated with the figure of Silvanus.

Tamica
Meaning and origin: she who is very sweet (English)
Significance: The name Tamica is often seen as a creative and unique choice, reflecting modern naming trends. It carries a sense of individuality and contemporary appeal.

Taryn
Meaning and origin: Rocky Hill (Modern)
Significance: Represents strength and stability, reflecting a resilient and grounded personality. Often associated with a strong connection to nature.

Tia
Meaning and origin: Aunt (Spanish)
Significance: Tia is a bright, diminutive form of names like Tiana.

Tinsley
Meaning and origin: Tynni's Meadow (Modern)
Significance: Symbolizes tranquility and grace, reflecting a serene and gentle personality. Often associated with a deep connection to nature and peaceful surroundings.

Tova
Meaning and origin: Good, Pleasant (Hebrew)
Significance: Represents positivity and kindness, reflecting a warm and cheerful personality. Often associated with a caring and nurturing nature.

Valencia
Meaning and origin: Strength; Valor (Latin)
Significance: Symbolizes bravery and resilience, reflecting a strong and courageous personality. Often associated with a sense of determination and fortitude.

Veda
Meaning and origin: Knowledge, Wisdom (Sanskrit)
Significance: Represents intelligence and insight, reflecting a wise and thoughtful personality. Often associated with a deep understanding of life and spiritual wisdom.

Yalena
Meaning and origin: Light (Slavic)
Significance: Symbolizes illumination and clarity, reflecting a bright and insightful personality. Often associated with wisdom and a guiding presence.

Yvaine
Meaning and origin: Evening Star (Scottish)
Significance: Symbolizes guidance and inspiration, reflecting a luminous and captivating personality. Often associated with a sense of wonder and mystery.

Vienna
Meaning and origin: From Vienna (Latin)
Significance: Symbolizes cultural richness and sophistication, reflecting a refined and elegant personality. Often associated with a love for art, music, and history.

Zia
Meaning and origin: Light; Splendor (Arabic)
Significance: Represents brightness and energy, reflecting a radiant and lively personality. Often associated with a positive and optimistic outlook on life.

Zinnia
Meaning and origin: Flower (Latin)
Significance: Symbolizes beauty and creativity, reflecting a vibrant and artistic personality. Often associated with a love for nature and a colorful outlook on life.

Ziva
Meaning and origin: Radiant (Hebrew)
Significance: Represents brightness and energy, reflecting a lively and spirited personality.

As we reach the end of our journey through the vibrant world of modern baby names, it is clear that contemporary choices offer a fresh and exciting way to celebrate your child's arrival. These names, rich with current cultural significance, provide a unique opportunity to craft an identity that is both personal and of-the-moment. Whether inspired by popular culture, innovative trends, or a blend of both, modern names can encapsulate the dynamic spirit of today's world. They offer a sense of individuality and creativity, setting the stage for your child's future with a name that stands out and resonates.

So, as you ponder the perfect name for your little one, remember the power of a name that is as unique and remarkable as they are. Embrace the new and the now and choose a modern name that will carry them confidently into the future. Your child's name is the first gift you give them, a symbol of your hopes and dreams for their life ahead. Make it count, and let it be as special as the wonderful journey you are about to embark on together. We have reached the end of our Contemporary names, Which I'm sure you have tons of options for your little one. In the next chapter, we're looking at names for twins! So, if you are expecting two or more little ones, be sure to stick around for the final chapter.

CHAPTER 11: TWIN NAMES

Deciding on names for twins presents a delightful opportunity for creativity, but there's also a unique consideration: How the names will sound together. While there's no single *right* way to name twins, choosing names that complement each other creates a sense of connection and harmony. This can be achieved through matching sounds (like Blake and Jake) or using names with similar themes or origins (like Luna and Stella). Even opting for completely different names can work beautifully if they share a balanced feel, like a longer name paired with a shorter one for example (Alexander and Leo). Ultimately, the goal is for the names to feel like a well-matched set, acknowledging the twins' special bond while allowing each child to have their own distinct identity.

The same goes for triplets or quadruplets. While this chapter specifically focuses on twins, feel free to add some names to the pairs or combine the pairs to create a set of names for your little ones.

Twin Boy Names

With two boys, there can often be a power struggle. However, by choosing names that complement each other, you can add positivity to their relationship. Here are a few name combinations that harmonize and complement each other, symbolizing the unbreakable bond between twin brothers.

Aaron and Adam
Meaning and origin: High mountain; Man (Hebrew)
Significance: Both names are of Hebrew origin and have strong biblical connections. Aaron, the older brother of Moses, symbolizes leadership and strength, while Adam, the first man created by God, represents humanity and creation.

Adrian and Aidan
Meaning and origin: Sea; Little fire (Latin and Irish)
Significance: Both names convey a sense of nature and passion. Adrian represents the vastness of the sea, while Aidan signifies warmth and energy.

Aiden and Caden
Meaning and origin: Fire; Battle (Celtic)
Significance: Both names have strong, powerful meanings with a rich Celtic heritage. Aiden, meaning "little fire," evokes a sense of warmth and vitality, while Caden, meaning "battle," symbolizes strength and resilience. Together, they create a harmonious and dynamic theme for twins, combining the elements of fire and warrior spirit. This pairing reflects a perfect balance of passion and determination, suggesting a bond of fiery energy and unyielding courage.

Alden and Ramon
Meaning and origin: Wise (British and Spanish)
Significance: These names represent someone who is wise and a good friend. Giving your boys these names signify a close connection to each other and an ability to lead wisely.

Alex and Andrew
Meaning and origin: Defender of the people; Manly (Greek)
Significance: Both names are of Greek origin and signify strength and protection. Alex is often associated with leadership, while Andrew symbolizes bravery and masculinity.

Andrew and Anthony
Meaning and origin: Manly; Priceless one (Greek and Latin)
Significance: Both names signify strength and value. Andrew represents bravery and masculinity, while Anthony signifies worth and nobility.

Arthur and Albert
Meaning and origin: Bear-like and Noble (Irish and German)
Significance: These two regal names embody power, leadership skills, and riches.

Ash and Rowan
Meaning and origin: One-dwelling and Red-one (British and Scottish)
Significance: Both are names of strong trees. With the same meaning, it creates a sense of belonging and connectedness between the two siblings.

Asher and Felix
Meaning and origin: Fortunate (Hebrew and Latin)
Significance: Both these names share a meaning, which is a beautiful way to complement one another without the names sounding the same. These boys are bound to be very blessed and fortunate to have one another.

Ashton and Austin
Meaning and origin: Ash tree town; Great (English and Latin)
Significance: Both names are of English origin and signify greatness and growth. Ashton represents connection to nature, while Austin signifies magnificence and strength.

Barclay and Benton
Meaning and origin: Clearing and Hill (Scottish and British)
Significance: The names both start with a "B" which creates a beautiful rhyming sound. This rhyming quality is a common feature in names chosen for twins, creating a sense of connection while still allowing the names to retain their individuality.

Benjamin and Braxton
Meaning and origin: Son of the right hand and Brock's settlement (Hebrew and British)
Significance: While they share some sounds, they have distinct beginnings ("Ben-" vs. "Brax-") and meanings, preventing them from being too matchy-matchy.

Blaise and Bruno
Meaning and origin: Fire; Brown (Latin and German)
Significance: Blaise evokes the imagery of fire and brilliance, while Bruno symbolizes strength and stability. Together, they reflect a dynamic combination of fiery energy and steadfastness.

Blake and Jake
Meaning and origin: Contrasting qualities; Supplanter (English and Hebrew)
Significance: Blake symbolizes contrasting qualities such as darkness and fairness, often associated with artists like William Blake. Jake, a diminutive of Jacob, represents the biblical patriarch known for his pivotal role in founding the twelve tribes of Israel.

Brady and Brett
Meaning and origin: Spirited; From Brittany (Irish and English)
Significance: Both names signify vitality and heritage. Brady represents energy and enthusiasm, while Brett signifies cultural pride and history.

Brandon and Landon
Meaning and origin: Hill covered with broom; Long hill (Old English)
Significance: Brandon symbolizes leadership and prominence, often seen as a guiding light or a beacon. Landon signifies stability and strength, representing enduring qualities and a firm foundation.

Brayden and Brandon
Meaning and origin: Broad hill; Broom hill (English)
Significance: Both names signify a connection to nature and the land. Brayden signifies expansiveness and strength, while Brandon represents resilience and growth.

Brock and Blake
Meaning and origin: Badger; Contrasting qualities (English)
Significance: Both names convey a sense of uniqueness. Brock signifies resilience and determination, while Blake symbolizes contrasting qualities such as darkness and fairness.

Bryce and Brooks
Meaning and origin: Speckled; Stream (Celtic and English)
Significance: Both names convey a sense of natural beauty and tranquility. Bryce represents uniqueness and charm, while Brooks signifies calmness and flow.

Caleb and Jacob
Meaning and origin: Whole-hearted; Supplanter (Hebrew)
Significance: Both names are of Hebrew origin and have deep biblical roots. Caleb, one of the twelve spies sent by Moses, represents faith and loyalty, while Jacob, the patriarch, symbolizes determination and strength.

Cameron and Carson
Meaning and origin: Crooked nose; Son of Carr (Scottish and Irish)
Significance: Both names are of Scottish origin and signify familial heritage and uniqueness. Cameron represents individuality and strength, while Carson signifies lineage and nobility.

Carter and Cooper
Meaning and origin: Cart driver; Barrel maker (English)
Significance: Both names are of English origin and are occupational surnames, reflecting industriousness and skill. Carter and Cooper both evoke images of craftsmanship and hard work.

Caspian and Cedric
Meaning and origin: From the Caspian Sea; Bounty (English and Celtic)
Significance: Caspian brings to mind vast, unexplored waters, while Cedric symbolizes abundance and leadership. Together, they embody a sense of adventure and prosperity.

Cassian and Felix
Meaning and origin: Empty-handed and Lucky (Latin)
Significance: Distinctive names with positive meanings. Cassian means empty-handed. In more modern translations, it can symbolize purity and humility. Felix means lucky and chosen. Together, these two names sound like a package deal.

Charlie and Riley
Meaning and origin: Freedom and Courage (German and Irish)
Significance: Both names have a similar length (two syllables) and feel casual, creating a sense of balance. The sounds also complement each other. Charlie's ending "ie" echoes the "e" sound in Riley, creating a subtle connection.

Charlie and Chase
Meaning and origin: Free man; Hunter (English and French)
Significance: Both names convey a sense of freedom and adventure. Charlie represents independence and spirit, while Chase signifies pursuit and determination.

Chase and Chance
Meaning and origin: Hunter; Good fortune (French)
Significance: Both names are of French origin and convey a sense of adventure and luck. Chase signifies pursuit and determination, while Chance represents serendipity and opportunity.

Christian and Christopher
Meaning and origin: Follower of Christ; Christ-bearer (Latin and Greek)
Significance: Both names signify a connection to faith and spirituality. Christian represents devotion and faith, while Christopher signifies carrying the spirit of Christ.

Cole and Colin
Meaning and origin: Victory of the people; Young creature (English and Gaelic)
Significance: Both names have a modern, youthful feel. Cole signifies strength and triumph, while Colin suggests youthfulness and vitality.

Colton and Carter
Meaning and origin: From the coal town; Cart driver (English)
Significance: Both names are of English origin and signify industriousness and craftsmanship. Colton represents a strong work ethic, while Carter signifies skill and hard work.

Connor and Caleb
Meaning and origin: Lover of hounds; Whole-hearted (Irish and Hebrew)
Significance: Both names convey loyalty and devotion. Connor represents love for nature and animals, while Caleb signifies faithfulness and commitment.

Cyrus and Samson
Meaning and origin: Sun (Persian and Hebrew)
Significance: These names directly translate to mean the sun, potentially symbolizing strength and power. While different in sound and origin, these names share meaning, which embodies the individuality yet togetherness of twins.

Damon and Dean
Meaning and origin: To tame; Valley (Greek and English)
Significance: Both names signify strength and tranquility. Damon represents control and calmness, while Dean signifies peacefulness and leadership.

Daniel and David
Meaning and origin: God is my judge; Beloved (Hebrew)
Significance: Both names are of Hebrew origin with significant biblical connections. Daniel symbolizes judgment and wisdom, while David represents belovedness and leadership.

Dashiell and Donovan
Meaning and origin: Page Boy; Dark Warrior (French and Irish)
Significance: Dashiell is associated with youthful energy and service, while Donovan signifies strength and valor. Together, they reflect a blend of spirited enthusiasm and warrior-like bravery.

Derek and Dustin
Meaning and origin: Ruler of the people; Brave warrior (German and English)
Significance: Both names signify leadership and courage. Derek represents authority and protection, while Dustin signifies bravery and resilience.

Dominic and Damien
Meaning and origin: Belonging to the Lord; To tame (Latin and Greek)
Significance: Both names signify strength and devotion. Dominic represents faith and divine connection, while Damien signifies calmness and control.

Dylan and Devin
Meaning and origin: Son of the sea; Poet (Welsh and Irish)
Significance: Both names have Celtic origins and convey a sense of artistic and natural beauty. Dylan signifies the power of the sea, while Devin represents creativity and inspiration.

Dashiell and Donovan
Meaning and origin: Page Boy; Dark Warrior (French and Irish)
Significance: Dashiell is associated with youthful energy and service, while Donovan signifies strength and valor. Together, they reflect a blend of spirited enthusiasm and warrior-like bravery.

Edward and Edwin
Meaning and origin: Wealthy guardian; Rich friend (English)
Significance: Both names signify prosperity and protection. Edward represents guardianship and wealth, while Edwin signifies friendship and fortune.

Eli and Ethan
Meaning and origin: Ascended; Strong (Hebrew)
Significance: Both names are of Hebrew origin and convey strength and resilience. Eli represents elevation and wisdom, while Ethan signifies firmness and endurance.

Elias and Ethan
Meaning and origin: Yahweh is God; Strong (Hebrew)
Significance: Both classic and biblical names have a similar "ee" sound. Together, these names represent someone of strong faith and who will be firm in their beliefs.

Elijah and Ezekiel
Meaning and origin: The Lord is my God; God strengthens (Hebrew)
Significance: Both names are of Hebrew origin and have deep biblical connections. Elijah represents prophetic strength, while Ezekiel signifies divine fortitude.

Emmett and Elliott
Meaning and origin: Universal; The Lord is my God (English and Hebrew)
Significance: Both names signify universality and divine connection. Emmett represents inclusiveness and unity, while Elliott signifies divine favor and strength.

Ethan and Evan
Meaning and origin: Strong; God is gracious (Hebrew and Welsh)
Significance: Both names suggest strength and grace. Ethan represents firmness and resilience, while Evan signifies kindness and divine favor.

Felix and Finley
Meaning and origin: Happy; Fair warrior (Latin and Irish)
Significance: Both names signify joy and valor. Felix represents happiness and good fortune, while Finley signifies bravery and fairness.

Finn and Flynn
Meaning and origin: Fair; Son of the red-haired one (Irish)
Significance: Both names are of Irish origin and evoke images of adventure and bravery. Finn represents fairness and heroism, while Flynn signifies a strong familial connection.

Finnegan and Fletcher
Meaning and origin: Fair; Arrow Maker (Irish and English)
Significance: Finnegan evokes a sense of fairness and brightness, while Fletcher symbolizes precision and craftsmanship. Together, they embody a blend of justice and skill.

Frederick and Milo
Meaning and origin: Peace (German)
Significance: The names Frederick and Milo refer to someone striving for peace while possessing the qualities of a strong leader. Both these names are equally strong, and together, they will work as a team to create peace wherever they go.

Gale and Caio
Meaning and origin: Windstorm and Rejoice (British and Latin)
Significance: Both names share a two-syllable structure with a strong consonant sound at the beginning and a softer ending. This creates a sense of balance and parallelism. They have a similar length and pronunciation style, making them feel like a cohesive pair.

Gavin and Grayson
Meaning and origin: White hawk; Son of the steward (Welsh and English)
Significance: Both names convey nobility and strength. Gavin symbolizes leadership and protection, while Grayson represents responsibility and honor.

Grady and Grant
Meaning and origin: Noble; Great (Irish and English)
Significance: Both names signify nobility and greatness. Grady represents honorable character, while Grant signifies generosity and leadership.

Graham and Garrett
Meaning and origin: Gravelly homestead; Spear strength (Scottish and German)
Significance: Both names convey a sense of stability and strength. Graham represents foundation and tradition, while Garrett signifies bravery and power.

Griffin and Gideon
Meaning and origin: Strong Lord; Hewer (Welsh and Hebrew)
Significance: Griffin symbolizes mythological strength and leadership, while Gideon represents cutting through obstacles with determination. Together, they reflect powerful leadership and tenacity.

Harrison and Henry
Meaning and origin: Son of Harry; Ruler of the home (English and German)
Significance: Both names signify leadership and heritage. Harrison signifies lineage and strength, while Henry represents authority and home.

Hawthorne and Holden
Meaning and origin: Lives where hawthorn hedges grow; Deep Valley (English)
Significance: Hawthorne evokes nature and protection, while Holden signifies depth and exploration. Together, they embody a blend of natural guardianship and intellectual curiosity.

Hayden and Hunter
Meaning and origin: Hill and Someone who hunts (British)
Significance: The names inherently refer to someone active, skilled in hunting, and resourceful. Together, they create a beautiful harmony of sharing a love for the outdoors, and the alliteration in the names sounds beautiful.

Henry and Harry
Meaning and origin: Estate ruler (German)
Significance: Both Henry and Harry share a strong sound connection. Harry is a well-known nickname for Henry, creating a sense of connection between the twins without having identical names. Both names also stem from the German name Heimrich, meaning "estate ruler." This gives them a common root and history.

Holden and Hudson
Meaning and origin: Hollow valley; Son of Hud (English)
Significance: Both names convey a sense of nature and strength. Holden represents tranquility and peace, while Hudson signifies dependability and resilience.

Hunter and Hudson
Meaning and origin: One who hunts; Son of Hud (English)
Significance: Both names are of English origin and evoke a sense of adventure and the outdoors. Hunter represents pursuit and skill, while Hudson signifies strength and dependability.

Ian and Ryan
Meaning and origin: God is gracious and little king (Scottish)
Significance: Both names have strong, positive meanings. Ian conveys a sense of divine favor, while Ryan suggests leadership and regality. Although not identical, they share a connection to power and strength, making them thematically linked.

Ian and Isaac
Meaning and origin: God is gracious; He will laugh (Scottish and Hebrew)
Significance: Both names signify divine favor and joy. Ian represents kindness and grace, while Isaac signifies joy and laughter.

Isaac and Isaiah
Meaning and origin: He will laugh; Salvation of the Lord (Hebrew)
Significance: Both names are of Hebrew origin with deep biblical roots. Isaac symbolizes joy and laughter, while Isaiah represents salvation and prophetic wisdom.

Jace and Jude
Meaning and origin: The Lord is salvation; Praised (Greek and Hebrew)
Significance: Both names signify divine connection and praise. Jace represents salvation and hope, while Jude signifies appreciation and honor.

Jaden and Jordan
Meaning and origin: Thankful; Flowing down (Hebrew)
Significance: Both names are of Hebrew origin and convey a sense of gratitude and fluidity. Jaden represents thankfulness, while Jordan signifies the famous river and spiritual journeys.

James and John
Meaning and origin: Supplanter; God is gracious (Hebrew)
Significance: Both names are of Hebrew origin with strong biblical ties. James symbolizes determination and resilience, while John represents kindness and divine grace.

Jameson and Jackson
Meaning and origin: Son of James; Son of Jack (English)
Significance: Both names signify familial heritage and strength. Jameson represents tradition and legacy, while Jackson signifies leadership and vigor.

Jason and Justin
Meaning and origin: Healer; Just, Fair (Greek and Latin)
Significance: Both names convey a sense of justice and care. Jason represents healing and protection, while Justin signifies fairness and righteousness.

Jasper and Ezra
Meaning and origin: Bringer of treasure and Helper (Persian and Hebrew)
Significance: Both have a modern feel with a touch of mystery. These two names go well together as both embody the qualities of helping others or bringing treasures to those around them. These twins are bound to be kind to each other and bring you to those around them.

Jayden and Jaylen
Meaning and origin: Thankful; Calm or Healer (Hebrew)
Significance: Jayden signifies gratitude and divine listening. Jaylen combines the elements of "Jay" and "Len," suggesting calmness and healing, embodying tranquility, and restoration.

Jeremiah and Josiah
Meaning and origin: Yahweh will exalt; Yahweh supports or heals (Hebrew)
Significance: Jeremiah, a major prophet known for his prophecies and lamentations, emphasizes faithfulness and divine purpose. Josiah, a king of Judah, symbolizes righteousness and reform through his religious reforms and efforts to restore the worship of Yahweh.

John and Shaun
Meaning and origin: Yahweh is gracious (Hebrew and Irish)
Significance: John is a central figure in the New Testament, including John the Baptist and John the Apostle, known for his writings and role as a forerunner of Jesus. Shaun, an Irish variant of Sean derived from John, carries the same significance, emphasizing divine grace and favor.

Jonah and Jude
Meaning and origin: Dove; Praised (Hebrew)
Significance: Both names signify peace and honor. Jonah represents peace and a messenger, while Jude signifies praise and respect.

Jordan and Justin
Meaning and origin: Flow down and Righteous (Hebrew and Latin)
Significance: They both start with the letter "J" and have two syllables. This creates a sense of balance and connection between the names. Both Jordan and Justin have been popular names for decades, offering a timeless feel.

Joseph and Joshua
Meaning and origin: He will add; The Lord is salvation (Hebrew)
Significance: Both names have strong biblical connections and signify divine favor. Joseph represents growth and addition, while Joshua signifies deliverance and leadership.

Kaiden and Karter
Meaning and origin: Companion; Cart driver (Celtic and English)
Significance: Both names signify companionship and industriousness. Kaiden represents friendship and loyalty, while Karter signifies skill and hard work.

Landon and Logan
Meaning and origin: Long hill; Small hollow (English and Scottish)
Significance: Both names convey a sense of nature and tranquility. Landon represents expansive landscapes, while Logan signifies peacefulness and security.

Leo and Liam
Meaning and origin: Lion; Strong-willed warrior (Latin and Irish)
Significance: Both names signify strength and courage. Leo represents bravery and leadership, while Liam signifies determination and warrior spirit.

Levi and Luke
Meaning and origin: Joined; Light (Hebrew and Greek)
Significance: Both names signify connection and illumination. Levi represents unity and attachment, while Luke signifies enlightenment and brightness.

Lincoln and Lawson
Meaning and origin: Town by the pool; Son of Lawrence (English)
Significance: Both names signify heritage and strength. Lincoln represents a historical and sturdy town, while Lawson signifies lineage and nobility.

Logan and Lucas
Meaning and origin: Small hollow; Light (Scottish and Latin)
Significance: Both names convey a sense of illumination and presence. Logan signifies a peaceful and secure place, while Lucas represents brightness and enlightenment.

Louis and Walter
Meaning and origin: Warrior (French and German)
Significance: Both these names embody the characteristics of someone brave and powerful. By providing both sons with a name that shares meaning, they will be closely connected and equal partners.

Mason and Morgan
Meaning and origin: Worker in stone; Sea-born (English and Welsh)
Significance: Both names convey a sense of craftsmanship and natural beauty. Mason signifies construction and strength, while Morgan represents the sea and mystery.

Matthew and Mark
Meaning and origin: Gift of God; Warlike (Hebrew and Latin)
Significance: Both names have strong biblical ties and signify divine favor and strength. Matthew represents a divine gift, while Mark signifies courage and resilience.

Maverick and Maddox
Meaning and origin: Independent One; Son of Madoc (American and Welsh)
Significance: Maverick signifies independence and nonconformity, while Maddox symbolizes generosity and good fortune. Together, they reflect a spirit of individualism and prosperity.

Max and Miles
Meaning and origin: Greatest; Soldier (Latin and English)
Significance: Both names signify strength and valor. Max represents greatness and achievement, while Miles signifies courage and determination.

Micah and Mitchell
Meaning and origin: Who is like God? (Hebrew)
Significance: Both names signify divine strength and protection. Micah represents humility before God, while Mitchell signifies faith and reverence.

Michael and Matthew
Meaning and origin: Who is like God? (Hebrew)
Significance: Both names are of Hebrew origin with deep biblical significance. Michael represents divine strength and protection, while Matthew signifies a divine gift and blessing.

Nathan and Nolan
Meaning and origin: He gave; Champion (Hebrew and Irish)
Significance: Both names convey a sense of generosity and heroism. Nathan represents giving and benevolence, while Nolan signifies leadership and valor.

Nathaniel and Daniel
Meaning and origin: Gift of God; God is my judge (Hebrew)
Significance: Nathaniel, a biblical name representing a blessing or gift from God, was one of the twelve apostles. Daniel is known as a prophet for his wisdom and faithfulness, central to the Book of Daniel.

Nicholas and Nathaniel
Meaning and origin: Victory of the people; Gift of God (Greek and Hebrew)
Significance: Both names signify divine favor and strength. Nicholas represents triumph and leadership, while Nathaniel signifies a divine gift and blessing.

Nolan and Noah
Meaning and origin: Champion; Rest, Comfort (Irish and Hebrew)
Significance: Both names signify strength and tranquility. Nolan represents leadership and bravery, while Noah signifies peace and salvation.

Oliver and Oscar
Meaning and origin: Olive tree; God's spear (Latin and English)
Significance: Both names convey a sense of peace and strength. Oliver represents peace and prosperity, while Oscar signifies valor and protection.

Orlando and Rodrigo
Meaning and origin: Famous (Spanish)
Significance: Both these names represent something famous. By sharing meaning, both boys will be equals and have a special connection thanks to their shared meaning.

Orson and Oscar
Meaning and origin: Bear; Divine Spear (Latin and Old English)
Significance: Orson symbolizes strength and courage like a bear, while Oscar represents divine protection and warrior spirit. Together, they embody a combination of robust power and sacred defense.

Owen and Leo
Meaning and origin: Warrior and Lion (Welsh and Latin)
Significance: These two names create a powerful duo and will surely be powerful leaders among their peers. They will also have a strong connection to one another and be incredibly loyal.

Parker and Preston
Meaning and origin: Park keeper; Priest's town (English)
Significance: Both names are of English origin and suggest a sense of duty and community. Parker signifies guardianship and care, while Preston represents spiritual guidance and nobility.

Patrick and Peter
Meaning and origin: Nobleman; Rock (Latin and Greek)
Significance: Both names signify strength and foundation. Patrick represents nobility and leadership, while Peter signifies stability and steadfastness.

Paxton and Parker
Meaning and origin: Peaceful town; Park keeper (English)
Significance: Both names signify tranquility and responsibility. Paxton represents a serene place, while Parker signifies guardianship and care.

Philip and Patrick
Meaning and origin: Lover of horses; Nobleman (Greek and Latin)
Significance: Both names signify nobility and strength. Philip represents affection and care, while Patrick signifies leadership and valor.

Riley and Ryan
Meaning and origin: Courageous; Little king (Irish)
Significance: Both names are of Irish origin and convey a sense of bravery and leadership. Riley represents courage and valor, while Ryan signifies royalty and strength.

River and Forest
Meaning and origin: Stream and Woodland (British and Latin)
Significance: Evocative names that connect to the outdoors. These names embody adventure, love for the outdoors, and kindness.

Robert and Richard
Meaning and origin: Bright fame; Brave ruler (German)
Significance: Both names signify strength and leadership. Robert represents renown and brilliance, while Richard signifies courage and authority.

Rowan and Ryan
Meaning and origin: Little red one; Little king (Irish)
Significance: Both names are of Irish origin and signify youthfulness and leadership. Rowan represents nature and vitality, while Ryan signifies royalty and strength.

Ryder and Riley
Meaning and origin: Horseman; Courageous (English and Irish)
Significance: Both names signify bravery and adventure. Ryder represents skill and daring, while Riley signifies valor and courage.

Sam and Sebastian
Meaning and origin: Heard by God; Venerable (Hebrew and Latin)
Significance: Both names signify honor and reverence. Sam represents divine communication and faith, while Sebastian signifies respect and nobility.

Samuel and Simon
Meaning and origin: Heard by God; Listener (Hebrew)
Significance: Both names are of Hebrew origin and signify a connection to the divine. Samuel represents divine communication and faith, while Simon signifies understanding and wisdom.

Sawyer and Spencer
Meaning and origin: Woodcutter; Steward (English)
Significance: Both names are of English origin and reflect industriousness and responsibility. Sawyer signifies craftsmanship and hard work, while Spencer represents stewardship and care.

Sean and Shane
Meaning and origin: God is gracious (Irish)
Significance: Both names are of Irish origin and convey a sense of divine favor. Sean and Shane both signify kindness and grace.

Seth and Scott
Meaning and origin: Appointed; Wanderer (Hebrew and English)
Significance: Both names signify purpose and exploration. Seth represents divine appointment and destiny, while Scott signifies wanderlust and adventure.

Shane and Shawn
Meaning and origin: God is gracious (Irish)
Significance: Both names are of Irish origin and signify divine favor and kindness. Shane and Shawn both represent grace and gentleness.

Silas and Jude
Meaning and origin: Forest and Praised (Greek and Hebrew)
Significance: Short yet impactful names with biblical roots, Silas and Jude, go well together and create the combined meaning of *forest of praise*, which embodies a place of worship and positive qualities.

Sullivan and Sawyer
Meaning and origin: Dark-eyed; Woodcutter (Irish and English)
Significance: Both names signify industriousness and charm. Sullivan signifies beauty and strength, while Sawyer represents craftsmanship and hard work

Sylvio and Atwood
Meaning and origin: Forest and one who lives near the woods (Latin and British)
Significance: These two names share a similar meaning, Together, they embody twins who are close to one another, share interests, and enjoy being together.

Tanner and Trevor
Meaning and origin: Leather worker; Large village (English and Welsh)
Significance: Both names signify industriousness and community. Tanner represents craftsmanship and skill, while Trevor signifies nobility and tradition.

Tate and Trent
Meaning and origin: Cheerful; Gushing waters (English)
Significance: Both names signify positivity and movement. Tate represents happiness and joy, while Trent signifies strength and dynamic energy.

Thaddeus and Thatcher
Meaning and origin: Courageous Heart; Roof Maker (Aramaic and English)
Significance: Thaddeus symbolizes bravery and compassion, while Thatcher evokes practicality and craftsmanship. Together, they represent a blend of courageous spirit and industrious skill.

Theo and Thomas
Meaning and origin: Divine gift; Twin (Greek and Aramaic)
Significance: Both names signify connection and favor. Theo represents a divine gift, while Thomas signifies companionship and duality.

Thor and Loki
Meaning and origin: Thunder and Mischief (Norse)
Significance: Thor and Loki are classic and known for their bond as brothers (although it started out a little shaky). These names are strong and represent intelligence and smarts.

Timothy and Tyler
Meaning and origin: Honoring God; Tile maker (Greek and English)
Significance: Both names convey a sense of reverence and craftsmanship. Timothy represents faith and devotion, while Tyler signifies skill and industriousness.

Tobias and Tristan
Meaning and origin: God is good; Tumult (Hebrew and Celtic)
Significance: Both names signify strength and resilience. Tobias represents divine goodness and favor, while Tristan signifies adventure and romanticism.

Tristan and Troy
Meaning and origin: Tumult; Foot soldier (Celtic and Greek)
Significance: Both names signify strength and resilience. Tristan represents adventure and romanticism, while Troy signifies bravery and historical valor.

Victor and Vincent
Meaning and origin: Conqueror; Victorious (Latin)
Significance: Both names signify triumph and success. Victor represents strength and achievement, while Vincent signifies conquest and resilience.

Warren and Wesley
Meaning and origin: Guard; Western meadow (English)
Significance: Both names are of English origin and convey a sense of protection and tranquility. Warren signifies defense and strength, while Wesley represents nature and peace.

Wesley and Wyatt
Meaning and origin: Western meadow; Strong fighter (English)
Significance: Both names are of English origin and convey a sense of courage and exploration. Wesley represents tranquility and nature, while Wyatt signifies bravery and strength.

William and Wyatt
Meaning and origin: Resolute protector; Strong fighter (English)
Significance: Both names signify strength and protection. William represents steadfastness and leadership, while Wyatt signifies bravery and valor.

Xavier and Xander
Meaning and origin: Bright; Defender of the people (Basque and Greek)
Significance: Both names convey a sense of brilliance and protection. Xavier represents enlightenment and wisdom, while Xander signifies defense and strength.

Zachary and Zane
Meaning and origin: The Lord has remembered; God is gracious (Hebrew)
Significance: Both names are of Hebrew origin and convey a sense of divine remembrance and favor. Zachary represents faithfulness and divine memory, while Zane signifies grace and kindness.

Twin Girl Names

When choosing names for your twin girls, it's important to say the names out loud and hear what they sound like as a team. In doing so, you'll subconsciously create an unbreakable bond between your two little girls, ensuring that they always have a little bestie with them. Here are names that resonate together with grace and beauty, mirroring the close relationship between twin sisters.

Abby and Gabby
Meaning and origin: My father is joy; God is my strength (Hebrew)
Significance: Abigail is known for her wisdom and beauty in the Hebrew Bible, becoming the wife of King David. Gabrielle, the feminine form of Gabriel, represents divine strength and support, with Gabriel being an archangel appearing in the books of Daniel and Luke.

Abigail and Amelia
Meaning and origin: Father's joy; Work of the Lord (Hebrew and Latin)
Significance: Both names convey a sense of joy and divine connection. Abigail represents happiness and delight, while Amelia signifies dedication and diligence.

Addison and Madison
Meaning and origin: Son of Adam; Son of Matthew or Maud (English)
Significance: Addison, originally a surname, symbolizes legacy and connection to the biblical figure Adam. Madison, also a surname turned first name, represents heritage and lineage.

Adira and Amara
Meaning and origin: Strong; Eternal (Hebrew and Latin)
Significance: Adira represents strength and resilience, while Amara signifies eternal beauty and grace. Together, they reflect a powerful combination of enduring strength and timeless elegance.

Alice and Amelia
Meaning and origin: Noble; Work of the Lord (German and Latin)
Significance: Both names convey a sense of nobility and dedication. Alice represents honor and grace, while Amelia signifies diligence and industriousness.

Alicia and Michelle
Meaning and origin: Noble and Gift from God (German and Hebrew)
Significance: Both names share a similar cadence and syllable count (three syllables each). This creates a pleasing sense of balance when said together.

Amanda and Miranda
Meaning and origin: Worthy of love; Admirable or Wonderful (Latin)
Significance: Amanda conveys endearment and admiration, while Miranda, popularized by Shakespeare's "The Tempest," signifies someone worthy of admiration and amazement.

Amy and May
Meaning and origin: Beloved and Month (French)
Significance: On top of sharing the same origin country, they also share a similar sound structure with one syllable. They also contain the same letters. This creates a sense of connection between the names.

Anna and Emma
Meaning and origin: Grace; Whole (Hebrew and German)
Significance: Both names signify completeness and favor. Anna represents kindness and grace, while Emma signifies wholeness and universal appeal.

Annabella and Isabella
Meaning and origin: Graceful beauty; God is my oath (Latin and Hebrew)
Significance: Annabella combines Anna (grace) and Bella (beautiful), conveying a sense of graceful beauty. Isabella, derived from Elizabeth, signifies strong faith and commitment to God.

Arianna and Brianna
Meaning and origin: Most holy; Strong; Noble (Greek and Irish)
Significance: Arianna, derived from the Greek mythological figure Ariadne, represents purity and sacredness. Brianna conveys strength and nobility, reflecting a proud and robust character.

Aurora and Ariel
Meaning and origin: Dawn; Lion of God (Latin and Hebrew)
Significance: Both names signify light and strength. Aurora represents the dawn, symbolizing new beginnings and hope, while Ariel signifies the lion of God, suggesting courage and protection.

Autumn and April
Meaning and origin: Fall season; Opening (Latin and Latin)
Significance: Both names signify the beauty of nature and change. Autumn represents richness and maturity, while April signifies renewal and freshness.

Ava and Aubrie
Meaning and origin: Bird and Elf-ruler (German)
Significance: Both names are two syllables long and end with a vowel sound. This creates a pleasing sense of balance and connection.

Avery and Addison
Meaning and origin: Elf counsel; Son of Adam (English)
Significance: Both names signify wisdom and strength. Avery signifies guidance and enchantment, while Addison represents tradition and strength

Bailey and Brooke
Meaning and origin: Bailiff; Small stream (English)
Significance: Both names convey a sense of duty and nature. Bailey represents guardianship and authority, while Brooke signifies tranquility and natural beauty.

Beatrice and Bianca
Meaning and origin: Bringer of joy; White (Latin and Italian)
Significance: Both names signify purity and happiness. Beatrice represents joy and happiness, while Bianca signifies purity and clarity.

Bella and Luna
Meaning and origin: Beautiful and Moon (Italian and Latin)
Significance: While both names have positive connotations (beauty and celestial wonder), they offer distinct meanings. This creates a connection between the twins while allowing them to have their own identities.

Bianca and Brianna
Meaning and origin: White; Noble (Italian and Celtic)
Significance: Both names signify purity and nobility. Bianca represents elegance and simplicity, while Brianna signifies strength and dignity.

Callie and Chloe
Meaning and origin: Beautiful voice; Blooming (Greek)
Significance: Both names evoke qualities of beauty and grace. Callie means beautiful voice, while Chloe signifies blooming or fertility.

Caroline and Charlotte
Meaning and origin: Free man; Free man (Latin and French)
Significance: Both names signify freedom and nobility. Caroline and Charlotte represent elegance, grace, and strong historical connections.

Cassidy and Chelsea
Meaning and origin: Clever; Port (Irish and Old English)
Significance: Both names signify intelligence and connection. Cassidy represents cleverness and wit, while Chelsea signifies a port or landing place, suggesting a sense of arrival and connection.

Celeste and Seraphine
Meaning and origin: Heavenly; Fiery (Latin)
Significance: Celeste symbolizes the heavens and divinity, while Seraphine embodies fiery passion and purity. Together, they evoke a celestial and ethereal harmony, blending serenity with intensity.

Chloe and Zoey
Meaning and origin: Blooming; Fertility, Life (Greek)
Significance: Chloe signifies growth and vitality, mentioned in the New Testament. Zoey, derived from the Greek word for life, embodies liveliness and energy.

Claire and Chloe
Meaning and origin: Clear; Blooming (French and Greek)
Significance: Both names signify clarity and natural beauty. Claire signifies brightness and clarity, while Chloe represents freshness and growth.

Clara and Cora
Meaning and origin: Bright; Maiden (Latin and Greek)
Significance: Both names signify clarity and youthfulness. Clara represents brightness and clarity, while Cora signifies a maiden or youthful vigor.

Crystal and Ruby
Meaning and origin: Purity and clarity and Fire and passion (Greek)
Significance: Both Crystal and Ruby are inspired by gemstones, creating a harmonious theme for the twins. This theme is visually appealing and evokes ideas of beauty, strength, and preciousness, which are all wonderful qualities to associate with your daughters.

Dahlia and Delilah
Meaning and origin: Flower named after botanist A. Dahl; Delicate (Scandinavian and Hebrew)
Significance: Both names have floral associations. Dahlia is named after the botanist A. Dahl and symbolizes elegance, while Delilah means delicate and gentle.

Daisy and Lily
Meaning and origin: Day's eye; Pure (English and Latin)
Significance: Both names are floral and convey purity and beauty. Daisy represents cheerfulness and simplicity, while Lily signifies purity and elegance.

Dakota and Delaney
Meaning and origin: Friend; From the alder grove (Native American and Irish)
Significance: Both names signify companionship and strength. Dakota represents friendship and unity, while Delaney signifies resilience and growth.

Delilah and Ophelia
Meaning and origin: Delicate and Helper (Hebrew and Greek)
Significance: Both names share a similar vowel sound, "ah," which creates a sense of balance and connection when spoken together. They are also both elegant-sounding and from a different era.

Danielle and Diana
Meaning and origin: God is my judge; Divine (Hebrew and Latin)
Significance: Both names signify divine favor and judgment. Danielle signifies God's judgment and wisdom, while Diana represents the Roman goddess of the hunt and moon, symbolizing independence, and strength.

Demi and Destiny
Meaning and origin: Half; Fate (French and English)
Significance: Both names signify purpose and inevitability. Demi represents being half or incomplete, while Destiny signifies fate and purpose.

Diane and Delilah
Meaning and origin: Divine; Delicate (Latin and Hebrew)
Significance: Both names signify femininity and beauty. Diane represents divine qualities, while Delilah signifies delicacy and allure.

Dream and Destiny
Meaning and origin: Ambition and imagination, Purpose, and fulfillment (British)
Significance: Both names carry a strong, symbolic meaning related to a person's path and future. Dream of represents aspirations and hopes, while Destiny signifies one's predetermined fate or course. Together, they create a sense of balance, acknowledging the interplay between personal desires (dreams) and the forces shaping one's life (destiny).

Eden and Elise
Meaning and origin: Paradise; Pledged to God (Hebrew and French)
Significance: Both names signify divine connection and beauty. Eden represents paradise and peace, while Elise signifies dedication and grace.

Eleanor and Emmeline
Meaning and origin: Bright, shining one; Hardworking (Greek and German)
Significance: Both names signify strength and diligence. Eleanor represents a bright and shining presence, while Emmeline signifies hard work and industriousness.

Eliza and Esme
Meaning and origin: God is my oath; Beloved (Hebrew and French)
Significance: Both names signify devotion and affection. Eliza represents a commitment to God, while Esme signifies being beloved or cherished.

Ella and Emma
Meaning and origin: Beautiful and Universal (German)
Significance: Both names are short (two syllables), start with the "ay" sound, have a double consonant, and end with "ah," creating a sense of connection.

Emily and Evelyn
Meaning and origin: Rival; Desired (Latin and English)
Significance: Both names signify aspiration and desire. Emily represents competitiveness and ambition, while Evelyn signifies charm and allure.

Fiona and Freya
Meaning and origin: Fair; Lady (Scottish and Norse)
Significance: Both names signify beauty and nobility. Fiona represents fairness and beauty, while Freya signifies a noble lady, symbolizing strength and leadership.

Freya and Fiona
Meaning and origin: Noble woman; Fair (Norse and Gaelic)
Significance: Freya represents love and beauty, while Fiona signifies fairness and purity. Together, they reflect a blend of divine beauty and graceful integrity.

Gabriella and Isabelle
Meaning and origin: God is my strength; God is my oath (Hebrew)
Significance: Gabriella, the feminine form of Gabriel, symbolizes divine strength and protection. Isabelle, derived from Elizabeth, signifies a strong commitment to God.

Gemma and Gia
Meaning and origin: Gemstone; Earth (Italian)
Significance: Both names have strong and grounded meanings. Gemma signifies gemstone or precious stone, while Gia means earth or land.

Giselle and Gloria
Meaning and origin: Pledge; Gloria (German and Latin)
Significance: Both names signify honor and praise. Giselle represents a pledge or promise, while Gloria signifies glory and magnificence.

Grace and Faith
Meaning and origin: Grace; Faith (Latin and English)
Significance: Both names signify virtues. Grace represents elegance and kindness, while Faith signifies trust and belief.

Gwen and Grace
Meaning and origin: Blessed; Grace (Welsh and Latin)
Significance: Both names signify kindness and favor. Gwen signifies purity and blessing, while Grace represents elegance and kindness.

Hailey and Hannah
Meaning and origin: Hay's meadow; Favor (British and Hebrew)
Significance: Both names convey a sense of nature and grace. Haley represents peace and tranquility, while Hannah signifies kindness and favor.

Hannah and Harper
Meaning and origin: Favor; Harp player (Hebrew and English)
Significance: Both names convey a sense of favor and artistry. Hannah represents grace and favor, while Harper signifies creativity and talent.

Harmony and Hope
Meaning and origin: Agreement; Expectation (Greek and English)
Significance: Both names convey positive sentiments. Harmony signifies agreement or peace, while Hope represents expectation and optimism.

Harper and Hazel
Meaning and origin: Harp player; Hazelnut tree (English)
Significance: Both names signify nature and creativity. Harper represents musical talent and creativity, while Hazel signifies a tree associated with wisdom and protection.

Hope and Faith
Meaning and origin: Optimism, anticipation; Belief, trust (British)
Significance: The names are thematically linked, referencing two of the three theological virtues: faith, hope, and charity. This creates a beautiful connection between the twins without being overly matchy-matchy.

Iris and Ivy
Meaning and origin: Rainbow; Faithfulness (Greek and English)
Significance: Both names signify beauty and steadfastness. Iris represents color and diversity, while Ivy signifies loyalty and dependability.

Isadora and Isabella
Meaning and origin: God's gift; God is my oath (Greek and Latin)
Significance: While not identical, the meanings share a sense of being blessed or cherished. Isadora signifies a gift, and Isabella signifies a devotion to God. They both convey a sense of something precious.

Isla and Ivy
Meaning and origin: Island; Faithfulness (Scottish and English)
Significance: Both names signify nature and loyalty. Isla represents tranquility and beauty, while Ivy signifies steadfastness and fidelity.

Jade and Jolie
Meaning and origin: Purity; Pretty (Spanish and French)
Significance: Both names share a similar structure with a soft "J" sound at the beginning, creating a pleasing aesthetic when said together.

Jenna and Julia
Meaning and origin: Fair one; Youthful (Arabic and Latin)
Significance: Both names signify beauty and youthfulness. Jenna represents fairness and charm, while Julia signifies vitality and youth.

Jocelyn and Juliana
Meaning and origin: Joyous; Youthful (German and Latin)
Significance: Both names convey joy and vitality. Jocelyn represents happiness and delight, while Juliana signifies youth and energy.

Josephine and Juliet
Meaning and origin: God will increase; Youthful (Hebrew and French)
Significance: Both names carry themes of vitality and promise. Josephine signifies God's blessing and increase, while Juliet symbolizes youthfulness and beauty.

Juliana and Julia
Meaning and origin: Youthful (Latin)
Significance: The names sound very similar, creating a clear connection between the twins. They also share the same origin and meaning, contributing to their unity even more.

Kate and Katherine
Meaning and origin: Pure (Greek)
Significance: Both names signify purity and strength. Kate and Katherine represent the same virtue of purity, with Katherine offering a more formal variant.

Kelsey and Kylie
Meaning and origin: Island of the ships; Boomerang (English and Australian)
Significance: Both names signify uniqueness and resilience. Kelsey represents adaptability and strength, while Kylie signifies return and perseverance.

Kylie and Miley
Meaning and origin: Boomerang; Proud chief (Australian; Irish)
Significance: Kylie signifies return and perseverance, while Miley signifies leadership and dignity.

Layla and Leila
Meaning and origin: Night; Dark beauty (Arabic)
Significance: Both names evoke images of beauty and mystery. Layla signifies the night, often associated with beauty and romance, while Leila denotes dark beauty and elegance.

Lillian and Lydia
Meaning and origin: Lily; From Lydia (Latin and Greek)
Significance: Both names signify beauty and heritage. Lillian represents purity and elegance, while Lydia signifies nobility and tradition.

Lily and Milly
Meaning and origin: Purity, Innocence; Industrious, Strong in work (English and German)
Significance: Lily symbolizes purity and renewal, often associated with the Virgin Mary. Milly conveys diligence and strength, reflecting a hardworking nature.

Lorelai and Legacy
Meaning and origin: Flowing; Something left behind (German and Latin)
Significance: While the meanings differ, they complement each other. Lorelai suggests a connection to nature and a flowing quality, while Legacy implies something enduring and passed on. Together, they represent a balance between the fleeting beauty of the present and the lasting impact one can have.

Lucy and Luna
Meaning and origin: Light; Moon (Latin)
Significance: Both names signify illumination and celestial beauty. Lucy represents brightness and clarity, while Luna signifies mystery and serenity.

Lyric and Melody
Meaning and origin: Singing to the lyre and Song (Greek)
Significance: Both names share a strong connection to music and share positive meanings. By choosing thematically linked names, you create a special connection between the twins without sacrificing individuality. They'll share a beautiful theme while still having distinct identities.

Mackenzie and Maddison
Meaning and origin: Son of Kenneth; Son of Maud (Scottish and English)
Significance: Both names originally denoted lineage. Mackenzie signifies "son of Kenneth," while Madison means "son of Matthew," although it is now used for girls as well.

Maddison and Morgan
Meaning and origin: Son of Maud; Sea protector (English and Welsh)
Significance: Both names signify strength and guardianship. Madison represents resilience and tradition, while Morgan signifies protection and courage.

Mercy and Miracle
Meaning and origin: Kindness and Compassion (Hebrew)
Significance: While the meanings differ slightly, they share a thematic link. Mercy emphasizes positive actions, while Miracle highlights the positive outcome of those actions. Together, they create a sense of the two girls leaving a positive mark on the world through their kindness.

Mia and Sophia
Meaning and origin: Mine, Beloved; Wisdom (Latin and Greek)
Significance: Mia conveys endearment and personal attachment. Sophia represents wisdom and insight, with deep philosophical and religious connotations.

Mila and Mia
Meaning and origin: Gracious; Mine, Beloved (Slavic and Latin)
Significance: Both names convey warmth and affection. Mia signifies endearment ("mine"), while Mila means gracious and dear.

Natalie and Nicole
Meaning and origin: Born on Christmas; Victory of the people (Latin and Greek)
Significance: Both names convey a sense of celebration and triumph. Natalie represents joy and festivity, while Nicole signifies strength and leadership.

Nerissa and Nereida
Meaning and origin: Sea nymph; Sea nymph (Greek)
Significance: Both names signify sea nymphs, representing the mystery and allure of the ocean. Together, they reflect a harmonious blend of mystical beauty and oceanic grace.

Nora and Natalie
Meaning and origin: Light; Born on Christmas (Latin)
Significance: Both names signify light and celebration. Nora represents illumination and wisdom, while Natalie signifies joy and festivity.

Olivia and Sophia
Meaning and origin: Olive tree; Wisdom (Latin and Greek)
Significance: Both names signify peace and intelligence. Olivia represents harmony and fruitfulness, while Sophia signifies wisdom and knowledge.

Ophelia and Octavia
Meaning and origin: Help; Eighth (Greek and Latin)
Significance: Ophelia represents assistance and compassion, while Octavia signifies strength and regality. Together, they evoke a sense of noble compassion and steadfast grace.

Paige and Piper
Meaning and origin: Page to a lord; Flute player (English)
Significance: Both names convey a sense of service and artistry. Paige represents loyalty and dedication, while Piper signifies musical talent and creativity.

Paisley and Piper
Meaning and origin: Decorated and Player of tunes (Scottish)
Significance: Both names share Scottish origins and evoke a sense of heritage. Each name carries its own meaning and creates a unique identity for each twin. Yet, when paired together, they create a connection that highlights their shared bond.

Paloma and Petra
Meaning and origin: Dove; Rock (Spanish and Greek)
Significance: Paloma symbolizes peace and gentleness, while Petra signifies strength and stability. Together, they reflect a harmonious blend of serene peace and solid strength.

Penelope and Piper
Meaning and origin: Weaver; Flute player (Greek and English)
Significance: Both names convey creativity and skill. Penelope represents artistry and resilience, while Piper signifies musical talent and creativity.

Peyton and Paige
Meaning and origin: Noble; Page to a lord (English and French)
Significance: Both names denote positions of honor. Peyton means noble or patrician, while Paige originally referred to a young servant or page.

Poppy and Ivy
Meaning and origin: Red flower and green plant (Latin and British)
Significance: Both names are derived from plants, creating a natural and cohesive theme for the twins. The two-syllable structure of both names also provides a sense of balance and simplicity when said together.

Quinn and Quinley
Meaning and origin: Descendant of Conn; Descendant of Caoinleán (Irish)
Significance: Both names denote lineage. Quinn means descendant of Conn, while Quinley means descendant of Caoinleán.

Racquel and Royal
Meaning and origin: Innocent; Regal (Spanish and English)
Significance: Both names carry connotations of status and dignity. Racquel signifies innocence or purity, while Royal denotes regal or majestic qualities.

Raven and Rebecca
Meaning and origin: Dark-haired; To tie or bind (English and Hebrew)
Significance: Both names carry strong symbolic meanings. Raven signifies a dark-haired beauty or intelligence, while Rebecca means "to tie" or "to bind," symbolizing connection and strength.

Reagan and Riley
Meaning and origin: Little king; Courageous (Irish)
Significance: Both names signify leadership and bravery. Reagan represents royalty and strength, while Riley signifies valor and determination.

Reese and Rachael
Meaning and origin: Enthusiasm; Ewe (Welsh and Hebrew)
Significance: Both names have distinct origins and meanings. Reese signifies enthusiasm or ardent, while Rachael means ewe (female sheep) in Hebrew.

Remy and Rosemary
Meaning and origin: Oarsman; Dew of the sea (French and Latin)
Significance: Both names have botanical references. Remy originally meant "oarsman" but is now associated with the herb name, while Rosemary denotes the herb known for its fragrance and symbolism.

Rhea and Rina
Meaning and origin: Flowing; Joyful (Greek and Hebrew)
Significance: Rhea represents the natural flow and continuity, while Rina signifies joy and happiness. Together, they evoke a sense of joyful continuity and flowing grace.

Rose and Ruby
Meaning and origin: Flower; Precious stone (Latin)
Significance: Both names are associated with beauty and rarity. Rose represents the flower known for its beauty and fragrance, while Ruby signifies a precious gemstone.

Ruby and Rose
Meaning and origin: Precious red stone; Flower (Latin and Latin)
Significance: Both names are associated with beauty and nature. Ruby represents passion and vitality, while Rose signifies elegance and timeless beauty.

Ruth and Ruby
Meaning and origin: Companion, friend; Red gemstone (Hebrew and Latin)
Significance: Both names signify loyalty and preciousness. Ruth signifies companionship and friendship, while Ruby represents passion and vitality due to its association with the vibrant red gemstone.

Sadie and Sophie
Meaning and origin: Princess; Wisdom (Hebrew and Greek)
Significance: Both names convey a sense of grace and intelligence. Sadie represents nobility and charm, while Sophie signifies wisdom and insight.

Sage and Sloane
Meaning and origin: Wise; Raider (English and Irish)
Significance: Both names have distinct characteristics. Sage signifies wisdom and knowledge, while Sloane originally meant "raider" and now evokes images of strength and determination.

Samantha and Savannah
Meaning and origin: Listener; Open plain (Aramaic and Spanish)
Significance: Both names signify openness and attentiveness. Samantha represents a listener, someone who is receptive and understanding, while Savannah signifies an open plain, suggesting freedom and expansiveness.

Sarah and Sydney
Meaning and origin: Princess; Wide Island (Hebrew and Old English)
Significance: Both names signify prominence and expansiveness. Sarah represents princess-like qualities and prominence, while Sydney signifies a wide island, suggesting a vast and open landscape.

Savannah and Sierra
Meaning and origin: Grassland and Mountain range (Spanish)
Significance: Both names evoke imagery of natural landscapes: Savannah with its vast grasslands and Sierra with its majestic mountain ranges. These names are not overly common but still recognizable and easy to pronounce.

Scarlett and Stella
Meaning and origin: Red; Star (English and Latin)
Significance: Both names signify vibrancy and brilliance. Scarlett represents passion and boldness, while Stella signifies brightness and aspiration.

Selene and Seraphina
Meaning and origin: Moon; Burning fire (Greek and Hebrew)
Significance: Both names evoke celestial and spiritual imagery. Selene represents the moon goddess in Greek mythology, while Seraphina signifies a burning fire or fiery angel in Hebrew tradition.

Serenity and Trinity
Meaning and origin: Peaceful; Three in one (Latin)
Significance: Serenity embodies tranquility and calm. Trinity represents the Christian doctrine of the Father, the Son, and the Holy Spirit.

Sienna and Serenity
Meaning and origin: Reddish brown; Peaceful (Italian and Latin)
Significance: Both names signify calmness and warmth. Sienna signifies a warm reddish-brown color, evoking a sense of earthiness and comfort, while Serenity represents a state of peace and tranquility.

Sierra and Simone
Meaning and origin: Mountain range; One who hears (Spanish and Hebrew)
Significance: Both names have geographical and personal meanings. Sierra denotes a mountain range, while Simone means one who hears, reflecting attentiveness and sensitivity.

Sophia and Stella
Meaning and origin: Wisdom; Star (Greek and Latin)
Significance: Both names signify illumination and insight. Sophia represents wisdom and knowledge, while Stella signifies a star, symbolizing guidance, and brilliance.

Tara and Tessa
Meaning and origin: Hill; Harvester (Irish and Greek)
Significance: Both names convey a sense of nature and productivity. Tara represents serenity and stability, while Tessa signifies hard work and diligence.

Taylor and Tiana
Meaning and origin: Tailor; Fairy queen (English and Latin)
Significance: Both names signify creativity and elegance. Taylor represents a tailor, suggesting craftsmanship and skill, while Tiana signifies a fairy queen, suggesting grace and charm.

Thea and Talia
Meaning and origin: Goddess; Dew of heaven (Greek and Hebrew)
Significance: Both names have celestial connections. Thea denotes a goddess or divine figure, while Talia signifies dew of heaven, symbolizing freshness, and purity.

Tia and Tamara
Meaning and origin: Aunt; Palm tree (Spanish and Hebrew)
Significance: Tia is a bright, diminutive form of names like Tiana. Tamara signifies biblical heritage, representing several women in the Bible.

Trinity and Tiffany
Meaning and origin: Three in one; Manifestation of God (Latin and Greek)
Significance: Both names signify divine presence and manifestation. Trinity represents the Christian doctrine of the Father, Son, and Holy Spirit, while Tiffany signifies a manifestation of God's presence and beauty.

Valentina and Veronica
Meaning and origin: Strong, healthy; True image (Latin and Greek)
Significance: Both names signify strength and truth. Valentina represents health and vigor, while Veronica signifies the true image or honest representation.

Valeria and Verena
Meaning and origin: Strong; True (Latin)
Significance: Valeria symbolizes strength and health, while Verena signifies truth and integrity. Together, they reflect a harmonious blend of robust strength and unwavering honesty.

Victoria and Vanessa
Meaning and origin: Victory; Butterfly (Latin and Greek)
Significance: Both names signify triumph and beauty. Victoria represents strength and success, while Vanessa signifies grace and transformation.

Violet and Victoria
Meaning and origin: Purple flower; Victory (Latin)
Significance: Both names signify strength and victory. Violet represents the purple flower, symbolizing modesty, and virtue, while Victoria signifies victory and triumph.

Vivian and Violet
Meaning and origin: Alive; Purple flower (Latin)
Significance: Both names convey vitality and beauty. Vivian means alive or lively, while Violet represents the purple flower known for its fragrance and elegance.

Willa and Winona
Meaning and origin: Resolute protection; Firstborn daughter (German and Sioux)
Significance: Willa represents determination and protection, while Winona signifies the pride of being the firstborn. Together, they evoke a sense of protective determination and cherished beginnings.

Willow and River
Meaning and origin: Grace and Movement (English)
Significance: Both names have a beautiful connection to nature. Willow refers to the graceful willow tree, while River evokes images of flowing water and life. This creates a harmonious theme for twins.

Winter and Willow
Meaning and origin: The season; Graceful tree (English)
Significance: Both names evoke images of nature and tranquility. Winter signifies the season of cold and stillness, while Willow symbolizes grace and flexibility.

Yara and Yvette
Meaning and origin: Butterfly; Yew (Arabic and French)
Significance: Both names have natural and elegant associations. Yara means butterfly, representing transformation and beauty, while Yvette means yew tree, symbolizing resilience, and strength.

Zara and Zaina
Meaning and origin: Princess; Beautiful (Arabic)
Significance: Zara represents royal splendor and grace, while Zaina signifies beauty and elegance. Together, they reflect a harmonious blend of regal beauty and majestic charm.

Zarah and Zoeye
Meaning and origin: Blooming flower and Life (Arabic and Greek)
Significance: The names share similar sounds, particularly the "z" at the beginning and the vowels at the end. This creates a pleasing sense of balance and connection when said together. However, Zarah offers a touch of elegance and royalty, while Zoeye emphasizes vitality and zest for life. This provides a subtle distinction between the twins.

Zoe and Zara
Meaning and origin: Life; Princess (Greek and Arabic)
Significance: Both names convey a sense of vitality and nobility. Zoe represents life and vibrancy, while Zara signifies elegance and regality.

Twin Boy and Girl Names

When selecting names for your twin boy and girl, it's crucial to consider how they harmonize when spoken together. By hearing their names as a pair, you forge a lasting connection between your little boy and girl, ensuring they grow up with a built-in best friend. Here are names that complement each other, reflecting the special bond between twin siblings.

Aaron and Abigail
Meaning and origin: Exalted, Strong; Father's joy (Hebrew)
Significance: Aaron represents strength and leadership, while Abigail embodies joy and delight. Together, they reflect a harmonious blend of power and happiness.

Aiden and Ava
Meaning and origin: Little fire; Life (Irish and Latin)
Significance: Aiden symbolizes passion, energy, and warmth, while Ava represents vitality and liveliness. Together, they embody a dynamic and spirited combination.

Alder and Aveline
Meaning and origin: Noble tree; Hazelnut (Old English and French)
Significance: Alder signifies strength and resilience like the sturdy tree, while Aveline represents delicacy and beauty akin to the hazelnut. Together, they symbolize a balanced blend of robustness and grace.

Asher and Astrid
Meaning and origin: Happy, Blessed; Divinely beautiful (Hebrew and Norse)
Significance: Asher symbolizes joy, blessing, and good fortune, while Astrid represents divine beauty, strength, and nobility. Together, they reflect a combination of happiness and grace.

Beckett and Briar
Meaning and origin: Beehive; Thorny patch (Old English and English)
Significance: Beckett conveys industriousness and community, akin to a beehive, while Briar evokes a sense of natural beauty and protection. Together, they reflect a combination of hard work and natural charm.

Benjamin and Bella
Meaning and origin: Son of the right hand; Beautiful (Hebrew and Latin)
Significance: Benjamin symbolizes strength, favor, and virtue, while Bella represents beauty and charm. Together, they embody a blend of valor and elegance.

Brandon and Brianna
Meaning and origin: Beacon hill; Noble (English and Irish)
Significance: Brandon symbolizes light, guidance, and leadership, while Brianna represents strength, nobility, and honor. Together, they embody a blend of direction and resilience.

Caleb and Chloe
Meaning and origin: Faithful, Devotion; Blooming (Hebrew and Greek)
Significance: Caleb symbolizes loyalty, commitment, and courage, while Chloe represents growth, fertility, and new beginnings. Together, they reflect a harmonious combination of steadfastness and vitality.

Cameron and Camila
Meaning and origin: Crooked nose; Young ceremonial attendant (Scottish and Latin)
Significance: Cameron symbolizes uniqueness, distinction, and individuality, while Camila represents service, grace, and dedication. Together, they reflect a harmonious balance of singularity and devotion.

Caspian and Callista
Meaning and origin: From the Caspian Sea; Most beautiful (Latin and Greek)
Significance: Caspian represents vastness and exploration, like the expansive sea, while Callista signifies unparalleled beauty. Together, they embody a fusion of adventure and aesthetic elegance.

Daniel and Delilah
Meaning and origin: God is my judge; Delicate (Hebrew)
Significance: Daniel symbolizes righteousness, wisdom, and courage, while Delilah represents beauty, delicacy, and allure. Together, they embody a blend of strength and charm.

Darius and Dahlia
Meaning and origin: Kingly; Flowering branch (Persian and Scandinavian)
Significance: Darius reflects royalty and leadership, while Dahlia represents beauty and grace in bloom. Together, they signify a regal yet blossoming union.

David and Diana
Meaning and origin: Beloved; Divine (Hebrew and Latin)
Significance: David symbolizes love, affection, and loyalty, while Diana represents divinity, purity, and grace. Together, they embody a perfect blend of devotion and celestial beauty.

Edward and Eliza
Meaning and origin: Wealthy guardian; God is my oath (English and Hebrew)
Significance: Edward symbolizes protection, prosperity, and guardianship, while Eliza represents faithfulness, commitment, and spirituality. Together, they reflect a harmonious combination of security and devotion.

Emrys and Elara
Meaning and origin: Immortal; Shining one (Welsh and Greek)
Significance: Emrys conveys timelessness and wisdom, while Elara represents radiance and celestial beauty. Together, they symbolize eternal wisdom and shining grace.

Ethan and Emma
Meaning and origin: Strong, Firm; Universal (Hebrew and German)
Significance: Ethan symbolizes strength, reliability, and endurance, while Emma represents universality, wholeness, and compassion. Together, they embody a powerful blend of resilience and inclusiveness.

Finnian and Faye
Meaning and origin: Fair; Fairy (Irish and English)
Significance: Finnian represents fairness and purity, while Faye evokes enchantment and magic. Together, they reflect a blend of purity and whimsical charm.

Frederick and Freya
Meaning and origin: Peaceful ruler; Lady (German and Norse)
Significance: Frederick symbolizes leadership, peace, and strength, while Freya represents beauty, love, and fertility. Together, they embody a blend of serene governance and enchanting grace.

Gabriel and Grace
Meaning and origin: God is my strength; Grace, Favor (Hebrew and Latin)
Significance: Gabriel symbolizes strength, divine support, and communication, while Grace represents elegance, kindness, and divine favor. Together, they reflect a harmonious blend of strength and elegance.

Gideon and Gemma
Meaning and origin: Mighty warrior; Precious stone (Hebrew and Italian)
Significance: Gideon symbolizes strength, courage, and leadership, while Gemma represents beauty, rarity, and value. Together, they reflect a harmonious balance of might and elegance.

Griffin and Giselle
Meaning and origin: Strong lord; Pledge (Welsh and German)
Significance: Griffin symbolizes strength and nobility, while Giselle represents a promise and dedication. Together, they embody powerful loyalty and commitment.

Harrison and Hazel
Meaning and origin: Son of Harry; Hazel tree (English)
Significance: Harrison symbolizes heritage, legacy, and strength, while Hazel represents natural beauty, wisdom, and protection. Together, they embody a blend of tradition and grace.

Hawthorne and Helena
Meaning and origin: Where hawthorn trees grow; Light (English and Greek)
Significance: Hawthorne signifies natural strength and protection, while Helena represents illumination and clarity. Together, they symbolize protective strength and enlightening presence.

Isaac and Isabella
Meaning and Origin: He will laugh; God is my oath (Hebrew)
Significance: Isaac symbolizes joy, laughter, and divine promise, while Isabella represents faithfulness, commitment, and spirituality. Together, they embody a harmonious combination of joy and devotion.

Isidore and Isla
Meaning and Origin: Gift of Isis; Island (Greek and Scottish)
Significance: Isidore reflects a divine gift, while Isla signifies tranquility and beauty of an island. Together, they represent a blend of divine favor and serene beauty.

Jack and Julia
Meaning and Origin: God is gracious; Youthful (Hebrew and Latin)
Significance: Jack symbolizes grace, kindness, and favor, while Julia represents youthfulness, beauty, and love. Together, they reflect a harmonious blend of benevolence and vibrancy.

Jack and Jill
Meaning and Origin: God is gracious; Sweetheart or Youthful (Hebrew and Latin)
Significance: Jack symbolizes grace and kindness, while Julia represents Sweet and youthfulness. Together, they reflect a blend of benevolence and vibrancy.

James and Juliet
Meaning and Origin: Supplanter; Youthful (Hebrew and Latin)
Significance: James symbolizes determination, strength, and adaptability, while Juliet represents youthfulness, beauty, and love. Together, they embody a harmonious blend of resilience and romance.

Jasper and Juniper
Meaning and Origin: Treasurer; Young (Persian and Latin)
Significance: Jasper signifies wealth and value, while Juniper represents youth and vibrancy. Together, they embody a union of richness and youthful energy.

Kai and Keira
Meaning and Origin: Sea; Little dark one (Hawaiian and Irish)
Significance: Kai symbolizes freedom, depth, and tranquility, while Keira represents beauty, mystery, and elegance. Together, they reflect a harmonious balance of serenity and allure.

Kian and Kaia
Meaning and Origin: Ancient; Sea (Irish and Hawaiian)
Significance: Kian symbolizes enduring strength and history, while Kaia represents the vast, life-giving sea. Together, they reflect ancient strength and boundless vitality.

Leon and Luna
Meaning and Origin: Lion; Moon (Greek and Latin)
Significance: Leon symbolizes courage, strength, and royalty, while Luna represents illumination, mystery, and tranquility. Together, they embody a blend of power and serene beauty.

Levi and Leah
Meaning and Origin: Joined, Attached; Weary, Delicate (Hebrew)
Significance: Levi, the third son of Jacob and Leah, is the ancestor of the Levites. Leah, the first wife of Jacob, mothered six of the twelve tribes.

Liam and Lily
Meaning and Origin: Strong-willed warrior; Pure, Passion (Irish and Latin)
Significance: Liam symbolizes strength, determination, and protection, while Lily represents purity, beauty, and renewal. Together, they reflect a harmonious blend of strength and grace.

Logan and Layla
Meaning and Origin: Little hollow; Night (Scottish and Arabic)
Significance: Logan symbolizes depth, resilience, and calmness, while Layla represents beauty, mystery, and allure. Together, they embody a combination of tranquility and enchantment.

Lucas and Lucy
Meaning and Origin: Light (Latin)
Significance: Both names signify illumination, clarity, and inspiration. Lucas and Lucy together reflect a harmonious blend of brightness and guidance, embodying the essence of light.

Lysander and Liora
Meaning and Origin: Liberator; Light (Greek and Hebrew)
Significance: Lysander symbolizes freedom and leadership, while Liora represents light and brightness. Together, they signify a blend of liberating power and illuminating grace.

Maxwell and Madeline
Meaning and Origin: Great stream; High tower (Scottish and Hebrew)
Significance: Maxwell symbolizes strength, stability, and resilience, while Madeline represents elevation, protection, and beauty. Together, they reflect a combination of steadfastness and grace.

Mason and Mia
Meaning and Origin: Worker in stone; Mine, Beloved (English and Scandinavian)
Significance: Mason symbolizes craftsmanship, strength, and reliability, while Mia represents endearment, affection, and love. Together, they embody a harmonious blend of skill and warmth.

Maddison and Mason
Meaning and Origin: Son of Maud; Stoneworker (English)
Significance: Maddison, originally a surname, has come to signify heritage and lineage. Mason signifies craftsmanship and building, often representing strength and structure.

Matthew and Mary
Meaning and Origin: Gift of Yahweh; Bitter, Beloved (Hebrew)
Significance: Matthew, one of the twelve apostles, authored the Gospel of Matthew. Mary, the mother of Jesus, is a central figure in Christianity.

Merrick and Mirabel
Meaning and Origin: Ruler of the sea; Wonderful (Welsh and Latin)
Significance: Merrick signifies strength and command over the sea, while Mirabel represents wonder and beauty. Together, they embody a harmonious blend of strength and splendor.

Nathan and Naomi
Meaning and Origin: He gave; Pleasantness (Hebrew)
Significance: Nathan was a prophet during King David's reign. Naomi, the mother-in-law of Ruth, is central to the Book of Ruth.

Nicholas and Natalia
Meaning and Origin: Victory of the people; Birthday of the Lord (Greek and Latin)
Significance: Nicholas symbolizes victory, leadership, and strength, while Natalia represents celebration, spirituality, and grace. Together, they embody a blend of triumph and festivity.

Noah and Nora
Meaning and Origin: Rest, Comfort; Light (Hebrew and Latin)
Significance: Noah symbolizes peace, rest, and stability, while Nora represents illumination, clarity, and inspiration. Together, they reflect a harmonious blend of serenity and enlightenment.

Oliver and Olivia
Meaning and Origin: Olive tree (Latin)
Significance: Both names signify peace, prosperity, and harmony. Oliver and Olivia together embody a harmonious balance of serenity and abundance, reflecting the essence of the olive tree.

Orion and Ophelia
Meaning and Origin: Hunter; Help (Greek)
Significance: Orion reflects strength and celestial prowess, while Ophelia represents assistance and support. Together, they symbolize strength in unity and celestial harmony.

Owen and Olivia
Meaning and Origin: Young warrior; Olive tree (Welsh and Latin)
Significance: Owen symbolizes youth, vigor, and bravery, while Olivia represents peace, prosperity, and harmony. Together, they reflect a harmonious blend of vitality and tranquility.

Paul and Phoebe
Meaning and Origin: Small, Humble; Bright, Pure (Latin and Greek)
Significance: Paul, the Apostle to the Gentiles, wrote many New Testament epistles. Phoebe, a deaconess mentioned in Romans, signifies brightness and purity.

Percival and Penelope
Meaning and Origin: Pierces the valley; Weaver (Old French and Greek)
Significance: Percival represents bravery and determination, while Penelope signifies patience and creativity. Together, they reflect courageous perseverance and artistic ingenuity.

Peter and Phoebe
Meaning and Origin: Rock; Bright, Shining (Greek)
Significance: Peter symbolizes strength, stability, and reliability, while Phoebe represents brightness, clarity, and inspiration. Together, they embody a blend of steadfastness and brilliance.

Quentin and Quilla
Meaning and Origin: Fifth; Goddess of the moon (Latin and Quechua)
Significance: Quentin represents uniqueness and order, while Quilla signifies celestial beauty and mystery. Together, they embody a harmonious blend of individuality and cosmic grace.

Rafferty and Rosalind
Meaning and Origin: Prosperity wielder; Pretty rose (Irish and Latin)
Significance: Rafferty symbolizes wealth and charm, while Rosalind represents beauty and delicate elegance. Together, they reflect a union of prosperity and floral grace.

Reuben and Ruby
Meaning and Origin: Behold, a son; Red gemstone (Hebrew and Latin)
Significance: Reuben symbolizes pride, blessing, and strength, while Ruby represents beauty, rarity, and value. Together, they embody a blend of joy and elegance.

Samuel and Sabrina
Meaning and Origin: God has heard; River Severn (Hebrew and Celtic)
Significance: Samuel symbolizes divine communication, faith, and gratitude, while Sabrina represents natural beauty, flow, and grace. Together, they reflect a harmonious balance of spirituality and elegance.

Sam and Sophia
Meaning and Origin: God has heard; Wisdom (Hebrew and Greek)
Significance: Sam symbolizes divine communication, faith, and gratitude, while Sophia represents wisdom, knowledge, and insight. Together, they embody a harmonious blend of spiritual awareness and intellectual depth.

Sebastian and Seraphina
Meaning and Origin: Venerable; Fiery (Greek and Hebrew)
Significance: Sebastian signifies dignity and reverence, while Seraphina represents passionate spirit. Together, they symbolize a blend of esteemed presence and fiery energy.

Simon and Susanna
Meaning and Origin: He has heard; Lily (Hebrew)
Significance: Simon, one of the twelve apostles, is also known as Peter. Susanna, mentioned in the Gospel of Luke, supported Jesus.

Timothy and Tamara
Meaning and Origin: Honoring God; Palm tree (Greek and Hebrew)
Significance: Timothy, a close companion of Paul, received two New Testament epistles. Tamara represents several women in the Bible.

Theodore and Thalia
Meaning and Origin: Gift of God; To blossom (Greek)
Significance: Theodore reflects divine blessing and favor, while Thalia signifies growth and flourishing. Together, they embody divine generosity and blossoming vitality.

Thomas and Tessa
Meaning and Origin: Twin; Harvester (Aramaic and Greek)
Significance: Thomas symbolizes duality, companionship, and reliability, while Tessa represents productivity, diligence, and nurturing. Together, they reflect a combination of loyalty and industriousness.

Tobias and Tabitha
Meaning and Origin: God is good; Gazelle (Hebrew and Aramaic)
Significance: Tobias symbolizes goodness, divine favor, and joy, while Tabitha represents grace, beauty, and swiftness. Together, they embody a blend of kindness and elegance.

Ulysses and Ursula
Meaning and Origin: Wrathful; Little bear (Greek and Latin)
Significance: Ulysses symbolizes adventurous spirit, resilience, and heroism, while Ursula represents strength, protection, and tenacity. Together, they embody a powerful blend of bravery and guardianship.

Uriah and Una
Meaning and Origin: God is my light; One (Hebrew and Latin)
Significance: Uriah symbolizes divine guidance, faith, and illumination, while Una represents uniqueness, unity, and singularity. Together, they reflect a combination of spiritual enlightenment and individuality.

Valerian and Vespera
Meaning and Origin: Strong, healthy; Evening star (Latin)
Significance: Valerian signifies vitality and robustness, while Vespera represents beauty and tranquility of the evening. Together, they embody a blend of strength and serene beauty.

Vance and Vera
Meaning and Origin: Marshland; Faith, Truth (English and Latin)
Significance: Vance symbolizes nature, strength, and resilience, while Vera represents truth, faith, and honesty. Together, they embody a harmonious balance of natural beauty and integrity.

Victor and Victoria
Meaning and Origin: Conqueror; Victory (Latin)
Significance: Both names signify triumph, success, and strength. Victor and Victoria together reflect a harmonious balance of achievement and resilience, embodying the essence of victory.

William and Willow
Meaning and Origin: Resolute protector; Willow tree (German and English)
Significance: William symbolizes protection, determination, and leadership, while Willow represents flexibility, grace, and natural beauty. Together, they reflect a blend of steadfastness and elegance.

Wyatt and Willow
Meaning and Origin: Brave in war; Willow tree (English)
Significance: Wyatt symbolizes courage, bravery, and leadership, while Willow represents flexibility, grace, and natural beauty. Together, they embody a blend of valor and elegance.

Xander and Xena
Meaning and Origin: Defender of the people; Guest, Stranger (Greek)
Significance: Xander symbolizes protection, strength, and leadership, while Xena represents hospitality, uniqueness, and adventure. Together, they embody a harmonious blend of guardianship and exploration.

Yusuf and Yara
Meaning and Origin: God increases; Small butterfly (Hebrew and Arabic)
Significance: Yusuf symbolizes growth, prosperity, and divine blessing, while Yara represents delicacy, beauty, and transformation. Together, they reflect a combination of abundance and grace.

Zachary and Zoe
Meaning and Origin: The Lord remembers; Life (Hebrew and Greek)
Significance: Zachary symbolizes remembrance, faithfulness, and divine favor, while Zoe represents vitality, energy, and liveliness. Together, they embody a harmonious blend of spiritual depth and vibrant life.

Zeke and Zara
Meaning and Origin: God strengths; Princess, Radiance, Blossom (Hebrew)
Significance: Zeke is closely linked to the name Zaki, but both represents striving to be pure and draws strength from faith. While, Zara is not a biblical character, the name signifies brightness and bloom.

If your twins consist of boys and girls, consider what makes these matches a great pair. Think of a boy and girl name with a similar origin or meaning or perhaps names of a classic duo. If that doesn't spark any creativity, you can always choose names individually and see if they match up together—chances are they will!

CONCLUSION

Congratulations, future parents! You've just embarked on a remarkable adventure: The creation of a brand-new life. Choosing a name for your precious child is one of the first and most exciting steps on this journey. We hope this book has been your delightful companion, offering a glimpse into the vast and vibrant world of names across cultures and eras.

Remember, finding the perfect name doesn't have to be all about ticking boxes or following tradition. It's about a spark of recognition, a feeling that resonates deep within. Does a name evoke a smile? Does it whisper promises of the person you hope your child will become?

Embrace the opportunity to be creative! Maybe a cherished family name gets a fresh twist, or perhaps a hidden gem from literature catches your eye. Don't shy away from something unique: The right name will feel effortlessly personal, a perfect fit for the little one growing inside you.

Above all, remember that a name is the first gift you bestow upon your child, a promise whispered at the very dawn of their life's story. Make it a name you cherish, one that carries the weight of your love and hopes.

In these chapters, we covered many different names, and if you still don't feel like you've found the perfect name, take a deep breath and know that it will come. Why not re-read the chapters you enjoyed the most and allow the names that you like to spark some creativity within you to perhaps create a brand-new name? You've got this!

If you found this book a valuable companion on your naming quest, we'd be incredibly grateful if you could consider leaving a review. Your voice can guide other expectant parents as they navigate the exciting world of choosing the perfect name for their child. Happy choosing, and all the very best as you embark on this extraordinary adventure called parenthood!

Grab your free Universal Baby Registry

scan me

REFERENCES

Advanced name search. (n.d.). Names.org. https://www.names.org/advanced-search/

Astoria, D. (2008). *The name book.* Bethany House.

Baby boy names that start with A. (2023, September 11). Babylist. https://www.babylist.com/hello-baby/baby-boy-names-that-start-with-a

Baby names. (n.d.). BabyCenter. https://www.babycenter.com/baby-names

Baby names and meanings. (2024, April 11). BabyNames.com. https://babynames.com/

Baby names from books. (n.d.). Nameberry. https://nameberry.com/list/375/baby-names-from-books/8

Bennett, G. (2022, December 22). *Uncommon baby names.* The Bump. https://www.thebump.com/b/uncommon-baby-names

Bennett, G. (2023, December 14). *88 vintage baby boy names.* The Bump. https://www.thebump.com/b/vintage-baby-boy-names

Bolton, L. (2013). *The complete book of baby names: The most names, most lists, most help to find the best name.* Sourcebooks, Inc.

The Bump's favorite fictional baby names. (n.d.). The Bump. https://www.thebump.com/b/fictional-baby-names

Cinelli, E. (2023, August 16). *50 mythological names for your new baby.* Parents. https://www.parents.com/50-mythological-baby-names-meanings-and-origins-5185053

Forry, L. E. (2024, January 29). *100 Greek mythology boy names for your little hero.* Family Education. https://www.familyeducation.com/pregnancy/boy-names/100-greek-mythology-boy-names

Girl twin names. (n.d.). Pinterest. https://za.pinterest.com/search/pins/?q=girl%20twins%20names&rs=rs&eq=&etslf=1385

Herzog, B. (2014, February 2). *70 best character names in literature.* The Why Not 100. https://thewhynot100.blogspot.com/2014/02/70-best-character-names-in-literature.html

Kihm, S. (2024, March 18). *International baby boy names.* Nameberry. https://nameberry.com/list/198/cool-boy-names-from-around-the-world

Lansky, B. (2015). *100,000 + baby names.* Da Capo Press.

Murray, D. (2023, August 16). *How to choose a name for your baby.* Parents. https://www.parents.com/baby-names-4014180

Nameberry. (n.d.). https://nameberry.com/

Nast, C. (2016, April 19). *The most unusual celebrity baby names.* Vogue. https://www.vogue.com/article/celebrity-baby-names-unusual-apple-blue-ivy-suri-pilot-inspektor

Online Etymology Dictionary. (2023). https://www.etymonline.com/

Redmond, P. (2024, April 1). *Vintage baby names.* Nameberry. https://nameberry.com/list/339/vintage-baby-names

Sole, E. (2024, January 31). *Here are 101 of the coolest celebrity baby names.* Today. https://www.today.com/parents/parents/celebrity-baby-names-rcna28653

Thakur, S. (2015, January 30). *100 best twin baby boy names with meanings*. Mom Junction. https://www.momjunction.com/articles/twin-baby-boy-names-with-meanings_00207840

Vance, A. (2023, November 2). *50 unique baby names*. Parents. https://www.parents.com/unique-baby-names-meanings-and-origins-5200719

Made in the USA
Columbia, SC
20 April 2025